DAN-19 DANTES SUBJECT STANDARDIZED TESTS (DSST)

*This is your
PASSBOOK for...*

Intermediate Algebra

*Test Preparation Study Guide
Questions & Answers*

COPYRIGHT NOTICE

This book is SOLELY intended for, is sold ONLY to, and its use is RESTRICTED to individual, bona fide applicants or candidates who qualify by virtue of having seriously filed applications for appropriate license, certificate, professional and/or promotional advancement, higher school matriculation, scholarship, or other legitimate requirements of education and/or governmental authorities.

This book is NOT intended for use, class instruction, tutoring, training, duplication, copying, reprinting, excerption, or adaptation, etc., by:

1) Other publishers
2) Proprietors and/or Instructors of "Coaching" and/or Preparatory Courses
3) Personnel and/or Training Divisions of commercial, industrial, and governmental organizations
4) Schools, colleges, or universities and/or their departments and staffs, including teachers and other personnel
5) Testing Agencies or Bureaus
6) Study groups which seek by the purchase of a single volume to copy and/or duplicate and/or adapt this material for use by the group as a whole without having purchased individual volumes for each of the members of the group
7) Et al.

Such persons would be in violation of appropriate Federal and State statutes.

PROVISION OF LICENSING AGREEMENTS – Recognized educational, commercial, industrial, and governmental institutions and organizations, and others legitimately engaged in educational pursuits, including training, testing, and measurement activities, may address request for a licensing agreement to the copyright owners, who will determine whether, and under what conditions, including fees and charges, the materials in this book may be used them. In other words, a licensing facility exists for the legitimate use of the material in this book on other than an individual basis. However, it is asseverated and affirmed here that the material in this book CANNOT be used without the receipt of the express permission of such a licensing agreement from the Publishers. Inquiries re licensing should be addressed to the company, attention rights and permissions department.

All rights reserved, including the right of reproduction in whole or in part, in any form or by any means, electronic or mechanical, including photocopying, recording, or by any information storage and retrieval system, without permission in writing from the Publisher.

Copyright © 2025 by
National Learning Corporation

212 Michael Drive, Syosset, NY 11791
(516) 921-8888 • www.passbooks.com
E-mail: info@passbooks.com

PASSBOOK® SERIES

THE *PASSBOOK® SERIES* has been created to prepare applicants and candidates for the ultimate academic battlefield – the examination room.

At some time in our lives, each and every one of us may be required to take an examination – for validation, matriculation, admission, qualification, registration, certification, or licensure.

Based on the assumption that every applicant or candidate has met the basic formal educational standards, has taken the required number of courses, and read the necessary texts, the *PASSBOOK® SERIES* furnishes the one special preparation which may assure passing with confidence, instead of failing with insecurity. Examination questions – together with answers – are furnished as the basic vehicle for study so that the mysteries of the examination and its compounding difficulties may be eliminated or diminished by a sure method.

This book is meant to help you pass your examination provided that you qualify and are serious in your objective.

The entire field is reviewed through the huge store of content information which is succinctly presented through a provocative and challenging approach – the question-and-answer method.

A climate of success is established by furnishing the correct answers at the end of each test.

You soon learn to recognize types of questions, forms of questions, and patterns of questioning. You may even begin to anticipate expected outcomes.

You perceive that many questions are repeated or adapted so that you can gain acute insights, which may enable you to score many sure points.

You learn how to confront new questions, or types of questions, and to attack them confidently and work out the correct answers.

You note objectives and emphases, and recognize pitfalls and dangers, so that you may make positive educational adjustments.

Moreover, you are kept fully informed in relation to new concepts, methods, practices, and directions in the field.

You discover that you are actually taking the examination all the time: you are preparing for the examination by "taking" an examination, not by reading extraneous and/or supererogatory textbooks.

In short, this PASSBOOK®, used directedly, should be an important factor in helping you to pass your test.

NONTRADITIONAL EDUCATION

Students returning to school as adults bring more varied experience to their studies than do the teenagers who begin college shortly after graduating from high school. As a result, there are numerous programs for students with nontraditional learning curves. Hundreds of colleges and universities grant degrees to people who cannot attend classes at a regular campus or have already learned what the college is supposed to teach.

You can earn nontraditional education credits in many ways:
- Passing standardized exams
- Demonstrating knowledge gained through experience
- Completing campus-based coursework, and
- Taking courses off campus

Some methods of assessing learning for credit are objective, such as standardized tests. Others are more subjective, such as a review of life experiences.

With some help from four hypothetical characters – Alice, Vin, Lynette, and Jorge – this article describes nontraditional ways of earning educational credit. It begins by describing programs in which you can earn a high school diploma without spending 4 years in a classroom. The college picture is more complicated, so it is presented in two parts: one on gaining credit for what you know through course work or experience, and a second on college degree programs. The final section lists resources for locating more information.

Earning High School Credit

People who were prevented from finishing high school as teenagers have several options if they want to do so as adults. Some major cities have back-to-school programs that allow adults to attend high school classes with current students. But the more practical alternatives for most adults are to take the General Educational Development (GED) tests or to earn a high school diploma by demonstrating their skills or taking correspondence classes.

Of course, these options do not match the experience of staying in high school and graduating with one's friends. But they are viable alternatives for adult learners committed to meeting and, often, continuing their educational goals.

GED Program

Alice quit high school her sophomore year and took a job to help support herself, her younger brother, and their newly widowed mother. Now an adult, she wants to earn her high school diploma – and then go on to college. Because her job as head cook and her family responsibilities keep her busy during the day, she plans to get a high school equivalency diploma. She will study for, and take, the GED tests. Every year, about half a million adults earn their high school credentials this way. A GED diploma is accepted in lieu of a high school one by more than 90 percent of employers, colleges, and universities, so it is a good choice for someone like Alice.

The GED testing program is sponsored by the American Council on Education and State and local education departments. It consists of examinations in five subject areas: Writing, science, mathematics, social studies, and literature and the arts. The tests also measure skills such as analytical ability, problem solving, reading comprehension, and ability to understand and apply information. Most of the questions are multiple choice; the writing test includes an essay section on a topic of general interest.

Eligibility rules for taking the exams vary, but some states require that you must be at least 18. Tests are given in English, Spanish, and French. In addition to standard print, versions in large print, Braille, and audiocassette are also available. Total time allotted for the tests is 7 1/2 hours.

The GED tests are not easy. About one-fourth of those who complete the exams every year do not pass. Passing scores are established by administering the tests to a sample of graduating high school seniors. The minimum standard score is set so that about one-third of graduating seniors would not pass the tests if they took them.

Because of the difficulty of the tests, people need to prepare themselves to take them. Often, they start by taking the Official GED Practice Tests, usually available through a local adult education center. Centers are listed in your phone book's blue pages under "Adult Education," "Continuing Education," or "GED." Adult education centers also have information about GED preparation classes and self-study materials. Classes are generally arranged to accommodate adults' work schedules. National Learning Corporation publishes several study guides that aim to thoroughly prepare test-takers for the GED.

School districts, colleges, adult education centers, and community organizations have information about GED testing schedules and practice tests. For more information, contact them, your nearest GED testing center, or:

GED Testing Service
One Dupont Circle, NW, Suite 250
Washington, DC 20036-1163
1(800) 62-MY GED (626-9433)
(202) 939-9490

Skills Demonstration

Adults who have acquired high school level skills through experience might be eligible for the National External Diploma Program. This alternative to the GED does not involve any direct instruction. Instead, adults seeking a high school diploma must demonstrate mastery of 65 competencies in 8 general areas: Communication; computation; occupational preparedness; and self, social, consumer, scientific, and technological awareness.

Mastery is shown through the completion of the tasks. For example, a participant could prove competency in computation by measuring a room for carpeting, figuring out the amount of carpet needed, and computing the cost.

Before being accepted for the program, adults undergo an evaluation. Tests taken at one of the program's offices measure reading, writing, and mathematics abilities. A take-home segment includes a self-assessment of current skills, an individual skill evaluation, and an occupational interest and aptitude test.

Adults accepted for the program have weekly meetings with an assessor. At the meeting, the assessor reviews the participant's work from the previous week. If the task has not been completed properly, the assessor explains the mistake. Participants continue to correct their errors until they master each competency. A high school diploma is awarded upon proven mastery of all 65 competencies.

Fourteen States and the District of Columbia now offer the External Diploma Program. For more information, contact:

    External Diploma Program
    One Dupont Circle, NW, Suite 250
    Washington, DC 20036-1193
    (202) 939-9475

Correspondence and Distance Study

Vin dropped out of high school during his junior year because his family's frequent moves made it difficult for him to continue his studies. He promised himself at the time he dropped out that he would someday finish the courses needed for his diploma. For people like Vin, who prefer to earn a traditional diploma in a nontraditional way, there are about a dozen accredited courses of study for earning a high school diploma by correspondence, or distance study. The programs are either privately run, affiliated with a university, or administered by a State education department.

Distance study diploma programs have no residency requirements, allowing students to continue their studies from almost any location. Depending on the course of study, students need not be enrolled full time and usually have more flexible schedules for finishing their work. Selection of courses ranges from vo-tech to college prep, and some programs place different emphasis on the types of diplomas offered. University affiliated schools, for example, allow qualified students to take college courses along with their high school ones. Students can then apply the college credits toward a degree at that university or transfer them to another institution.

Taking courses by distance study is often more challenging and time consuming than attending classes, especially for adults who have other obligations. Success depends on each student's motivation. Students usually do reading assignments on their own. Written exercises, which they complete and send to an instructor for grading, supplement their reading material.

A list of some accredited high schools that offer diplomas by distance study is available free from the Distance Education and Training Council, formerly known as the National Home Study Council. Request the "DETC Directory of Accredited Institutions" from:

    The Distance Education and Training Council
    1601 18th Street, NW.
    Washington, DC 20009-2529
    (202) 234-5100

Some publications profiling nontraditional college programs include addresses and descriptions of several high school correspondence ones. See the Resources section at the end of this article for more information.

Getting College Credit For What You Know

Adults can receive college credit for prior coursework, by passing examinations, and documenting experiential learning. With help from a college advisor, nontraditional students should assess their skills, establish their educational goals, and determine the number of college credits they might be eligible for.

Even before you meet with a college advisor, you should collect all your school and training records. Then, make a list of all knowledge and abilities acquired through experience, no matter how irrelevant they seem to your chosen field. Next, determine your educational goals: What specific field do you wish to study? What kind of a degree do you want? Finally, determine how your past work fits into the field of study. Later on, you will evaluate educational programs to find one that's right for you.

People who have complex educational or experiential learning histories might want to have their learning evaluated by the Regents Credit Bank. The Credit Bank, operated by Regents College of the University of the State of New York, allows people to consolidate credits earned through college, experience, or other methods. Special assessments are available for Regents College enrollees whose knowledge in a specific field cannot be adequately evaluated by standardized exams. For more information, contact the Regents Credit Bank at:

Regents College
7 Columbia Circle
Albany, NY 12203-5159
(518) 464-8500

Credit For Prior College Coursework

When Lynette was in college during the 1970s, she attended several different schools and took a variety of courses. She did well in some classes and poorly in others. Now that she is a successful business owner and has more focus, Lynette thinks she should forget about her previous coursework and start from scratch. Instead, she should start from where she is.

Lynette should have all her transcripts sent to the colleges or universities of her choice and let an admissions officer determine which classes are applicable toward a degree. A few credits here and there may not seem like much, but they add up. Even if the subjects do not seem relevant to any major, they might be counted as elective credits toward a degree. And comparing the cost of transcripts with the cost of college courses, it makes sense to spend a few dollars per transcript for a chance to save hundreds, and perhaps thousands, of dollars in books and tuition.

Rules for transferring credits apply to all prior coursework at accredited colleges and universities, whether done on campus or off. Courses completed off campus, often called extended learning, include those available to students through independent study and correspondence. Many schools have extended learning programs; Brigham Young University, for example, offers more than 300 courses through its Department of Independent Study. One type of extended learning is distance learning, a form of correspondence study by technological means such as television, video and audio, CD-ROM, electronic mail, and computer tutorials. See the Resources section at the end of this article for more information about publications available from the National University Continuing Education Association.

Any previously earned college credits should be considered for transfer, no matter what the subject or the grade received. Many schools do not accept the transfer of courses graded below a C or ones taken more than a designated number of years ago. Some colleges and universities also have limits on the number of credits that can be transferred and applied toward a degree. But not all do. For example, Thomas Edison State College, New Jersey's State college for adults, accepts the transfer of all 120 hours of credit required for a baccalaureate degree – provided all the credits are transferred from regionally accredited schools, no more than 80 are at the junior college level, and the student's grades overall and in the field of study average out to C.

To assign credit for prior coursework, most schools require original transcripts. This means you must complete a form or send a written, signed request to have your transcripts released directly to a college or university. Once you have chosen the schools you want to apply to, contact the schools you attended before. Find out how much each transcript costs, and ask them to send your transcripts to the ones you are applying to. Write a letter that includes your name (and names used during attendance, if different) and dates of attendance, along with the names and addresses of the schools to which your transcripts should be sent. Include payment and mail to the registrar at the schools you have attended. The registrar's office will process your request and send an official transcript of your coursework to the colleges or universities you have designated.

Credit For Noncollege Courses

Colleges and universities are not the only ones that offer classes. Volunteer organizations and employers often provide formal training worth college credit. The American Council on Education has two programs that assess thousands of specific courses and make recommendations on the amount of college credit they are worth. Colleges and universities accept the recommendations or use them as guidelines.

One program evaluates educational courses sponsored by government agencies, business and industry, labor unions, and professional and voluntary organizations. It is the Program on Noncollegiate Sponsored Instruction (PONSI). Some of the training seminars Alice has participated in covered topics such as food preparation, kitchen safety, and nutrition. Although she has not yet earned her GED, Alice can earn college credit because of her completion of these formal job-training seminars. The number of credits each seminar is worth does not hinge on Alice's current eligibility for college enrollment.

The other program evaluates courses offered by the Army, Navy, Air Force, Marines, Coast Guard, and Department of Defense. It is the Military Evaluations Program. Jorge has never attended college, but the engineering technology classes he completed as part of his military training are worth college credit. And as an Army veteran, Jorge is eligible for a service that takes the evaluations one step further. The Army/American Council on Education Registry Transcript System (AARTS) will provide Jorge with an individualized transcript of American Council on Education credit recommendations for all courses he completed, the military occupational specialties (MOS's) he held, and examinations he passed while in the Army. All Army and National Guard enlisted personnel and veterans who enlisted after October 1981 are eligible for the transcript. Similar services are being considered by the Navy and Marine Corps.

To obtain a free transcript, see your Army Education Center for a 5454R transcript request form. Include your name, Social Security number, basic active service date, and complete address where you want the transcript sent. Mail your request to:
AARTS Operations Center
415 McPherson Ave.
Fort Leavenworth, KS 66027-1373

Recommendations for PONSI are published in *The National Guide to Educational Credit for Training Programs;* military program recommendations are in *The Guide to the Evaluation of Educational Experiences in the Armed Forces.* See the Resources section at the end of this article for more information about these publications.

Former military personnel who took a foreign language course through the Defense Language Institute may request course transcripts by sending their name, Social Security number, course title, duration of the course, and graduation date to:

Commandant, Defense Language Institute
Attn: ATFL-DAA-AR
Transcripts
Presidio of Monterey
Monterey, CA 93944-5006

Not all of Jorge's and Alice's courses have been assessed by the American Council on Education. Training courses that have no Council credit recommendation should still be assessed by an advisor at the schools they want to attend. Course descriptions, class notes, test scores, and other documentation may be helpful for comparing training courses to their college equivalents. An oral examination or other demonstration of competency might also be required.

There is no guarantee you will receive all the credits you are seeking – but you certainly won't if you make no attempt.

Credit By Examination

Standardized tests are the best-known method of receiving college credit without taking courses. These exams are often taken by high school students seeking advanced placement for college, but they are also available to adult learners. Testing programs and colleges and universities offer exams in a number of subjects. Two U.S. Government institutes have foreign language exams for employees that also may be worth college credit.

It is important to understand that receiving a passing score on these exams does not mean you get college credit automatically. Each school determines which test results it will accept, minimum scores required, how scores are converted for credit, and the amount of credit, if any, to be assigned. Most colleges and universities accept the American Council on Education credit recommendations, published every other year in the 250-page *Guide to Educational Credit by Examination*. For more information, contact:

The American Council on Education
Credit by Examination Program
One Dupont Circle, Suite 250
Washington, DC 20036-1193
(202) 939-9434

Testing programs:

You might know some of the five national testing programs by their acronyms or initials: CLEP, ACT PEP: RCE, DANTES, AP, and NOCTI. (The meanings of these initialisms are explained below.) There is some overlap among programs; for example, four of them have introductory accounting exams. Since you will not be awarded credit more than once for a specific subject, you should carefully evaluate each program for the subject exams you wish to take. And before taking an exam, make sure you will be awarded credit by the college or university you plan to attend.

CLEP (College-Level Examination Program), administered by the College Board, is the most widely accepted of the national testing programs; more than 2,800 accredited schools award credit for passing exam scores. Each test covers material taught in basic undergraduate courses. There are five general exams – English composition, humanities, college mathematics, natural sciences, and social sciences and history – and many subject exams. Most exams are entirely multiple-choice, but English composition exams may include an essay section. For more information, contact:

    CLEP
    P.O. Box 6600
    Princeton, NJ 08541-6600
    (609) 771-7865

ACT PEP: RCE (American College Testing Proficiency Exam Program: Regents College Examinations) tests are given in 38 subjects within arts and sciences, business, education, and nursing. Each exam is recommended for either lower- or upper-level credit. Exams contain either objective or extended response questions, and are graded according to a standard score, letter grade, or pass/fail. Fees vary, depending on the subject and type of exam. For more information or to request free study guides, contact:

    ACT PEP: Regents College Examinations
    P.O. Box 4014
    Iowa City, IA 52243
    (319) 337-1387
    (New York State residents must contact Regents College directly.)

DANTES (Defense Activity for Nontraditional Education Support) standardized tests are developed by the Educational Testing Service for the Department of Defense. Originally administered only to military personnel, the exams have been available to the public since 1983. About 50 subject tests cover business, mathematics, social science, physical science, humanities, foreign languages, and applied technology. Most of the tests consist entirely of multiple-choice questions. Schools determine their own administering fees and testing schedules. For more information or to request free study sheets, contact:

    DANTES Program Office
    Mail Stop 31-X
    Educational Testing Service
    Princeton, NJ 08541
    1(800) 257-9484

The AP (Advanced Placement) Program is a cooperative effort between secondary schools and colleges and universities. AP exams are developed each year by committees of college and high school faculty appointed by the College Board and assisted by consultants from the Educational Testing Service. Subjects include arts and languages, natural sciences, computer science, social sciences, history, and mathematics. Most tests are 2 or 3 hours long and include both multiple-choice and essay questions. AP courses are available to help students prepare for exams, which are offered in the spring. For more information about the Advanced Placement Program, contact:

    Advanced Placement Services
    P.O. Box 6671
    Princeton, NJ 08541-6671
    (609) 771-7300

NOCTI (National Occupational Competency Testing Institute) assessments are designed for people like Alice, who have vocational-technical skills that cannot be evaluated by other tests. NOCTI assesses competency at two levels: Student/job ready and teacher/experienced worker. Standardized evaluations are available for occupations such as auto-body repair, electronics, mechanical drafting, quantity food preparation, and upholstering. The tests consist of multiple-choice questions and a performance component. Other services include workshops, customized assessments, and pre-testing. For more information, contact:

NOCTI
500 N. Bronson Ave.
Ferris State University
Big Rapids, MI 49307
(616) 796-4699

Colleges and universities:
Many colleges and universities have credit-by-exam programs, through which students earn credit by passing a comprehensive exam for a course offered by the institution. Among the most widely recognized are the programs at Ohio University, the University of North Carolina, Thomas Edison State College, and New York University.

Ohio University offers about 150 examinations for credit. In addition, you may sometimes arrange to take special examinations in non-laboratory courses offered at Ohio University. To take a test for credit, you must enroll in the course. If you plan to transfer the credit earned, you also need written permission from an official at your school. Books and study materials are available, for a cost, through the university. Exams must be taken within 6 months of the enrollment date; most last 3 hours. You may arrange to take the exam off campus if you do not live near the university.

Ohio University is on the quarter-hour system; most courses are worth 4 quarter hours, the equivalent of 3 semester hours. For more information, contact:

Independent Study
Tupper Hall 302
Ohio University
Athens, OH 45701-2979
1(800) 444-2910
(614) 593-2910

The University of North Carolina offers a credit-by-examination option for 140 independent study (correspondence) courses in foreign languages, humanities, social sciences, mathematics, business administration, education, electrical and computer engineering, health administration, and natural sciences. To take an exam, you must request and receive approval from both the course instructor and the independent studies department. Exams must be taken within six months of enrollment, and you may register for no more than two at a time. If you are not near the University's Chapel Hill campus, you may take your exam under supervision at an accredited college, university, community college, or technical institute. For more information, contact:

Independent Studies
CB #1020, The Friday Center
UNC-Chapel Hill
Chapel Hill, NC 27599-1020
1(800) 862-5669 / (919) 962-1134

The Thomas Edison College Examination Program offers more than 50 exams in liberal arts, business, and professional areas. Thomas Edison State College administers tests twice a month in Trenton, New Jersey; however, students may arrange to take their tests with a proctor at any accredited American college or university or U.S. military base. Most of the tests are multiple choice; some also include short answer or essay questions. Time limits range from 90 minutes to 4 hours, depending on the exam. For more information, contact:

Thomas Edison State College
TECEP, Office of Testing and Assessment
101 W. State Street
Trenton, NJ 08608-1176
(609) 633-2844

New York University's Foreign Language Program offers proficiency exams in more than 40 languages, from Albanian to Yiddish. Two exams are available in each language: The 12-point test is equivalent to 4 undergraduate semesters, and the 16-point exam may lead to upper level credit. The tests are given at the university's Foreign Language Department throughout the year.

Proof of foreign language proficiency does not guarantee college credit. Some colleges and universities accept transcripts only for languages commonly taught, such as French and Spanish. Nontraditional programs are more likely than traditional ones to grant credit for proficiency in other languages.

For an informational brochure and registration form for NYU's foreign language proficiency exams, contact:

New York University
Foreign Language Department
48 Cooper Square, Room 107
New York, NY 10003
(212) 998-7030

Government institutes:

The Defense Language Institute and Foreign Service Institute administer foreign language proficiency exams for personnel stationed abroad. Usually, the tests are given at the end of intensive language courses or upon completion of service overseas. But some people – like Jorge, who knows Spanish – speak another language fluently and may be allowed to take a proficiency exam in that language before completing their tour of duty. Contact one of the offices listed below to obtain transcripts of those scores. Proof of proficiency does not guarantee college credit, however, as discussed above.

To request score reports from the Defense Language Institute for Defense Language Proficiency Tests, send your name, Social Security number, language for which you were tested, and, most importantly, when and where you took the exam to:

Commandant, Defense Language Institute
Attn: ATFL-ES-T
DLPT Score Report Request
Presidio of Monterey
Monterey, CA 93944-5006

To request transcripts of scores for Foreign Service Institute exams, send your name, Social Security number, language for which you were tested, and dates or year of exams to:

Foreign Service Institute
Arlington Hall
4020 Arlington Boulevard
Rosslyn, VA 22204-1500
Attn: Testing Office (Send your request to the attention of the testing office of the foreign language in which you were tested)

Credit For Experience

Experiential learning credit may be given for knowledge gained through job responsibilities, personal hobbies, volunteer opportunities, homemaking, and other experiences. Colleges and universities base credit awards on the knowledge you have attained, not for the experience alone. In addition, the knowledge must be college level; not just any learning will do. Throwing horseshoes as a hobby is not likely to be worth college credit. But if you've done research on how and where the sport originated, visited blacksmiths, organized tournaments, and written a column for a trade journal – well, that's a horseshoe of a different color.

Adults attempting to get credit for their experience should be forewarned: Having your experience evaluated for college credit is time-consuming, tedious work – not an easy shortcut for people who want quick-fix college credits. And not all experience, no matter how valuable, is the equivalent of college courses.

Requesting college credit for your experiential learning can be tricky. You should get assistance from a credit evaluations officer at the school you plan to attend, but you should also have a general idea of what your knowledge is worth. A common method for converting knowledge into credit is to use a college catalog. Find course titles and descriptions that match what you have learned through experience, and request the number of credits offered for those courses.

Once you know what credit to ask for, you must usually present your case in writing to officials at the college you plan to attend. The most common form of presenting experiential learning for credit is the portfolio. A portfolio is a written record of your knowledge along with a request for equivalent college credit. It includes an identification and description of the knowledge for which you are requesting credit, an explanatory essay of how the knowledge was gained and how it fits into your educational plans, documentation that you have acquired such knowledge, and a request for college credit. Required elements of a portfolio vary by schools but generally follow those guidelines.

In identifying knowledge you have gained, be specific about exactly what you have learned. For example, it is not enough for Lynette to say she runs a business. She must identify the knowledge she has gained from running it, such as personnel management, tax law, marketing strategy, and inventory review. She must also include brief descriptions about her knowledge of each to support her claims of having those skills.

The essay gives you a chance to relay something about who you are. It should address your educational goals, include relevant autobiographical details, and be well organized, neat, and convey confidence. In his essay, Jorge might first state his goal of becoming an engineer. Then he would explain why he joined the Army, where he got hands-on training and experience in developing and servicing electronic equipment.

This, he would say, led to his hobby of creating remote-controlled model cars, of which he has built 20. His conclusion would highlight his accomplishments and tie them to his desire to become an electronic engineer.

Documentation is evidence that you've learned what you claim to have learned. You can show proof of knowledge in a variety of ways, including audio or video recordings, letters from current or former employers describing your specific duties and job performance, blueprints, photographs or artwork, and transcripts of certifying exams for professional licenses and certification – such as Alice's certification from the American Culinary Federation. Although documentation can take many forms, written proof alone is not always enough. If it is impossible to document your knowledge in writing, find out if your experiential learning can be assessed through supplemental oral exams by a faculty expert.

Earning a College Degree

Nontraditional students often have work, family, and financial obligations that prevent them from quitting their jobs to attend school full time. Can they still meet their educational goals? Yes.

More than 150 accredited colleges and universities have nontraditional bachelor's degree programs that require students to spend little or no time on campus; over 300 others have nontraditional campus-based degree programs. Some of those schools, as well as most junior and community colleges, offer associate's degrees nontraditionally. Each school with a nontraditional course of study determines its own rules for awarding credit for prior coursework, exams, or experience, as discussed previously. Most have charges on top of tuition for providing these special services.

Several publications profile nontraditional degree programs; see the Resources section at the end of this article for more information. To determine which school best fits your academic profile and educational goals, first list your criteria. Then, evaluate nontraditional programs based on their accreditation, features, residency requirements, and expenses. Once you have chosen several schools to explore further, write to them for more information. Detailed explanations of school policies should help you decide which ones you want to apply to.

Get beyond the printed word – especially the glowing words each school writes about itself. Check out the schools you are considering with higher education authorities, alumni, employers, family members, and friends. If possible, visit the campus to talk to students and instructors and sit in on a few classes, even if you will be completing most or all of your work off campus. Ask school officials questions about such things as enrollment numbers, graduation rate, faculty qualifications, and confusing details about the application process or academic policies. After you have thoroughly investigated each prospective college or university, you can make an informed decision about which is right for you.

Accreditation

Accreditation is a process colleges and universities submit to voluntarily for getting their credentials. An accredited school has been investigated and visited by teams of observers and has periodic inspections by a private accrediting agency. The initial review can take two years or more.

Regional agencies accredit entire schools, and professional agencies accredit either specialized schools or departments within schools. Although there are no national accrediting standards, not just any accreditation will do. Countless "accreditation associations" have been invented by schools, many of which have no academic programs and sell phony degrees, to accredit themselves. But 6 regional and about 80 professional accrediting associations in the United States are recognized by the U.S. Department of Education or the Commission on Recognition of Postsecondary Accreditation. When checking accreditation, these are the names to look for. For more information about accreditation and accrediting agencies, contact:

Institutional Participation Oversight Service Accreditation and State Liaison Division
U.S. Department of Education
ROB 3, Room 3915
600 Independence Ave., SW
Washington, DC 20202-5244
(202) 708-7417

Because accreditation is not mandatory, lack of accreditation does not necessarily mean a school or program is bad. Some schools choose not to apply for accreditation, are in the process of applying, or have educational methods too unconventional for an accrediting association's standards. For the nontraditional student, however, earning a degree from a college or university with recognized accreditation is an especially important consideration. Although nontraditional education is becoming more widely accepted, it is not yet mainstream. Employers skeptical of a degree earned in a nontraditional manner are likely to be even less accepting of one from an unaccredited school.

Program Features

Because nontraditional students have diverse educational objectives, nontraditional schools are diverse in what they offer. Some programs are geared toward helping students organize their scattered educational credits to get a degree as quickly as possible. Others cater to those who may have specific credits or experience but need assistance in completing requirements. Whatever your educational profile, you should look for a program that works with you in obtaining your educational goals.

A few nontraditional programs have special admissions policies for adult learners like Alice, who plan to earn their GEDs but want to enroll in college in the meantime. Other features of nontraditional programs include individualized learning agreements, intensive academic counseling, cooperative learning and internship placement, and waiver of some prerequisites or other requirements – as well as college credit for prior coursework, examinations, and experiential learning, all discussed previously.

Lynette, whose primary goal is to finish her degree, wants to earn maximum credits for her business experience. She will look for programs that do not limit the number of credits awarded for equivalency exams and experiential learning. And since well-documented proof of knowledge is essential for earning experiential learning credits, Lynette should make sure the program she chooses provides assistance to students submitting a portfolio.

Jorge, on the other hand, has more credits than he needs in certain areas and is willing to forego some. To become an engineer, he must have a bachelor's degree; but because he is accustomed to hands-on learning, Jorge is interested in getting experience as he gains more technical skills. He will concentrate on finding schools with strong cooperative education, supervised fieldwork, or internship programs.

Residency Requirements

Programs are sometimes deemed nontraditional because of their residency requirements. Many people think of residency for colleges and universities in terms of tuition, with in-state students paying less than out-of-state ones. Residency also may refer to where a student lives, either on or off campus, while attending school.

But in nontraditional education, residency usually refers to how much time students must spend on campus, regardless of whether they attend classes there. In some nontraditional programs, students need not ever step foot on campus. Others require only a very short residency, such as one day or a few weeks. Many schools have standard residency requirements of several semesters but schedule classes for evenings or weekends to accommodate working adults.

Lynette, who previously took courses by independent study, prefers to earn credits by distance study. She will focus on schools that have no residency requirement. Several colleges and universities have nonresident degree completion programs for adults with some college credit. Under the direction of a faculty advisor, students devise a plan for earning their remaining credits. Methods for earning credits include independent study, distance learning, seminars, supervised fieldwork, and group study at arranged sites. Students may have to earn a certain number of credits through the degree-granting institution. But many programs allow students to take courses at accredited schools of their choice for transfer toward their degree.

Alice wants to attend lectures but has an unpredictable schedule. Her best course of action will be to seek out short residency programs that require students to attend seminars once or twice a semester. She can take courses that are televised and videotape them to watch when her schedule permits, with the seminars helping to ensure that she properly completes her coursework. Many colleges and universities with short residency requirements also permit students to earn some credits elsewhere, by whatever means the student chooses.

Some fields of study require classroom instruction. As Jorge will discover, few colleges and universities allow students to earn a bachelor's degree in engineering entirely through independent study. Nontraditional residency programs are designed to accommodate adults' daytime work schedules. Jorge should look for programs offering evening, weekend, summer, and accelerated courses.

Tuition and Other Expenses

The final decisions about which schools Alice, Jorge, and Lynette attend may hinge in large part on a single issue: Cost. And rising tuition is only part of the equation. Beginning with application fees and continuing through graduation fees, college expenses add up.

Traditional and nontraditional students have some expenses in common, such as the cost of books and other materials. Tuition might even be the same for some courses, especially for colleges and universities offering standard ones at unusual times. But for nontraditional programs, students may also pay fees for services such as credit or transcript review, evaluation, advisement, and portfolio assessment.

Students are also responsible for postage and handling or setup expenses for independent study courses, as well as for all examination and transcript fees for transferring credits. Usually, the more nontraditional the program, the more detailed the fees. Some schools charge a yearly enrollment fee rather than tuition for degree completion candidates who want their files to remain active.

Although tuition and fees might seem expensive, most educators tell you not to let money come between you and your educational goals. Talk to someone in the financial aid department of the school you plan to attend or check your library for publications about financial aid sources. The U.S. Department of Education publishes a guide to Federal aid programs such as Pell Grants, student loans, and work-study. To order the free 74-page booklet, *The Student Guide: Financial Aid from the U.S. Department of Education,* contact:

Federal Student Aid Information Center
P.O. Box 84
Washington, DC 20044
1 (800) 4FED-AID (433-3243)

Resources

Information on how to earn a high school diploma or college degree without following the usual routes is available from several organizations and in numerous publications. Information on nontraditional graduate degree programs, available for master's through doctoral level, though not discussed in this article, can usually be obtained from the same resources that detail bachelor's degree programs.

National Learning Corporation publishes study guides for all of these exams, for both general examinations and tests in specific subject areas. To order study guides, or to browse their catalog featuring more than 5,000 titles, visit NLC online at www.passbooks.com, or contact them by phone at (800) 632-8888.

Organizations

Adult learners should always contact their local school system, community college, or university to learn about programs that are readily available. The following national organizations can also supply information:

American Council on Education
One Dupont Circle
Washington, DC 20036-1193
(202) 939-9300

Within the American Council on Education, the Center for Adult Learning and Educational Credentials administers the National External Diploma Program, the GED Program, the Program on Noncollegiate Sponsored Instruction, the Credit by Examination Program, and the Military Evaluations Program.

DANTES Subject Standardized Tests

INTRODUCTION

The DANTES (Defense Activity for Non-Traditional Education Support) subject standardized tests are comprehensive college and graduate level examinations given by the Armed Forces, colleges and graduate schools as end-of-subject course evaluation final examinations or to obtain college equivalency credits in the various subject areas tested.

The DANTES Examination Program enables students to obtain college credit for what they have learned on the job, through self-study, personal interest, correspondence courses or by any other means. It is used by colleges and universities to award college credit to students who demonstrate that they know as much as students completing an equivalent college course. It is a cost-efficient, time-saving way for students to use their knowledge to accomplish their educational goals.

Most schools accept the American Council on Education (ACE) recommendations for the minimum score required and the amount of credit awarded, but not all schools do. Be sure to check the policy regarding the score level required for credit and the number of credits to be awarded.

Not all tests are accepted by all institutions. Even when a test is accepted by an institution, it may not be acceptable for every program at that institution. Before considering testing, ascertain the acceptability of a specific test for a particular course.

Colleges and universities that administer DANTES tests may administer them to any applicant – or they may administer the tests only to students registered at their institution. Decisions about who will be allowed to test are made by the school. Students should contact the test center to determine current policies and schedules for DANTES testing.

Colleges and universities authorized to administer DANTES tests usually do so throughout the calendar year. Each school sets its own fee for test administration and establishes its own testing schedule. Contact the representative at the administering school directly to make arrangements for testing.

Checklist For Students

- ✓ Visit **www.getcollegecredit.com** to obtain a list of tests, fact sheets, test preparation materials, participating colleges and universities, and much more.

- ✓ Contact your school advisor to confirm that the DSST you selected will fit into your curriculum.

- ✓ Consult the ***DSST Candidate Information Bulletin*** for answers to specific questions.

- ✓ Contact the test site to schedule your test.

- ✓ Prepare for your examination by using the fact sheet as a guide.

- ✓ Take the test.

If you would like a score report sent to your college or university, it is a good idea to bring the four-digit code with you. You must write the DSST Test Center Code for that institution on your answer sheet at the time of testing. DSST Test Center Codes are noted in the DSST Participating Colleges and Universities listing on the Web site.

If you prefer to send a score report to an institution at a later date, there is a transcript fee of $20 for each transcript ordered.

Thomson Prometric
DSST Program
2000 Lenox Drive, Third Floor
Lawrenceville, NJ 08648

Toll-free: 877-471-9860
609-895-5011

E-mail: pnj-dsst@thomson.com

MAKING A COLLEGE DEGREE WITHIN YOUR REACH

Today, there are many educational alternatives to the classroom—you can learn from your job, your reading, your independent study, and special interests you pursue. You may already have learned the subject matter covered by some college-level courses.

The DSST Program is a nationally recognized testing program that gives you the opportunity to receive college credit for learning acquired outside the traditional college classroom. Colleges and universities throughout the United States administer the program, developed by Thomson Prometric, year-round. Annually, over 90,000 DSSTs are administered to individuals who are interested in continuing their education. Take advantage of the DSST testing program; it speeds the educational process and provides the flexibility adults need, making earning a degree more feasible.

Since requirements differ from college to college, please check with the credit-awarding institution before taking a DSST. More than 1,800 colleges and universities currently award credit for DSSTs, and the number is growing every day. You can choose from 37 test titles in the areas of Social Science, Business, Mathematics, Applied Technology, Humanities, and Physical Science. A brief description of each examination is found on the pages that follow.

Reach Your Career Goals Through DSSTs

Use DSSTs to help you earn your degree, get a promotion, or simply demonstrate that you have college-level knowledge in subjects relevant to your work.

Save Time...

You don't have to sit through classes when you have previously acquired the knowledge or experience for most of what is being taught and can learn the rest yourself. You might be able to bypass introductory-level courses in subject areas you already know.

Save Money...

DSSTs save you money because the classes you bypass by earning credit through the DSST Program are classes you won't have to pay for on your way to earning your degree. You can use the money instead to take more advanced courses that can be more challenging and rewarding.

Improve Your Chances for Admission to College

Each college has its own admission policies; however, having passing scores for DSSTs on your transcript can provide strong evidence of how well you can perform at the college level.

Gain Confidence Performing at a College Level

Many adults returning to college find that lack of confidence is often the greatest hurdle to overcome. Passing a DSST demonstrates your ability to perform on a college level.

Make Up for Courses You May Have Missed

You may be ready to graduate from college and find that you are a few credits short of earning your degree. By using semester breaks, vacation time, or leisure time to study independently, you can prepare to take one or more DSSTs, fulfill your academic requirements, and graduate on time.

If You Cannot Attend Regularly Scheduled Classes...

If your lifestyle or responsibilities prevent you from attending regularly scheduled classes, you can earn your college degree from a college offering an external degree program. The DSST Program allows you to earn your degree by study and experience outside the traditional classroom.

Many colleges and universities offer external degree or distance learning programs. For additional information, contact the college you plan to attend or:

Center for Lifelong Learning
American Council on Education
One DuPont Circle NW, Suite 250
Washington, DC 20036
202-939-9475
www.acenet.edu
(Select "Center for Lifelong Learning" under "Programs & Services"
for more information)

Fact Sheets

For each test, there is a Fact Sheet that outlines the topics covered by each test and includes a list of sample questions, a list of recommended references of books that would be useful for review, and the number of credits awarded for a passing score as recommended by the American Council on Education (ACE). *Please note that some schools require scores that are higher than the minimum ACE-recommended passing score.* It is suggested that you check with your college or university to determine what score they require in order to earn credit. You can obtain Fact Sheets by:
- Downloading them from www.getcollegecredit.com
- E-mailing a request to pnj-dsst@thomson.com
- Completing a Candidate Publications Order Form

DSST Online Practice Tests

DSST online practice tests contain items that reflect a *partial range of difficulty* identified in the Content Outline section on each Fact Sheet. There is an online DSST Practice Test in the following categories:
- Mathematics
- Social Science
- Business
- Physical Science
- Applied Technology
- Humanities

Although the online DSST Practice Test questions do not indicate the full range of difficulty you would find in an actual DSST test, they will help you assess your knowledge level. Each online DSST Practice Test can be purchased by visiting www.getcollegecredit.com and clicking on DSST Practice Exams.

TAKING DSST EXAMINATIONS

Earning College Credit for DSST Examinations

To find out if the college of your choice awards credit for passing DSST scores, contact the admissions office or counseling and testing office. The college can also provide information on the scores required for awarding credit, the number of credit hours awarded, and any courses that can be bypassed with satisfactory scores.

It is important that you contact the institution of your choice as early as possible since credit-awarding policies differ among colleges and universities.

Where to Take DSSTs

DSSTs are administered at colleges and universities nationwide. Each location determines the frequency and scheduling of test administrations. To obtain the most current list of participating DSST colleges and universities:
- Visit and download the information from www.getcollegecredit.com
- E-mail pnj-dsst@thomson.com

Scheduling Your Examination

Please be aware that some colleges and universities provide DSST testing services to enrolled students only. After you have selected a college or university that administers DSSTs, you will need to contact them to schedule your test date.

The fee to take a DSST is $60 per test. This fee entitles you to two score reports after the test is scored. One will be sent directly to you and the other will be sent to the college or university that you designate on your answer sheet. You may pay the test fee with a certified check or U.S. money order made payable to Thomson Prometric or you may charge the test fee to your Visa, MasterCard or American Express credit card. Note: The credit card statement will reflect a charge from Thomson Prometric for all DSST examinations. *(Declined credit card charges will be assessed an additional $25 processing fee.)*

In addition, the test site may also require a test administration fee for each examination, to be paid directly to the institution. Contact the test site to determine its administration fee and payment policy.

Other Testing Arrangements

If you are unable to find a participating DSST college or university in your area, you may want to contact the testing office of a local accredited college or university to determine whether a representative from that office will agree to administer the test(s) for you.

The school's representative should then contact the DSST Program at 866-794-3497 to arrange for this administration. If you are unable to locate a test site, contact Thomson Prometric for assistance at pnj-dsst@thomson.com or 866-794-3497.

Testing Accommodations for Students with Disabilities

Thomson Prometric is committed to serving test takers with disabilities by providing services and reasonable testing accommodations as set forth in the provisions of the *Americans with Disabilities Act* (ADA). If you have a disability, as prescribed by the ADA, and require special testing services or arrangements, please contact the test administrator at the test site. You will be asked to submit to the test administrator documentation of your disability and your request for special accommodations. The test administrator will then forward your documentation along with your request for testing accommodations to Thomson Prometric for approval.

Please submit your request as far in advance of your test date as possible so that the necessary accommodations can be made. Only test takers with documented disabilities are eligible for special accommodations.

On the Day of the Examination

It is important to review this information and to have the correct identification present on the day of the examination:
- Arrive on time as a courtesy to the test administrator.
- Bring a valid form of government-issued identification that includes a current photo and your signature (acceptable documents include a driver's license, passport, state-issued identification card or military identification). *Anyone who fails to present valid identification will not be allowed to test.*
- Bring several No. 2 (soft-lead) sharpened pencils with good erasers, a watch, and a black pen if you will be writing an essay.
- Do not bring books or papers.
- Do not bring an alarm watch that beeps, a telephone, or a phone beeper into the testing room.
- The use of nonprogrammable calculators, slide rules, scratch paper and/or other materials is permitted for some of the tests.

DSST SCORING POLICIES

Your DSST examination scores are reported only to you, unless you request that they be sent elsewhere. If you want your scores sent to your college, you must provide the correct DSST code number of the school on your answer sheet at the time you take the test. See the *DSST Directory of Colleges and Universities* on the Web site www.getcollegecredit.com.

If your institution is not listed, contact Thomson Prometric at 866-794-3497 to establish a code number. (Some schools may require a student to be enrolled prior to receiving a score report.)

Receiving Your Score Report

Allow approximately four weeks after testing to receive your score report.

Calling DSST Customer Service before the required four-week score processing time has elapsed will not expedite the processing of your scores. Due to privacy and security requirements, scores will not be reported to students over the telephone under any circumstance.

Scoring of Principles of Public Speaking Speeches

The speech portion of the *Principles of Public Speaking* examination will be sent to speech raters who are faculty members at accredited colleges that currently teach or have previously taught the course. Scores for the *Principles of Public Speaking* examination are available six to eight weeks from receipt by Thomson Prometric. If you take the *Principles of Public Speaking* examination and fail (either the objective, speech portion, or both), you must follow the retesting policy waiting period of six months (180 days) before retaking the entire exam.

Essays

The essays for *Ethics in America* and *Technical Writing* are <u>optional</u> and thus are not scored by raters. The essays are forwarded to the college or university that you designate, along with your score report, for their use in determining the award of credit. <u>Before taking the *Ethics in America* or *Technical Writing* examinations, check with your college or university to determine whether the essay is required.</u>

NOTE: *Principles of Public Speaking* speech topic cassette tapes and essays are kept on file at Thomson Prometric for one year from the date of administration.

How to Get Transcripts

There is a $20 fee for each transcript you request. Payment must be in the form of a certified check, U.S. money order payable to Thomson Prometric, or credit card. Personal checks and debit cards are NOT an acceptable method of payment. One transcript may include scores for one or more examinations taken. To request a transcript, download the Transcript Order Form from www.getcollegecredit.com.

DESCRIPTION OF THE DSST EXAMINATIONS

Mathematics

• **Fundamentals of College Algebra** covers mathematical concepts such as fundamental algebraic operations; linear, absolute value; quadratic equations, inequalities, radials, exponents and logarithms, factoring polynomials and graphing. The use of a nonprogrammable, handheld calculator is permitted.

• **Principles of Statistics** tests the understanding of the various topics of statistics, both qualitatively and quantitatively, and the ability to apply statistical methods to solve a variety of problems. The topics included in this test are descriptive statistics; correlation and regression; probability; chance models and sampling and tests of significance. The use of a nonprogrammable, handheld calculator is permitted.

Social Science

• **Art of the Western World** deals with the history of art during the following periods: classical; Romanesque and Gothic; early Renaissance; high Renaissance, Baroque; rococo; neoclassicism and romanticism; realism, impressionism and post-impressionism; early twentieth century; and post-World War II.

• **Western Europe Since 1945** tests the knowledge of basic facts and terms and the understanding of concepts and principles related to the areas of the historical background of the aftermath of the Second World War and rebuilding of Europe; national political systems; issues and policies in Western European societies; European institutions and processes; and Europe's relations with the rest of the world.

• **An Introduction to the Modern Middle East** emphasizes core knowledge (including geography, Judaism, Christianity, Islam, ethnicity); nineteenth-century European impact; twentieth-century Western influences; World Wars I and II; new nations; social and cultural changes (1900-1960) and the Middle East from 1960 to present.

• **Human/Cultural Geography** includes the Earth and basic facts (coordinate systems, maps, physiography, atmosphere, soils and vegetation, water); culture and environment, spatial processes (social processes, modern economic systems, settlement patterns, political geography); and regional geography.

- **Rise and Fall of the Soviet Union** covers Russia under the Old Regime; the Revolutionary Period; New Economic Policy; Pre-war Stalinism; The Second World War; Post-war Stalinism; The Khrushchev Years; The Brezhnev Era; and reform and collapse.

- **A History of the Vietnam War** covers the history of the roots of the Vietnam War; the First Vietnam War (1946-1954); pre-war developments (1954-1963); American involvement in the Vietnam War; Tet (1968); Vietnamizing the War (1968-1973); Cambodia and Laos; peace; legacies and lessons.

- **The Civil War and Reconstruction** covers the Civil War from presecession (1861) through Reconstruction. It includes causes of the war; secession; Fort Sumter; the war in the east and in the west; major battles; the political situation; assassination of Lincoln; end of the Confederacy; and Reconstruction.

- **Foundations of Education** includes topics such as contemporary issues in education; past and current influences on education (philosophies, democratic ideals, social/economic influences); and the interrelationships between contemporary issues and influences.

- **Life-span Developmental Psychology** covers models and theories; methods of study; ethical issues; biological development; perception, learning and memory; cognition and language; social, emotional, and personality development; social behaviors, family life cycle, extrafamilial settings; singlehood and cohabitation; occupational development and retirement; adjustment to life stresses; and bereavement and loss.

- **Drug and Alcohol Abuse** includes such topics as drug use in society; classification of drugs; pharmacological principles; alcohol (types, effects of, alcoholism); general principles and use of sedative hypnotics, narcotic analgesics, stimulants, and hallucinogens; other drugs (inhalants, steroids); and prevention/treatment.

- **General Anthropology** deals with anthropology as a discipline; theoretical perspectives; physical anthropology; archaeology; social organization; economic organization; political organization; religion; and modernization and application of anthropology.

- **Introduction to Law Enforcement** includes topics such as history and professional movement of law enforcement; overview of the U.S. criminal justice system; police systems in the U.S.; police organization, management, and issues; and U.S. law and precedents.

- **Criminal Justice** deals with criminal behavior (crime in the U.S., theories of crime, types of crime); the criminal justice system (historical origins, legal foundations, due process); police; the court system (history and organization, adult court system, juvenile court, pre-trial and post-trial processes); and corrections.

- **Fundamentals of Counseling** covers historical development (significant influences and people); counselor roles and functions; the counseling relationship; and theoretical approaches to counseling.

Business
- **Principles of Finance** deals with financial statements and planning; time value of money; working capital management; valuation and characteristics; capital budgeting; cost of capital; risk and return; and international financial management. The use of a nonprogrammable, handheld calculator is permitted.

- **Principles of Financial Accounting** includes topics such as general concepts and principles, accounting cycle and classification; transaction analysis; accruals and deferrals; cash and internal control; current accounts; long- and short-term liabilities; capital stock; and financial statements. The use of a nonprogrammable, handheld calculator is permitted.

- **Human Resource Management** covers general employment issues; job analysis; training and development; performance appraisals; compensation issues; security issues; personnel legislation and regulation; labor relations and current issues; an overview of the Human Resource Management Field; Human Resource Planning; Staffing; training and development; compensation issues; safety and health; employee rights and discipline; employment law; labor relations and current issues and trends.

- **Organizational Behavior** deals with the study of organizational behavior (scientific approaches, research designs, data collection methods); individual processes and characteristics; interpersonal and group processes and characteristics; organizational processes and characteristics; and change and development processes.

- **Principles of Supervision** deals with the roles and responsibilities of the supervisor; management functions (planning, organization and staffing, directing at the supervisory level); and other topics (legal issues, stress management, union environments, quality concerns).

- **Business Law II** covers topics such as sales of goods; debtor and creditor relations; business organizations; property; and commercial paper.

- **Introduction to Computing** includes topics such as history and technological generations; hardware/software; applications to information technology; program development; data management; communications and connectivity; and computing and society. The use of a nonprogrammable, handheld calculator is permitted.

- **Management Information Systems** covers systems theory, analysis and design of systems, hardware and software; database management; telecommunications; management of the MIS functional area and informational support.

- **Introduction to Business** deals with economic issues affecting business; international business; government and business; forms of business ownership; small business, entrepreneurship and franchise; management process; human resource management; production and operations; marketing management; financial management; risk management and insurance; and management and information systems.

- **Money and Banking** covers the role and kinds of money; commercial banks and other financial intermediaries; central banking and the Federal Reserve system; money and macroeconomics activity; monetary policy in the U.S.; and the international monetary system.

- **Personal Finance** includes topics such as financial goals and values; budgeting; credit and debt; major purchases; taxes; insurance; investments; and retirement and estate planning. The use of auxiliary materials, such as calculators and slide rules, is NOT permitted.

- **Business Mathematics** deals with basic operations with integers, fractions, and decimals; round numbers; ratios; averages; business graphs; simple interest; compound interest and annuities; net pay and deductions; discounts and markups; depreciation and net worth; corporate securities; distribution of ownership; and stock and asset turnover.

Physical Science
• **Astronomy** covers the history of astronomy, celestial mechanics; celestial systems; astronomical instruments; the solar system; nature and evolution; the galaxy; the universe; determining astronomical distances; and life in the universe.

• **Here's to Your Health** covers mental health and behavior; human development and relationships; substance abuse; fitness and nutrition; risk factors, disease, and disease prevention; and safety, consumer awareness, and environmental concerns.

• **Environment and Humanity** deals with topics such as ecological concepts (ecosystems, global ecology, food chains and webs); environmental impacts; environmental management and conservation; and political processes and the future.

• **Principles of Physical Science I** includes physics: Newton's Laws of Motion; energy and momentum; thermodynamics; wave and optics; electricity and magnetism; chemistry: properties of matter; atomic theory and structure; and chemical reactions.

• **Physical Geology** covers Earth materials; igneous, sedimentary, and metamorphic rocks; surface processes (weathering, groundwater, glaciers, oceanic systems, deserts and winds, hydrologic cycle); internal Earth processes; and applications (mineral and energy resources, environmental geology).

Applied Technology
• **Technical Writing** covers topics such as theory and practice of technical writing; purpose, content, and organizational patterns of common types of technical documents; elements of various technical reports; and technical editing. Students have the option to write a short essay on one of the technical topics provided. Thomson Prometric will not score the essay; however, for determining the award of credit, a copy of the essay will be forwarded to the college or university you've designated along with the score report or transcript.

Humanities
• **Ethics in America** deals with ethical traditions (Greek views, Biblical traditions, moral law, consequential ethics, feminist ethics); ethical analysis of issues arising in interpersonal and personal-societal relationships and in professional and occupational roles; and relationships between ethical traditions and the ethical analysis of situations. Students have the option to write an essay to analyze a morally problematic situation in terms of issues relevant to a decision and arguments for alternative positions. Thomson Prometric will not score the essay; however, for determining the award of credit, a copy of the essay will be forwarded to the college or university you've designated along with the score report or transcript.

• **Introduction to World Religions** covers topics such as dimensions and approaches to religion; primal religions; Hinduism; Buddhism; Confucianism; Taoism; Judaism; Christianity; and Islam.

• **Principles of Public Speaking** consists of two parts: Part One consists of multiple-choice questions covering considerations of Principles of Public Speaking; audience analysis; purposes of speeches; structure/organization; content/supporting materials; research; language and style; delivery; communication apprehension; listening and feedback; and criticism and evaluation. Part Two requires the student to record an impromptu persuasive speech that will be scored.

FREQUENTLY ASKED QUESTIONS ABOUT DSSTs

In order to pass the test, must I study from one of the recommended references?

The recommended references are a listing of books that were being used as textbooks in college courses of the same or similar title at the time the test was developed. Appropriate textbooks for study are not limited to those listed in the fact sheet. If you wish to obtain study resources to prepare for the examination, you may reference either the current edition of the listed titles or textbooks currently used at a local college or university for the same class title. It is recommended that you reference more than one textbook on the topics outlined in the fact sheet. You should begin by checking textbook content against the content outline included on the front page of the DSST fact sheet before selecting textbooks that cover the text content from which to study. Textbooks may be found at the campus bookstore of a local college or university offering a course on the subject.

Is there a penalty for guessing on the tests?

There is no penalty for guessing on DSSTs, so you should mark an answer for each question.

How much time will I have to complete the test?

Many DSSTs can be completed within 90 minutes; however, additional time can be allowed if necessary.

What should I do if I find a test question irregularity?

Continue testing and then report the irregularity to the test administrator after the test. This may be done by asking that the test administrator note the irregularity on the Supervisor's Irregularity Report or you can write to Thomson Prometric, DSST Program, 2000 Lenox Drive, Third Floor, Lawrenceville, NJ 08648, and indicate the form and question number(s) or circumstances as well as your name and address.

When will I receive my score report?

Allow approximately four weeks from the date of testing to receive your score report. Allow six to eight weeks to receive a score report for the *Principles of Public Speaking* examination.

Will my test scores be released without my permission?

Your test score will not be released to anyone other than the school you designate on your answer sheet unless you write to us and ask us to send a transcript elsewhere. Instructions about how to do this can be found on your score report. Your scores may be used for research purposes, but individual scores are never made public nor are individuals identified if research findings are made public.

If I do not achieve a passing score on the test, how long must I wait until I can take the test again?

If you do not receive a score on the test that will enable you to obtain credit for the course, you may take the test again after six months (180 days). Please do not attempt to take the test before six months (180 days) have passed because you will receive a score report marked *invalid* and your test fee will not be refunded.

Can my test scores be canceled?
   The test administrator is required to report any irregularities to Thomson Prometric. <u>The consequence of bringing unauthorized materials into the testing room, or giving or receiving help, will be the forfeiture of your test fee and the invalidation of test scores.</u> The DSST Program reserves the right to cancel scores and not issue score reports in such situations.

What can I do if I feel that my test scores were not accurately reported?
   Thomson Prometric recognizes the extreme importance of test results to candidates and has a multi-step quality-control procedure to help ensure that reported scores are accurate. If you have reason to believe that your score(s) were not accurately reported, you may request to have your answer sheet reviewed and hand scored.
   The fees for this service are:
   • $20 fee if requested within six months of the test date
   • $30 fee if requested more than six months from the test date
   • $30 fee if a re-evaluation of the *Principles of Public Speaking* speech is requested

   The fee for this service can be paid by credit card or by certified check or U.S. money order payable to Thomson Prometric. Submit your request for score verification along with the appropriate fee or credit card information (credit card number and expiration date) to Thomson Prometric, DSST Program, 2000 Lenox Drive, Third Floor, Lawrenceville, NJ 08648. Include your full name, the test title, the date you took the test, and your Social Security number. Candidates will be notified if a scoring discrepancy is discovered within four weeks of receipt of the request.

What does ACE recommendation mean?
   The ACE recommendation is the minimum passing score recommended by the American Council on Education for any given test. It is equivalent to the average score of students in the DSST norming sample who received a grade of C for the course. Some schools require a score higher than the ACE recommendation.

Who is NLC?
   National Learning Corporation (NLC) has been successfully preparing candidates for 40 years for over 5,000 exams. NLC publishes Passbook® study guides to help candidates prepare for all DANTES and CLEP exams and almost every other type of exam from high school through adult career.
   Go to our website — www.passbooks.com — or call (800) 632-8888 for information about ordering our Passbooks.

To get detailed information on the DSST program and DSST preparation materials, visit www.getcollegecredit.com.

If you are interested in taking the DSST exams, call 877-471-9860 or e-mail pnj-dsst@thomson.com.

HOW TO TAKE A TEST

You have studied long, hard and conscientiously.

With your official admission card in hand, and your heart pounding, you have been admitted to the examination room.

You note that there are several hundred other applicants in the examination room waiting to take the same test.

They all appear to be equally well prepared.

You know that nothing but your best effort will suffice. The "moment of truth" is at hand: you now have to demonstrate objectively, in writing, your knowledge of content and your understanding of subject matter.

You are fighting the most important battle of your life—to pass and/or score high on an examination which will determine your career and provide the economic basis for your livelihood.

What extra, special things should you know and should you do in taking the examination?

I. YOU MUST PASS AN EXAMINATION

A. WHAT EVERY CANDIDATE SHOULD KNOW
Examination applicants often ask us for help in preparing for the written test. What can I study in advance? What kinds of questions will be asked? How will the test be given? How will the papers be graded?

B. HOW ARE EXAMS DEVELOPED?
Examinations are carefully written by trained technicians who are specialists in the field known as "psychological measurement," in consultation with recognized authorities in the field of work that the test will cover. These experts recommend the subject matter areas or skills to be tested; only those knowledges or skills important to your success on the job are included. The most reliable books and source materials available are used as references. Together, the experts and technicians judge the difficulty level of the questions.
Test technicians know how to phrase questions so that the problem is clearly stated. Their ethics do not permit "trick" or "catch" questions. Questions may have been tried out on sample groups, or subjected to statistical analysis, to determine their usefulness.
Written tests are often used in combination with performance tests, ratings of training and experience, and oral interviews. All of these measures combine to form the best-known means of finding the right person for the right job.

II. HOW TO PASS THE WRITTEN TEST

A. BASIC STEPS

1) Study the announcement

How, then, can you know what subjects to study? Our best answer is: "Learn as much as possible about the class of positions for which you've applied." The exam will test the knowledge, skills and abilities needed to do the work.

Your most valuable source of information about the position you want is the official exam announcement. This announcement lists the training and experience qualifications. Check these standards and apply only if you come reasonably close to meeting them. Many jurisdictions preview the written test in the exam announcement by including a section called "Knowledge and Abilities Required," "Scope of the Examination," or some similar heading. Here you will find out specifically what fields will be tested.

2) Choose appropriate study materials

If the position for which you are applying is technical or advanced, you will read more advanced, specialized material. If you are already familiar with the basic principles of your field, elementary textbooks would waste your time. Concentrate on advanced textbooks and technical periodicals. Think through the concepts and review difficult problems in your field.

These are all general sources. You can get more ideas on your own initiative, following these leads. For example, training manuals and publications of the government agency which employs workers in your field can be useful, particularly for technical and professional positions. A letter or visit to the government department involved may result in more specific study suggestions, and certainly will provide you with a more definite idea of the exact nature of the position you are seeking.

3) Study this book!

III. KINDS OF TESTS

Tests are used for purposes other than measuring knowledge and ability to perform specified duties. For some positions, it is equally important to test ability to make adjustments to new situations or to profit from training. In others, basic mental abilities not dependent on information are essential. Questions which test these things may not appear as pertinent to the duties of the position as those which test for knowledge and information. Yet they are often highly important parts of a fair examination. For very general questions, it is almost impossible to help you direct your study efforts. What we can do is to point out some of the more common of these general abilities needed in public service positions and describe some typical questions.

1) General information

Broad, general information has been found useful for predicting job success in some kinds of work. This is tested in a variety of ways, from vocabulary lists to questions about current events. Basic background in some field of work, such as sociology or economics, may be sampled in a group of questions. Often these are principles which have become familiar to most persons through exposure rather than through formal training. It is difficult to advise you how to study for these questions; being alert to the world around you is our best suggestion.

2) Verbal ability

An example of an ability needed in many positions is verbal or language ability. Verbal ability is, in brief, the ability to use and understand words. Vocabulary and grammar tests are typical measures of this ability. Reading comprehension or paragraph interpretation questions are common in many kinds of civil service tests. You are given a paragraph of written material and asked to find its central meaning.

IV. KINDS OF QUESTIONS

1. Multiple-choice Questions

Most popular of the short-answer questions is the "multiple choice" or "best answer" question. It can be used, for example, to test for factual knowledge, ability to solve problems or judgment in meeting situations found at work.

A multiple-choice question is normally one of three types:
- It can begin with an incomplete statement followed by several possible endings. You are to find the one ending which best completes the statement, although some of the others may not be entirely wrong.
- It can also be a complete statement in the form of a question which is answered by choosing one of the statements listed.
- It can be in the form of a problem – again you select the best answer.

Here is an example of a multiple-choice question with a discussion which should give you some clues as to the method for choosing the right answer:

When an employee has a complaint about his assignment, the action which will best help him overcome his difficulty is to
- A. discuss his difficulty with his coworkers
- B. take the problem to the head of the organization
- C. take the problem to the person who gave him the assignment
- D. say nothing to anyone about his complaint

In answering this question, you should study each of the choices to find which is best. Consider choice "A" – Certainly an employee may discuss his complaint with fellow employees, but no change or improvement can result, and the complaint remains unresolved. Choice "B" is a poor choice since the head of the organization probably does not know what assignment you have been given, and taking your problem to him is known as "going over the head" of the supervisor. The supervisor, or person who made the assignment, is the person who can clarify it or correct any injustice. Choice "C" is, therefore, correct. To say nothing, as in choice "D," is unwise. Supervisors have and interest in knowing the problems employees are facing, and the employee is seeking a solution to his problem.

2. True/False

3. Matching Questions

Matching an answer from a column of choices within another column.

V. RECORDING YOUR ANSWERS

Computer terminals are used more and more today for many different kinds of exams.

For an examination with very few applicants, you may be told to record your answers in the test booklet itself. Separate answer sheets are much more common. If this separate answer sheet is to be scored by machine – and this is often the case – it is highly important that you mark your answers correctly in order to get credit.

VI. BEFORE THE TEST

YOUR PHYSICAL CONDITION IS IMPORTANT

If you are not well, you can't do your best work on tests. If you are half asleep, you can't do your best either. Here are some tips:

1) Get about the same amount of sleep you usually get. Don't stay up all night before the test, either partying or worrying—DON'T DO IT!
2) If you wear glasses, be sure to wear them when you go to take the test. This goes for hearing aids, too.
3) If you have any physical problems that may keep you from doing your best, be sure to tell the person giving the test. If you are sick or in poor health, you relay cannot do your best on any test. You can always come back and take the test some other time.

Common sense will help you find procedures to follow to get ready for an examination. Too many of us, however, overlook these sensible measures. Indeed, nervousness and fatigue have been found to be the most serious reasons why applicants fail to do their best on civil service tests. Here is a list of reminders:

- Begin your preparation early – Don't wait until the last minute to go scurrying around for books and materials or to find out what the position is all about.
- Prepare continuously – An hour a night for a week is better than an all-night cram session. This has been definitely established. What is more, a night a week for a month will return better dividends than crowding your study into a shorter period of time.
- Locate the place of the exam – You have been sent a notice telling you when and where to report for the examination. If the location is in a different town or otherwise unfamiliar to you, it would be well to inquire the best route and learn something about the building.
- Relax the night before the test – Allow your mind to rest. Do not study at all that night. Plan some mild recreation or diversion; then go to bed early and get a good night's sleep.
- Get up early enough to make a leisurely trip to the place for the test – This way unforeseen events, traffic snarls, unfamiliar buildings, etc. will not upset you.
- Dress comfortably – A written test is not a fashion show. You will be known by number and not by name, so wear something comfortable.
- Leave excess paraphernalia at home – Shopping bags and odd bundles will get in your way. You need bring only the items mentioned in the official notice you received; usually everything you need is provided. Do not bring reference books to the exam. They will only confuse those last minutes and be taken away from you when in the test room.

- Arrive somewhat ahead of time – If because of transportation schedules you must get there very early, bring a newspaper or magazine to take your mind off yourself while waiting.
- Locate the examination room – When you have found the proper room, you will be directed to the seat or part of the room where you will sit. Sometimes you are given a sheet of instructions to read while you are waiting. Do not fill out any forms until you are told to do so; just read them and be prepared.
- Relax and prepare to listen to the instructions
- If you have any physical problem that may keep you from doing your best, be sure to tell the test administrator. If you are sick or in poor health, you really cannot do your best on the exam. You can come back and take the test some other time.

VII. AT THE TEST

The day of the test is here and you have the test booklet in your hand. The temptation to get going is very strong. Caution! There is more to success than knowing the right answers. You must know how to identify your papers and understand variations in the type of short-answer question used in this particular examination. Follow these suggestions for maximum results from your efforts:

1) Cooperate with the monitor

The test administrator has a duty to create a situation in which you can be as much at ease as possible. He will give instructions, tell you when to begin, check to see that you are marking your answer sheet correctly, and so on. He is not there to guard you, although he will see that your competitors do not take unfair advantage. He wants to help you do your best.

2) Listen to all instructions

Don't jump the gun! Wait until you understand all directions. In most civil service tests you get more time than you need to answer the questions. So don't be in a hurry. Read each word of instructions until you clearly understand the meaning. Study the examples, listen to all announcements and follow directions. Ask questions if you do not understand what to do.

3) Identify your papers

Civil service exams are usually identified by number only. You will be assigned a number; you must not put your name on your test papers. Be sure to copy your number correctly. Since more than one exam may be given, copy your exact examination title.

4) Plan your time

Unless you are told that a test is a "speed" or "rate of work" test, speed itself is usually not important. Time enough to answer all the questions will be provided, but this does not mean that you have all day. An overall time limit has been set. Divide the total time (in minutes) by the number of questions to determine the approximate time you have for each question.

5) Do not linger over difficult questions

If you come across a difficult question, mark it with a paper clip (useful to have along) and come back to it when you have been through the booklet. One caution if you do this – be sure to skip a number on your answer sheet as well. Check often to be sure that you have not lost your place and that you are marking in the row numbered the same as the question you are answering.

6) Read the questions

Be sure you know what the question asks! Many capable people are unsuccessful because they failed to read the questions correctly.

7) Answer all questions

Unless you have been instructed that a penalty will be deducted for incorrect answers, it is better to guess than to omit a question.

8) Speed tests

It is often better NOT to guess on speed tests. It has been found that on timed tests people are tempted to spend the last few seconds before time is called in marking answers at random – without even reading them – in the hope of picking up a few extra points. To discourage this practice, the instructions may warn you that your score will be "corrected" for guessing. That is, a penalty will be applied. The incorrect answers will be deducted from the correct ones, or some other penalty formula will be used.

9) Review your answers

If you finish before time is called, go back to the questions you guessed or omitted to give them further thought. Review other answers if you have time.

10) Return your test materials

If you are ready to leave before others have finished or time is called, take ALL your materials to the monitor and leave quietly. Never take any test material with you. The monitor can discover whose papers are not complete, and taking a test booklet may be grounds for disqualification.

VIII. EXAMINATION TECHNIQUES

1) Read the general instructions carefully. These are usually printed on the first page of the exam booklet. As a rule, these instructions refer to the timing of the examination; the fact that you should not start work until the signal and must stop work at a signal, etc. If there are any special instructions, such as a choice of questions to be answered, make sure that you note this instruction carefully.

2) When you are ready to start work on the examination, that is as soon as the signal has been given, read the instructions to each question booklet, underline any key words or phrases, such as least, best, outline, describe and the like. In this way you will tend to answer as requested rather than discover on reviewing your paper that you listed without describing, that you selected the worst choice rather than the best choice, etc.

3) If the examination is of the objective or multiple-choice type – that is, each question will also give a series of possible answers: A, B, C or D, and you are called upon to select the best answer and write the letter next to that answer on your answer paper – it is advisable to start answering each question in turn. There may be anywhere from 50 to 100 such questions in the three or four hours allotted and you can see how much time would be taken if you read through all the questions before beginning to answer any. Furthermore, if you

come across a question or group of questions which you know would be difficult to answer, it would undoubtedly affect your handling of all the other questions.

4) If the examination is of the essay type and contains but a few questions, it is a moot point as to whether you should read all the questions before starting to answer any one. Of course, if you are given a choice – say five out of seven and the like – then it is essential to read all the questions so you can eliminate the two that are most difficult. If, however, you are asked to answer all the questions, there may be danger in trying to answer the easiest one first because you may find that you will spend too much time on it. The best technique is to answer the first question, then proceed to the second, etc.

5) Time your answers. Before the exam begins, write down the time it started, then add the time allowed for the examination and write down the time it must be completed, then divide the time available somewhat as follows:
   - If 3-1/2 hours are allowed, that would be 210 minutes. If you have 80 objective-type questions, that would be an average of 2-1/2 minutes per question. Allow yourself no more than 2 minutes per question, or a total of 160 minutes, which will permit about 50 minutes to review.
   - If for the time allotment of 210 minutes there are 7 essay questions to answer, that would average about 30 minutes a question. Give yourself only 25 minutes per question so that you have about 35 minutes to review.

6) The most important instruction is to read each question and make sure you know what is wanted. The second most important instruction is to time yourself properly so that you answer every question. The third most important instruction is to answer every question. Guess if you have to but include something for each question. Remember that you will receive no credit for a blank and will probably receive some credit if you write something in answer to an essay question. If you guess a letter – say "B" for a multiple-choice question – you may have guessed right. If you leave a blank as an answer to a multiple-choice question, the examiners may respect your feelings but it will not add a point to your score. Some exams may penalize you for wrong answers, so in such cases only, you may not want to guess unless you have some basis for your answer.

7) Suggestions
   a. Objective-type questions
      1. Examine the question booklet for proper sequence of pages and questions
      2. Read all instructions carefully
      3. Skip any question which seems too difficult; return to it after all other questions have been answered
      4. Apportion your time properly; do not spend too much time on any single question or group of questions
      5. Note and underline key words – all, most, fewest, least, best, worst, same, opposite, etc.
      6. Pay particular attention to negatives
      7. Note unusual option, e.g., unduly long, short, complex, different or similar in content to the body of the question
      8. Observe the use of "hedging" words – probably, may, most likely, etc.

9. Make sure that your answer is put next to the same number as the question
10. Do not second-guess unless you have good reason to believe the second answer is definitely more correct
11. Cross out original answer if you decide another answer is more accurate; do not erase until you are ready to hand your paper in
12. Answer all questions; guess unless instructed otherwise
13. Leave time for review

b. Essay questions
1. Read each question carefully
2. Determine exactly what is wanted. Underline key words or phrases.
3. Decide on outline or paragraph answer
4. Include many different points and elements unless asked to develop any one or two points or elements
5. Show impartiality by giving pros and cons unless directed to select one side only
6. Make and write down any assumptions you find necessary to answer the questions
7. Watch your English, grammar, punctuation and choice of words
8. Time your answers; don't crowd material

8) Answering the essay question

Most essay questions can be answered by framing the specific response around several key words or ideas. Here are a few such key words or ideas:

M's: manpower, materials, methods, money, management
P's: purpose, program, policy, plan, procedure, practice, problems, pitfalls, personnel, public relations

a. Six basic steps in handling problems:
1. Preliminary plan and background development
2. Collect information, data and facts
3. Analyze and interpret information, data and facts
4. Analyze and develop solutions as well as make recommendations
5. Prepare report and sell recommendations
6. Install recommendations and follow up effectiveness

b. Pitfalls to avoid
1. Taking things for granted – A statement of the situation does not necessarily imply that each of the elements is necessarily true; for example, a complaint may be invalid and biased so that all that can be taken for granted is that a complaint has been registered
2. Considering only one side of a situation – Wherever possible, indicate several alternatives and then point out the reasons you selected the best one
3. Failing to indicate follow up – Whenever your answer indicates action on your part, make certain that you will take proper follow-up action to see how successful your recommendations, procedures or actions turn out to be
4. Taking too long in answering any single question – Remember to time your answers properly

EXAMINATION SECTION

EXAMINATION SECTION
TEST 1

DIRECTIONS: Each question or incomplete statement is followed by several suggested answers or completions. Select the one that BEST answers the question or completes the statement. *PRINT THE LETTER OF THE CORRECT ANSWER IN THE SPACE AT THE RIGHT.*

1. If $x = 2$ and $y = 5$, which of the following is TRUE? 1._____
   - A. $x + y > 8$
   - B. $x + y < 8$
   - C. $x + y \neq 7$
   - D. $x + y = 3$

2. The expression $(3a - 7b)^2$ equals 2._____
   - A. $9a^2 - 42ab + 49b^2$
   - B. $9a^2 - 42ab - 49b^2$
   - C. $9a^2 - 49b^2$
   - D. $9a^2 - 21ab + 49b^2$

3. The three children in the Brown family were born in consecutive years. The sum of their ages is now 24 years. Which of the following equations expresses the above? 3._____
   - A. $n + (n+1) = n + 2$
   - B. $n + (n+2) + (n+4) = 24$
   - C. $n(n+1)(n+2) = 24$
   - D. $n + (n+1) + (n+2) = 24$

4. *Twice the sum of the numbers x and y added to three times their product* would be written as 4._____
   - A. $2xy + 3(x+y)$
   - B. $2(x+y) + 3xy$
   - C. $5x + 5y$
   - D. $2x + y + 3xy$

5. The symbol $\{1, 2, 3\}$ represents 5._____
   - A. an infinite set
   - B. a finite set
   - C. a cardinal number
   - D. the number three

6. The product of 4^6 times 4^{-2} equals 6._____
   - A. 4^{-8}
   - B. 4^{-4}
   - C. 4^4
   - D. 16^4

7. The expression $(27a^3b^9)^{1/3}$ equals 7._____
   - A. $3ab^3$
   - B. $9ab^3$
   - C. $9ab^6$
   - D. $3a^9b^{27}$

8. The value of $|-3|$ is 8._____
   - A. less than -3
   - B. -3
   - C. 0
   - D. 3

9. If John can shovel the snow from a drive in 20 minutes and Bob can shovel it in 30 minutes, how long will it take them working together? _____ minutes. 9._____
   - A. 6
   - B. 10
   - C. 12
   - D. 50

10. Three times a positive real number is less than 3. The solution set is 10._____
    - A. $\{1\}$
    - B. $\{3\}$
    - C. $\{1, 2, 3\}$
    - D. $\{x \text{ such that } 0 < x < 1\}$

11. The graph of the relation $y = 3 + 2x - x^2$ is shown at the right. Which one of the following statements about the graph is NOT true? The

   A. x-intercepts are -1 and +3
   B. point (1, 4) is called a maximum point
   C. curve is called a hyperbola
   D. y-intercept is +3

11.____

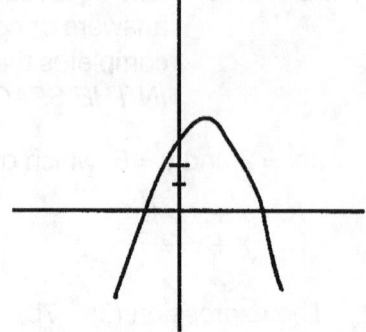

12. The expression $\dfrac{3}{\sqrt{2}+\sqrt{5}}$ may be written with a rational denominator by multiplying

   A. *both* numerator and denominator by $\sqrt{10}$
   B. *only* the denominator by $\sqrt{2}-\sqrt{5}$
   C. *both* numerator and denominator by the expression $\sqrt{2}+\sqrt{5}$
   D. *both* numerator and denominator by the expression $\sqrt{2}-\sqrt{5}$

12.____

13. At a constant temperature, the volume of a gas is inversely proportional to the pressure. If the pressure is multiplied by 3 while the temperature is unchanged, then the volume is _____ by 3.

   A. decreased   B. divided   C. increased   D. multiplied

13.____

14. Which of the following is an arithmetic progression?

   A. 4, 7, 10, 13,...
   B. 4, 7, 8, 11,...
   C. 4, 8, 16, 32,...
   D. 4, 5, 7, 10,...

14.____

15. What is the resulting equation when the value of x in the linear equation below is substituted in the quadratic equation below?

$$x^2 + 2y^2 = 10$$
$$x + y = 3$$

   A. $3 - y + 2y^2 = 10$
   B. $(3+y)^2 + 2y^2 = 10$
   C. $(3-y)^2 + 2y^2 = 10$
   D. $(3-y+2y)^2 = 10$

15.____

16. One factor of $12x^2 + 7x - 10$ is

   A. $4x + 5$ B. $4x - 5$ C. $3x - 5$ D. $3x + 2$

16.____

17. If $S = \pi r^2 + 2\pi rh$, then h equals

   A. $\dfrac{S + \pi r^2}{2\pi r}$
   B. $\dfrac{S - \pi r^2}{2\pi r}$
   C. $S - \dfrac{r}{2}$
   D. $S - \pi r^2 - 2\pi rh$

17.____

18. The equation $3x^2 - 75x = 0$ has   18.____

    A. only one solution, 25
    B. two solutions, 0 and 5
    C. two solutions, 0 and 25
    D. three solutions, 0, +5, and -5

19. If $2x + 3 > x - 1$, then   19.____

    A. $x > -4$ B. $x > -2$ C. $x > 2$ D. $x > 4$

20. The graphs whose equations are $x^2 + y^2 = 4$ and $x - y + 6 = 0$ are shown at the right. What is the common solution of the two equations?   20.____

    A. (-6,0) and (0,6)
    B. (0,0)
    C. (2,0), (0,2), and (0,-2)
    D. There is none

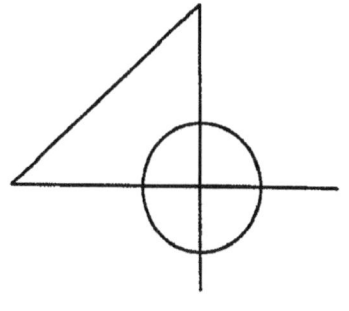

21. What are the factors of $8x^3 + 27y^3$?   21.____

    A. $(2x+3y)(4x^2+6xy+9y^2)$
    B. $(2x+3y)(2x^2-xy+3y^2)$
    C. $(2x+3y)(4x^2-6xy+9y^2)$
    D. $(2x+3y)(4x^2-12xy+9y^2)$

22. Which of the following facts would be applied in solving the equation $(x-a)(x-b)(x-c) = 0$?   22.____

    A. Both sides of an equation may be divided by any number except zero.
    B. The product of two or more factors is zero only if one or more factors is equal to zero.
    C. Both sides of an equation may be multiplied by any number.
    D. If equals are subtracted from equals, the results are equal.

23. If log 3.62 is given as .5587 and log 3.63 as .5599, what is the APPROXIMATE value of log 3.626?   23.____

    A. .5580   B. .5592   C. .5594   D. .5595

24. The fraction $\dfrac{x + 2i}{x - 3i}$ can be simplified by multiplying both numerator and denominator by   24.____

    A. $x - 3i$ B. $x + 3$ C. $x + 3i$ D. $x + i$

25. The roots of $2x^2 - 5x - 1 = 0$ are   25.____

    A. $\dfrac{5 \pm \sqrt{33}}{4}$ B. $\dfrac{5 \pm \sqrt{17}}{4}$ C. $\dfrac{-5 \pm \sqrt{33}}{44}$ D. $\dfrac{-2 \pm \sqrt{33}}{4}$

KEY (CORRECT ANSWERS)

1. B
2. A
3. D
4. B
5. B

6. C
7. A
8. D
9. C
10. D

11. C
12. D
13. B
14. A
15. C

16. A
17. B
18. C
19. A
20. D

21. C
22. B
23. C
24. C
25. A

SOLUTIONS TO PROBLEMS

1. If $x = 2$ and $y = 5$, then $x + y = 7 < 8$

2. $(3a-7b)^2 = 9a^2 - 21ab - 21ab + 49b^2 = 9a^2 - 42ab + 49b^2$

3. If n = age of youngest child, the other two children's ages are n+1 and n+2. Then, $n + (n+1) + (n+2) = 24$

4. Twice the sum of x and y is written as $2(x+y)$. Three times the product of x and y is written as $3xy$. The sum of these two expressions is $2(x+y) + 3xy$

5. $\{1, 2, 3\}$ is a finite set of three elements.

6. $4^6 \cdot 4^{-2} = 4^4$

7. $(27a^3b^9)^{\frac{1}{3}} = \sqrt[3]{27a^3b^9} = 3ab^3$

8. $|-3| = 3$. The symbol $|-3|$ means the absolute (positive) value of -3

9. Let x = time in minutes working together. Then, $\frac{x}{20} + \frac{x}{30} = 1$ Multiplying the equation by 60, $3x + 2x = 60$. Solving, $x = 12$

10. If three times a positive real number is less than 3, then the actual number is less than 1. Thus, $0 < x < 1$

11. The curve associated with $y = 3 + 2x - x^2$ is called a parabola

12. $\frac{3}{\sqrt{2}+\sqrt{5}}$ will have a rational denominator if both numerator and denominator are multiplied by $\sqrt{2}-\sqrt{5}$ to become $\frac{3(\sqrt{2}-\sqrt{5})}{-3}$

13. Since volume is inversely proportional to pressure, we can write $PV = K$, K a constant. If P is multiplied by 3, then V must be divided by 3. (Temperature is constant)

14. 4, 7, 10, 13, ... is an arithmetic progression since there is a constant difference between consecutive terms

15. Since $x+y=3$, $x = 3 - y$. Then, $x^2 + 2y^2 = 10$ becomes $(3-y)^2 + 2y^2 = 10$

16. $12x^2 + 7x - 10$ factors as $(4x+5)(3x-2)$

17. $S = \pi r^2 + 2\pi rh$. Then, $S - \pi r^2 = 2\pi rh$. Finally, $h = (S - \pi r^2)/2\pi r$

18. $3x^2 - 75x = 0$. Then, $3x(x-25) = 0$. Then the two solutions are $x = 0$ and $x = 25$

19. $2x + 3 > x - 1$. Adding $-x - 3$ to each side, $x > -4$

20. There is no common solution for $x^2 + y^2 = 4$ and $x - y + 6 = 0$

21. $8x^3 + 27y^3 = (2x+3y)(4x^2-6xy+9y^2)$. The general factoring of $A^3 + B^3$ is $(A+B)(A^2-AB+B^2)$. Here $A = 2x$, $B = 3y$

22. If $(x-a)(x-b)(x-c) = 0$, then one or more factors must equal zero, so that $x - a = 0$ or $x-b = 0$ or $x - c = 0$

23. $\text{Log } 3.626 \approx \text{Log } 3.62 + .6(\text{Log } 3.63 - \text{Log } 3.62) \approx$

    $.5587 + .6(.5599 - .5587) = .55942 \approx .5594$
    This is called linear interpolation.

24. To simplify $\dfrac{x + 2i}{x - 3i}$, multiply numerator and denominator by $x+3i$
    This will yield $(x^2+5ix-6)/(x^2+9)$

25. $2x^2 - 5x - 1 = 0$. Then, $x = (5 \pm \sqrt{25 - 4(2)(-1)}) / 4 = (5 \pm \sqrt{33}) / 4$

TEST 2

DIRECTIONS: Each question or incomplete statement is followed by several suggested answers or completions. Select the one that BEST answers the question or completes the statement. *PRINT THE LETTER OF THE CORRECT ANSWER IN THE SPACE AT THE RIGHT.*

1. If $x + 2 = x+2 = \sqrt{x^2 + 6}$, then x equals

   A. $-2\frac{1}{2}$ B. $-\frac{1}{2}$ C. $+\frac{1}{2}$ D. $+2\frac{1}{2}$

   1.____

2. The sum of |-4| + |+2| equals

   A. -6   B. -2   C. +2   D. +6

   2.____

3. The expression x + 7 = 7 + x illustrates the _____ property.

   A. commutative   B. transitive
   C. distributive   D. associative

   3.____

4. In the system of real numbers, zero is called the

   A. additive inverse   B. multiplicative identity
   C. reciprocal   D. additive identity

   4.____

5. The slope of the line at the right is

   A. $\frac{1}{4}$

   B. $\frac{1}{2}$

   C. 2

   D. 4

   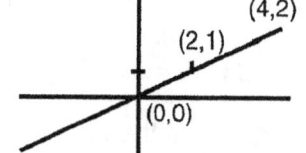

   5.____

6. If A = {1, 2, 3, 4} and B = {1, 3}, then

   A. $A \subset B$ B. $B \subset A$
   C. A = B   D. B is the complement of A

   6.____

7. A geometric progression is one in which every term after the first is formed by

   A. adding all the terms preceding it
   B. subtracting a fixed number from the preceding term
   C. adding a fixed number to the preceding term
   D. multiplying the preceding term by a fixed number

   7.____

8. Which one of the following points does NOT lie on the curve whose equation is $y = 2x^2 + x - 3$?

   A. (0, 3)   B. (0, -3)   C. (1, 0)   D. (-1, -2)

   8.____

7

9. The expression $\dfrac{\frac{1}{a}+\frac{1}{b}}{\frac{2}{ab}}$ equals

   A. $\dfrac{a}{2}+b$ B. $a+b$ C. $\dfrac{a+b}{2}$ D. $2(a+b)$

10. How many permutations of 3 letters each may be made with the letters a, b, c, d?

    A. 3   B. 4   C. 6   D. 24

11. If $\dfrac{x}{y}=5$, what is the value of $\dfrac{x-4y}{y}$

    A. $5-4y$ B. y C. 1   D. -1

12. An example of the associative property is

    A. $(xy)z=x(yz)$ B. $a+b=b+a$
    C. $ab=ba$ D. $x(a+b)=xa+xb$

13. In the process of solving $\sqrt{2x-1}=\sqrt{2x}-7$, we get which of the following?

    A. $2x+1=2x-7$
    B. $2x-2\sqrt{2x}+1=2x-7$
    C. $4x^2-4x+1=4x^2-28x+49$
    D. $2x-1=2x-7$

14. The graph at the right includes all the points outside but not on the circle.
    This is the graph of

    A. $x^2+y^2>4$
    B. $x^2+y^2<4$
    C. $x^2+y^2\geq 4$
    D. $x^2+y^2\leq 4$

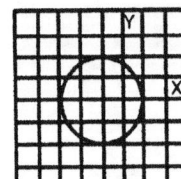

15. What is the range if the domain of the relationship $y=|x|$ is $\{-3,-2,-1,0,1,2,3\}$?

    A. $\{-3,-2,-1,0,1,2,3\}$ B. {all real numbers less than 3}
    C. $\{0,1,2,3\}$ D. null set

16. The product of $(a+bi)(2a-3bi)$ equals

    A. $2a^2+3b^2-abi$ B. $2a^2+3b^2+abi$
    C. $2a^2-3b^2-abi$ D. $2a^2-3b^2+abi$

17. $\dfrac{6 \pm \sqrt{36-24}}{4}$ can be expressed as

   A. $\dfrac{3 \pm \sqrt{12}}{2}$ B. $\dfrac{3}{2} \pm \sqrt{3}$ C. $\dfrac{3 \pm 2\sqrt{3}}{2}$ D. $\dfrac{3 \pm \sqrt{3}}{2}$

18. The roots of $ax^2 + bx + c = 0$ are NOT real if

   A. c is negative
   B. $b^2 - 4ac >$ zero
   C. $b^2 = 4ac$
   D. $b^2 - 4ac <$ zero

19. The sum of $\dfrac{x+1}{x-2} + \dfrac{x+2}{2-x}$ equals

   A. $\dfrac{1}{x-2}$ B. $\dfrac{1}{2-x}$ C. $\dfrac{2x+3}{x-2}$ D. $\dfrac{x-3}{(x-2)^2}$

20. The graph at the right consisting only of four points is the graph of $y = 2x$ where the domain of x is

   A. x real and -1 x 2
   B. $\{-2, 0, 2, 4\}$
   C. $\{-1, 0, 1, 2\}$
   D. x rational and $-1 \leq x \leq 2$

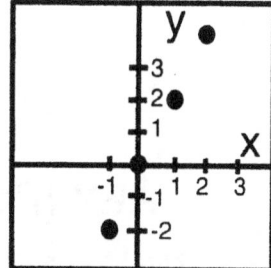

21. Which of the following represents the value of y in the system of equations below?
   $2x - y + 3z = 8$
   $x + y + z = 2$
   $3x + 2y + z = 5$

   A. $\dfrac{\begin{vmatrix} 2 & -1 & 3 \\ 1 & 1 & 1 \\ 3 & 2 & 1 \end{vmatrix}}{\begin{vmatrix} 2 & 8 & 3 \\ 1 & 2 & 1 \\ 3 & 5 & 1 \end{vmatrix}}$
   B. $\dfrac{\begin{vmatrix} 2 & 8 & 3 \\ 1 & 2 & 1 \\ 3 & 5 & 1 \end{vmatrix}}{\begin{vmatrix} 2 & -1 & 3 \\ 1 & 1 & 1 \\ 3 & 2 & 1 \end{vmatrix}}$
   C. $\begin{vmatrix} 2 & 8 & 3 \\ 1 & 2 & 1 \\ 3 & 5 & 1 \end{vmatrix}$
   D. $\begin{vmatrix} 2 & -1 & 3 \\ 1 & 1 & 1 \\ 3 & 2 & 1 \end{vmatrix} - \begin{vmatrix} 2 & 8 & 3 \\ 1 & 2 & 1 \\ 3 & 5 & 1 \end{vmatrix}$

22. If x pencils cost m cents, the formula for the cost c of y pencils is

   A. $c = \dfrac{my}{x}$ B. $c = \dfrac{mx}{y}$ C. $c = mxy$ D. $c = \dfrac{m}{x} + y$

23. Use the factor theorem to determine which of the following is a factor of $x^3 - 5x^2 - 2x + 4$.

    A. $x + 2$ B. $x - 2$ C. $x - 1$ D. $x + 1$

24. The trigonometric ratio cosine of angle θ is defined as

    A. $\dfrac{y}{r}$

    B. $\dfrac{x}{r}$

    C. $\dfrac{y}{x}$

    D. $\dfrac{r}{y}$

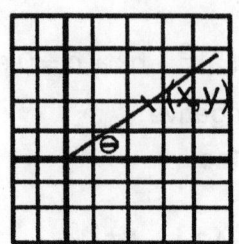

25. If $S = \{1, 2, 3\}$ and $T = \{3, 4, 5\}$, then

    A. $5 \, \varepsilon \, S$ B. $S \cup T = 3$ C. $5 \, \varepsilon \, T$ D. $S \cup T = T$

KEY (CORRECT ANSWERS)

1.	C	11.	C
2.	D	12.	A
3.	A	13.	B
4.	D	14.	A
5.	B	15.	C
6.	B	16.	A
7.	D	17.	D
8.	A	18.	D
9.	C	19.	B
10.	D	20.	C

21. B
22. A
23. D
24. B
25. C

SOLUTIONS TO PROBLEMS

1. $x+2 = \sqrt{x^2+6}$. Squaring both sides, $x^2 + 4x + 4 = x^2 + 6$. Then, $4x = 2$, so $x = 1/2$

2. $|-4| + |+2| = 4+2 = 6$

3. $x+7=7+x$ illustrates the commutative property of addition.

4. Zero is considered the additive identity since $n+0 = n$ for any real number n

5. Slope $= \dfrac{2-0}{4-0} = \dfrac{1}{2}$

6. If A = {1, 2, 3, 4} and B = {1, 3}, then B is a subset of A. This is written $B \subset A$

7. In a geometric progression, each term (except the 1st) is a constant multiplier of the previous term. Example: 3, 12, 48, 192,..

8. The point (0,3) does NOT lie on the curve with equation $y = 2x^2 + x - 3$ since $3 \neq 2(0) + 0 - 3$

9. $(\dfrac{1}{a}+\dfrac{1}{b})/\dfrac{2}{ab} = \dfrac{b+a}{ab} \cdot \dfrac{ab}{2} = \dfrac{b+a}{2} = \dfrac{a+b}{2}$

10. The number of permutations using 3 letters out of 4 is (4)(3)(2) = 24

11. $\dfrac{x}{y} = 5$, then x = 5y. Thus, (x-4y)/y = (5y-4y)/y = 1

12. (xy)(z) = (x)(yz) illustrates the associative property of multiplication.

13. $\sqrt{2x}-1 = \sqrt{2x-7}$. In squaring both sides, we get: $2x - 2\sqrt{2x} + 1 = 2x - 7$. The solution is x = 8

14. $x^2 + y^2 > 4$ describes all points outside the circle with center at (0,0) and a radius of 2

15. If y = |x| and x = -3, -2, -1, 0, 1, 2, 3, then the corresponding y values are 3, 2, 1, 0, 1, 2, 3. The range is {0,1,2,3}

16. $(a+bi)(2a-3bi) = 2a^2 - 3abi + 2abi - 3b^2 i^2 = 2a^2 - abi + 3b^2$

17. $(6 \pm \sqrt{36-24})/4 = (6 \pm 2\sqrt{3})/4 = (3 \pm \sqrt{3})/2$
    NOTE: $\sqrt{12} = \sqrt{4}\sqrt{3} = 2\sqrt{3}$

18. If $b^2 - 4ac < 0$, then the roots of $ax^2 + bx + c = 0$ are not real. They are complex roots.

19. $\dfrac{x+1}{x-2}+\dfrac{x+2}{2-x}=\dfrac{x+1}{x-2}+\dfrac{-x-1}{x-2}=\dfrac{-1}{x-2}=\dfrac{1}{2-x}$

20. In the graph, the x values are -1, 0, 1, and 2

21. For the system 2x-y+3z=8, x+y+z=2, 3x+2y+z=5, the determinants for the value of y is given by:

    $$\dfrac{\begin{vmatrix} 2 & 8 & 3 \\ 1 & 2 & 1 \\ 3 & 5 & 1 \end{vmatrix}}{\begin{vmatrix} 2 & -1 & 3 \\ 1 & 1 & 1 \\ 3 & 2 & 1 \end{vmatrix}}$$

    which equals $\dfrac{7}{-7} = -1$

22. $\dfrac{x}{m}=\dfrac{y}{c}$ Then, xc = my. Finally, $c = \dfrac{my}{x}$

23. Since -1 makes the expression $x^3 - 5x^2 - 2x + 4$ equal to 0, x+1 must be a factor of $x^3 - 5x^2 - 2x + 4$. Actually, $x^3 - 5x^2 - 2x + 4 = (x+1)(x^2-6x+4)$

24. Cosine θ = adjacent side/hypotenuse = $\dfrac{x}{r}$, where $r = \sqrt{x^2+y^2}$

25. Given S = {1, 2, 3} and T = {3, 4, 5}, 5 ε T is a correct statement.

EXAMINATION SECTION
TEST 1

DIRECTIONS: Each question or incomplete statement is followed by several suggested answers or completions. Select the one that BEST answers the question or completes the statement. *PRINT THE LETTER OF THE CORRECT ANSWER IN THE SPACE AT THE RIGHT.*

1. What is the equation of the locus of points P such that the sum of the distances from P to the two points (5,0) and (-5,0) is always 14 units?

   A. $24x^2 + 49y^2 = 1176$
   B. $24x^2 + 25y^2 = 600$
   C. $49x^2 + 24y^2 = 1176$
   D. $25x^2 + 24y^2 = 600$

   1._____

2. If f = {(0,3), (1,5), (2,7)} and g = {(0,-1), (1,0), (2,3)}, then f - 2g is equal to

   A. {(0,8), (1,5), (2,1)}
   B. {(0,4), (1,5), (2,4)}
   C. {(0,8), (1,5), (2,4)}
   D. {(0,5), (-1,5), (-2,1)}

   2._____

3. The line segment joining A(1,-4,3) to B(5,6,-1) in space is extended its own length through B to D.
   If the coordinates of D are (x_1, y_1, z_1), then $z_1 =$

   A. 5   B. -5   C. 1   D. -5/2

   3._____

4. The center and radius of the sphere whose equation is $x^2 + 4x + y^2 - 2y + z^2 = 59$ are, respectively,

   A. (2, -1, 0) and 4
   B. (2, -1, 0) and 8
   C. (-2, 1, 0) and 4
   D. (-2, 1, 0) and 8

   4._____

5. Given the following sets: the set of
   I. positive integers under addition
   II. integers under multiplication
   III. non-zero rational numbers under addition
   IV. non-zero rational numbers under multiplication
   Which one of the above sets forms a group?

   A. I   B. II   C. III   D. IV

   5._____

6. If the roots of a quadratic equation, $ax^2 + bx + c = 0$, are x_1 and x_2, then

   A. $x_1 + x_2 = -\frac{b}{a}$ and $x_1 \cdot x_2 = \frac{c}{a}$

   B. $x_1 + x_2 = \frac{a}{b}$ and $x_1 \cdot x_2 = \frac{a}{c}$

   C. $x_1 + x_2 = \frac{b}{a}$ and $x_1 \cdot x_2 = -\frac{c}{a}$

   D. $x_1 + x_2 = -\frac{c}{a}$ and $x_1 \cdot x_2 = \frac{b}{a}$

   6._____

7. $\dfrac{a^{-1}b^{-1}}{a^{-3}-b^{-3}}$ where $a \neq b$, equals which one of the following expressions?

   A. $\dfrac{a^2 b^2}{a^3 - b^3}$ B. $\dfrac{a^3 - b^3}{a^2 b^2}$ C. $\dfrac{b^3 - a^3}{a^2 b^2}$ D. $\dfrac{a^2 b^2}{b^3 - a^3}$

8. If an automobile travels at the rate of m miles per hour for p hours, and n miles per hour for q hours, then its average rate, in miles per hour, for the entire distance is which one of the following?

   A. $\dfrac{m+n}{2}$ B. $\dfrac{m}{p}+\dfrac{n}{q}$ C. $\dfrac{mp+nq}{2}$ D. $\dfrac{mp+nq}{p+q}$

9. If log 2 = .30 and log 3 = .48, then log 72 equals which one of the following?

   A. 1.38 B. 1.56 C. 1.86 D. 2.34

10. If the determinant $\begin{vmatrix} 2 & -x & 1 \\ 2 & -3 & 1 \\ -4 & 3 & 1 \end{vmatrix}$ is equal to zero, then x equals

    A. 1 B. 2 C. 3 D. -3

11. If $(x+iy)(2x-iy) = 4$, where x and y are real numbers and $i = \sqrt{-1}$ then which one of the following is always TRUE?

    A. $2x^2-y^2=4$
    B. $xy = 4$
    C. $xy = 0$
    D. $2x^2 + y^2 = 0$

12. If $x^3 + kx + 48$ is divisible by $(x-2)$, then it is also divisible by which one of the following binomials?

    A. x-1 B. x-3 C. x-4 D. x-6

13. If the sum of two of the roots of $9x^3 - 45x^2 - 4x + k = 0$ is 0, then the value of k is

    A. 0 B. 5 C. 10 D. 20

14. The real values of x such that $x^2 - x - 2 > 0$ can be described in which of the following ways?

    A. Either x < -1 or x > 2
    B. -1 < x < 2
    C. Either x < -2 or x > 1
    D. -2 < x < 1

15. The non-terminating, repeating decimal 2.525252... can be written as a rational fraction. When reduced to lowest terms, the sum of the numerator and denominator of this fraction equals

    A. 141   B. 299   C. 349   D. 399

16. If x is a real number, then $\sqrt{x^2}$ equals which one of the following?

    A. x   B. -x   C. ±x   D. $|x|$

17. If U is the set of real numbers, which one of the following is NOT in the domain of the function defined by $xy + 2x - 4 - 3y = 0$?

    A. 2   B. -3   C. 3   D. -2

18. If $f(X) = X + \frac{1}{X}, X \neq 0$ then $f(1+\frac{1}{y})$, $y \neq 0$, $y \neq -1$ equals

    A. $y + \frac{1}{y} + 1$ B. $\frac{2y^2 + 2y + 1}{y(y+1)}$

    C. $y^2 + \frac{2}{y} + 1$ D. $\frac{y^2 + 2y + 1}{y^2 + 1}$

19. The value of x which satisfies the equation is

    A. $\frac{1+\sqrt{3201}}{20}$ B. $2\frac{1}{3}$ C. 3   D. 1000

20. If U is the set of real numbers, then the graph of $\{(x,y) \mid (2x+3y < 12\}$ is the half-plane
    A. above the line $2x + 3y = 12$
    B. to the right of the line $2x + 3y = 12$
    C. below the x-axis
    D. below the line $2x + 3y = 12$

KEY (CORRECT ANSWERS)

1. A	6. A	11. C	16. D
2. D	7. D	12. C	17. C
3. B	8. D	13. D	18. C
4. D	9. C	14. A	19. D
5. D	10. C	15. C	20. D

SOLUTIONS TO PROBLEMS

1. Let P be located at (x,y). Then, $\sqrt{(x-5)^2 + (y-0)^2} + \sqrt{(x+5)^2 + (y-0)^2} = 14$
   Simplified, this equation becomes $24x^2 + 49y^2 = 1176$, which represents an ellipse. (Ans. A)

2. $2g = \{(0,-2), (2,0), (4,6)\}$. Thus, $f - 2g = \{(0,5), (-1,5), (-2,1)\}$, (Ans. D)

3. Since B is the midpoint of $\overline{AD}$, $-1 = \dfrac{3+z_1}{2}$, $z_1 = -5$. (Ans. B)

4. Rewrite $x^2 + 4x + y^2 - 2y + z^2 = 59$ as $(x+2)^2 + (y-1)^2 + (z-0)^2 = 64$. The center of the sphere is (-2,1,0) and the radius = 8. (Ans. D)

5. A group must have associativity, closure, identity element, and inverses. The non-zero rational numbers under multiplication would satisfy each requirement. The identity element = 1 and for each x, the number $\dfrac{1}{x}$ = inverse (Ans. D)

6. The sum of roots = $-\dfrac{b}{a}$, and the product of roots = $\dfrac{c}{a}$. (Ans. A)

7. $a^{-1} \cdot b^{-1} = \dfrac{1}{ab}$. $a^{-3} - b^{-3} = \dfrac{1}{a^3} - \dfrac{1}{b^3} = (b^3 - a^3)/a^3 b^3$
   Thus, the original fraction can be written as:
   $\dfrac{1}{ab} \div [(b^3 - a^3)/a^3 b^3] = a^2 b^2 / (b^3 - a^3)$. (Ans. D)

8. Total distance = mp + nq. Total time = p + q.
   Average rate = (mp+nq)/(p+q). (Ans. D)

9. Log 72 = Log (9·8) = Log 9 + Log 8 = 2 Log 3 + 3 Log 2 = 1.86 (Ans. C)

10. $-6 + 4x + 6 - (12 - 2x + 6) = 0$. Solving, x = 3. (Ans. C)

11. $(x+iy)(2x-iy) = 2x^2 + ixy + y^2 = 4$. This implies that xy = 0. (Ans. C)

12. 2 must be a solution of $x^3 + kx + 48 = 0$. Thus, $2^3 + (k)(2) + 48 = 0$, and so k = -28. The original polynomial equation is $x^3 - 28x + 48 = 0$. Since 4 is also a solution to this equation, x-4 is a factor. (Ans. C)

13. If k = 20, $9x^3 - 45x^2 - 4x + 20 = 0$ becomes $9x^2(x-5) - 4(x-5) = 0$. This equation further simplifies to $(3x-2)(3x+2)(x-5) = 0$, and two of the roots are $\dfrac{2}{3}$ and $-\dfrac{2}{3}$. (Ans. D)

14. $x^2 - x - 2 > 0$ means $(x-2)(x+1) > 0$, which implies both $x - 2 > 0$ and $x + 1 > 0$ or both $x - 2 < 0$ and $x + 1 < 0$. The solution is $x > 2$ or $x < -1$. (Ans. A)

15. Let $N = 2.\overline{52}$. Then, $100N = 252.\overline{52}$. By subtraction, $99N = 250$ and $N = \dfrac{250}{99}$. The sum of the numerator and denominator is 349. (Ans. C)

16. $\sqrt{x^2}$ always $= |x|$ whether $x \geq 0$ or $x < 0$. (Ans. D)

17. If x were 3, we would have 3y+6-4-3y=0, which leads to the contradiction 2=0. (Ans. C)

18. $f(1+\dfrac{1}{y}) = 1+\dfrac{1}{y}+[1\div(1+\dfrac{1}{y})] = 1+\dfrac{1}{y}+\dfrac{y}{y+1} = \dfrac{2y^2+2y+1}{y(y+1)}$

19. $\text{Log } x^2 = 2 \text{ Log } x$ and $\text{Log}\dfrac{x}{10} = \text{Log} x - \text{Log} 10 = \text{Log } x - 1$.
    Rewrite the original equation as $2 \text{ Log } x + \text{Log } x - 1 = 8$. This becomes $3 \text{ Log } x = 9$, which has the solution $x = 1000$. (Ans. D)

20. 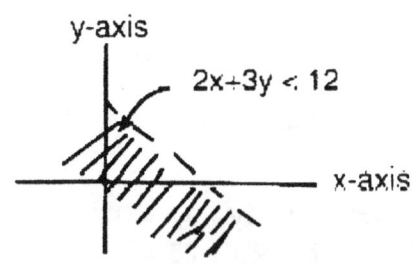   Since $2x + 3y < 12$ becomes $y < -\dfrac{2}{3}x + 4$, its graph lies below $2x + 3y = 12$. (Ans. D)

TEST 2

DIRECTIONS: Each question or incomplete statement is followed by several suggested answers or completions. Select the one that BEST answers the question or completes the statement. *PRINT THE LETTER OF THE CORRECT ANSWER IN THE SPACE AT THE RIGHT.*

1. Of the following sets of ordered pairs, the one set that is NOT a function is   1.___

   A. {(0,1), (1,1), (2,1), (3,1), (4,1)}
   B. {(0,0), (1,1), (2,2), (3,3), (4,4)}
   C. {(-1,-2), (0,-1), (1,0), (2,1), (3,3)}
   D. {(-1,1, (-1,-1), (0,0), (1,1), (1,-1)}

2. The set of real numbers which satisfies |2x-3| = 5 is   2.___

   A. {4}   B. {-1}   C. {-1,4}   D. the empty set

3. The equation of the line parallel to the line 2y = 3x - 5 and passing through the midpoint of the line segment whose end points are at (-5,6) and (1,4) is which one of the following?   3.___

   A. 2x - 3y + 19 = 0   B. 3x - 2y + 4 = 0
   C. 2y - 3x + 16 = 0   D. 3x - 2y + 16 = 0

4. The radius of the circle $x^2 + 8x + y^2 - 10y - 8 = 0$ is   4.___

   A. $\sqrt{8}$ B. $\sqrt{41}$ C. 7   D. 8

5. Which one of the following is the equation of the parabola with vertex at (3, 2) and focus at (3, 4)?   5.___

   A. $y^2 - 6y - 4x + 17 = 0$ B. $x^2 - 6x - 4y + 17 = 0$
   C. $x^2 - 6x - 8y + 25 = 0$ D. $y^2 - 6y - 8x + 25 = 0$

6. The number of negative real roots of the equation $x^3 + 3x = 5$ is   6.___

   A. 0   B. 1   C. 2   D. 3

7. All of the following are correct EXCEPT   7.___

   A. $\log(x^{-a}) = -a \log x$ B. $\log \sqrt[a]{x} = \frac{1}{a}\log x$
   C. $\log(x^{-a}) = -a \log x^a$ D. $\log \frac{x}{a} = \log x - \log a$

8. The MAXIMUM number of subsets which a set of eight different elements has is   8.___

   A. 8   B. 8^2 C. 256   D. 512

9. The ordered pairs of numbers which make both inequalities x + y > 2 and x - y < 1 true lie in quadrants   9.___

   A. 2 and 3   B. 1 and 4   C. 1 and 2   D. 3 and 4

10. In the universe of real numbers, the one of the following in which the relation is a function is

    A. $\{(x,y) | y = |x-5|\}$ B. $\{(x,y) | x = |2-y|\}$
    C. $\{(x,y) | y > x + 2\}$ D. $\{(x,y) | x = -5\}$

11. $\{x | x < 4\} \cap \{x | x > -3\}$ equals

    A. $\{-3 < x < 4\}$ B. $\{4 < x < -3\}$
    C. $\{x > -3\}$ D. $\{x < 4\}$

12. If $\log_{10} 2 = .30$, $\log_{10} 3 = .48$, and $\log_{10} 5 = .70$, the value of $\log_{10} \dfrac{(675)^3}{\sqrt[5]{576}}$ is

    A. 2.29   B. 5.76   C. 7.97   D. 9.07

13. If a, b, and c are in arithmetic progression, and b, c, and d are in geometric progression, a equals

    A. $b(2-d)$ B. $\dfrac{c(2c-d)}{d}$ C. $\dfrac{c^2}{d} - c$ D. $c(2c-1)$

14. The number of terms in the expansion of $(a+b+c)^4$ is

    A. 7   B. 12   C. 15   D. 16

15. If $x + 2y + (2x-y)i = 5 - 2i$, then

    A. $x = 5$ and $y = -2$ B. $x = 3$ and $y = 1$
    C. $x = \dfrac{4}{5}$ and $y = \dfrac{16}{5}$ D. $x = \dfrac{1}{5}$ and $y = \dfrac{12}{5}$

16. The solution of the inequalities $6y < 7y + 4$ and $2 - 3y \geq -1$ is

    A. $-4 < y \leq 1$ B. $-3 < y\ 2$
    C. $-5 < y \leq 4$ D. none of these

17. The third term of the expansion of $(3 + 2x)^{\frac{1}{2}}$ is

    A. $-\dfrac{\sqrt{3}}{18} x^2$ B. $-\dfrac{x}{\sqrt{3}}$ C. $\dfrac{\sqrt{3}}{54} x^3$ D. $\sqrt[2]{3x}$

18. If $p = \dfrac{A[1-(1+i)^{-n}]}{i}$, n equals

A. $\dfrac{\log A - \log ip}{\log(1+i)}$

B. $\dfrac{\log(1+i)}{\log A - \log(A-ip)}$

C. $\dfrac{\log A \log(A-ip)}{\log(1+i)}$

D. $\dfrac{\log A - \log(A-ip)}{\log(1+i)}$

19. When a and b are positive integers, a - b can be factored for all values of a and b, if the domain of the factors is the

    A. integers
    B. rational numbers
    C. numbers with bases other than 10
    D. real numbers

20. If one root of the equation $x^3 - kx^2 + 17x - 13 = 0$ is $2 + 3i$, another root is

    A. -1   B. +1   C. -13   D. +13

KEY (CORRECT ANSWERS)

1. D	6. A	11. A	16. A
2. C	7. B	12. C	17. A
3. D	8. C	13. B	18. D
4. C	9. C	14. C	19. B
5. C	10. A	15. D	20. B

SOLUTIONS TO PROBLEMS

1. {(-1,1), (-1,-1), (0,0), (1,1), (1,-1)} is NOT a function since it can be shown that for at least one given x, there corresponds more than one y-value. For example, when x = -1, y can equal either 1 or -1. (Ans. D)

2. $|2x-3| = 5$ means $2x-3 = 5$ or $2x-3 = -5$. Solving these equations, we get 4, -1. (Ans. C)

3. The midpoint of the segment connecting (-5, 6) and (1, 4) is (-2, 5). The line's slope = which is the same as the of the line $2y = 3x-5$. Equation of the required line is

   $y - 5 = \frac{3}{2}(x+2)$, which can be written as $3x - 2y + 16 = 0$. (Ans. D)

4. Rewrite as $(x^2+8x+16) + (y^2-10y+25) - 8 - 16 - 25 = 0$, which simplifies to $(x+4)^2 + (y-5)^2 = 49$. Thus, the radius = 7. (Ans. C)

5. The directrix is the x-axis. Any point (x, y) on the parabola must be the same distance to the x-axis as (x, y) is to (3, 4). Thus, $\sqrt{(x-3)^2 + (y-4)^2} = y$. This simplifies to $x^2 - 6x - 8y + 25 = 0$. (Ans. C)

6. The only possible rational roots of $x^3 + 3x - 5 = 0$ are 1, -1, 5, and -5; however, none of these numbers check the equation. By graphing, it can be seen that the one irrational root is +. (Ans. A)

7. $-\text{Log} x^a = \text{Log} x^{-a} = \text{Log} \frac{1}{x^a}$. However, $\text{Log}(-x^a)$ is not defined if $-x^a$ is a negative quantity. (Ans. B)

8. The maximum number of subsets associated with a set of n elements is 2^n. Thus, for a set of 8 elements, $2^8 = 256$ is the maximum number of subsets. (Ans. C)

9. 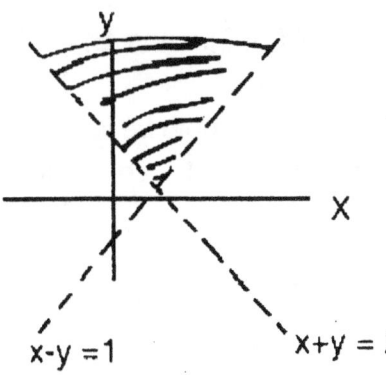 The shaded area represents the intersection of $x + y > 2$ and $x - y < 1$. (Ans. C)

10. $\{(x,y): y = |x-5|\}$ is a function since for each value of x, only one value of y is obtained. (Ans. A)

11. The intersection refers to the set of numbers common to both conditions, which is $-3 < x < 4$. (Ans. A)

5 (#2)

12. $\text{Log}\dfrac{(675)^3}{\sqrt[5]{576}} = 3\text{Log}\,675 - \dfrac{1}{5}\text{Log}\,576$. But, $675 = 5^2 \cdot 3^3$ and $576 = 2^6 \cdot 3^2$. Log $675 = 2$ Log $5 + 3$ Log $3 = 2.84$. Log $576 = 6$ Log $2 + 2$ Log $3 = 2.76$

    Thus, $3\text{Log}\,675 - \dfrac{1}{5}\text{Log}\,576 = 3(2.84) - \dfrac{1}{5}(2.76) = 7.97$. (Ans. C)

13. $c - b = b - a$ if a, b, c are in arithmetic progression. $b:c = c:d$ if b, c, d are in geometric progression.
    Thus, $a = 2b - c$, and since $b = c^2/d$, $a = 2c^2/d - c$ or $c(2c-d)/d$. (Ans. B)

14. $(a+b+c)^4 = [(a+b)+c]^4 = (a+b)^4 + 4(a+b)^3 c + 6(a+b)^2 c^2 + 4(a+b)c + c^4$, for which the number of terms $= 5+4+3+2+1 = 15$. (Ans. C)

15. Equating the real parts, $x + 2y = 5$. Equating the imaginary parts, $2x - y = -2$. Solving,

    $x = \dfrac{1}{5}$ and $y = \dfrac{12}{5}$. (Ans. D)

16. $6y < 7y + 4$ becomes $y > -4$ and $2 - 3y \geq -1$ becomes $y \leq 1$.
    The solution of the intersection is $-4 < y \leq 1$. (Ans. A)

17. The third term $= \dfrac{(\frac{1}{2})(-\frac{1}{2})(3)^{-\frac{3}{2}}(2x)^2}{2} = \dfrac{-\sqrt{3}x^2}{18}$. (Ans. A)

18. $Pi = A - A(1+i)^{-n}$. Then, $(A-Pi)/A = (1+i)^{-n}$.
    Log $(A-Pi)$ - Log $A = -n$ Log $(1+i)$. Finally,
    $n = [\text{Log } A - \text{Log } (A-iP)]/\text{Log } (1+i)$ (Ans. D)

19. If we allow $n = 1 \cdot n$ to be considered a factoring for an integer n, then either choice A or B is correct. However, if $1 \cdot n$ is disallowed, then choice B is the only correct answer. For example, if $a = 7$ and $b = 2$, $a - b = 5$ and (to illustrate) $5 = (4)(\dfrac{5}{4})$. (Ans. B)

20. A second root must be $2 - 3i$ and so $x - 2 - 3i$ and $x - 2 + 3i$ must both be factors of $x^3 - kx^2 + 17x - 13 = 0$. Now, the product of these two factors is $x^2 - 4x + 13$, so that the third factor must be $x - 1$. The last root is therefore 1.
    (The value of k is 5.) (Ans. B)

TEST 3

DIRECTIONS: Each question or incomplete statement is followed by several suggested answers or completions. Select the one that BEST answers the question or completes the statement. *PRINT THE LETTER OF THE CORRECT ANSWER IN THE SPACE AT THE RIGHT.*

1. Two numbers have an arithmetic mean of 17 and a geometric mean of 15. Hence, the quadratic equation of which the numbers are roots is

   A. $x^2 + 15x + 17 = 0$
   B. $x^2 + 34x + 225 = 0$
   C. $x^2 - 34x + 225 = 0$
   D. $x^2 - 17x + 255 = 0$

   1.____

2. Assume three consecutive integers represented by (x-1), x, and (x+1). Which one of the following represents an equation which will determine these integers, provided it is known that the sum of the reciprocals of the integers is 47/60?

   A. $47x^3 + 180x^2 + 47x - 60 = 0$
   B. $47x^3 + 39x^2 - 266x - 120 = 0$
   C. $47x^3 - 180x^2 - 47x + 60 = 0$
   D. $47x^3 - 39x^2 + 266x - 120 = 0$

   2.____

3. The equation of a line perpendicular to the line $3x + 2y = 5$ and having an x intercept of -3 is

   A. $3x + 2y + 9 = 0$
   B. $2x - 3y + 6 = 0$
   C. $2x - 3y = 9$
   D. $3x + 2y + 6 = 0$

   3.____

4. By Kepler's Law, the square of the time for a complete revolution of a planet is proportioned to the cube of its mean distance from the sun.
   If Planet X were 9 times as far from the sun as Earth, its time, in years, for one complete revolution would be

   A. 9
   B. 15
   C. 21
   D. 27

   4.____

5. Of the following, the illustration of a denumerable set is the set of _____ numbers.

   A. rational
   B. irrational
   C. real
   D. transcendental

   5.____

6. In the universe of real numbers, the one of the following in which the relation is a function is

   A. $\{(x,y) | x = y^2 - 1\}$
   B. $\{(x,y)\ y = x^2 + 1\}$
   C. $\{(x,y) | y = \pm\sqrt{16 - x^2}\}$
   D. $\{(x,y)\ y < x - 2)$

   6.____

7. If A = ( ) and B = ( ), then A Ω B, the
      (a, b, c)   (b, c, d)
   intersection of A and B, equals

   A. ( )
      (a,b,c,d)
   B. ( )
      (b,c)
   C. ⌀
   D. ( )
      (d)

   7.____

23

8. In a Venn diagram, shown at the right, in which the circle A represents the set of rhombi and B the set of rectangles, the section C represents the set of

   A. squares
   B. trapezoids
   C. parallelograms
   D. quadrilaterals

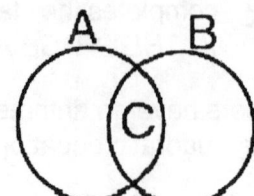

9. Of the following, the length of the vector that could CORRECTLY be used to represent the number $3 - i\sqrt{2}$ in the complex plane is _____.

   A. 11 B. $\sqrt{11}$ C. $3 - \sqrt{2}$ D. $\sqrt{5}$

10. Of the following, the statement which is FALSE is

    A. $\sqrt[b]{x^a} = x^{\frac{a}{b}}$
    B. $\sqrt[b]{x} \div \sqrt[b]{y} = \sqrt[b]{\frac{x}{y}}$
    C. $\sqrt[b]{x} + \sqrt[b]{y} = \sqrt[b]{x+y}$
    D. $\sqrt[b]{x} \cdot \sqrt[b]{y} = \sqrt[b]{xy}$

11. If $\frac{1}{x} - \frac{1}{y} = \frac{1}{z}$ then z equals

    A. $\frac{xy}{y-x}$ B. $\frac{xy}{y-x}$ C. $\frac{y-x}{xy}$ D. $\frac{x-y}{xy}$

12. The sum of the first n odd integers is

    A. $2n^2$ B. $2n^2 + 1$ C. n^2 D. $n^2 + 1$

13. The value of $5x^0 + 3x^{\frac{3}{4}} 4x^{-\frac{1}{2}}$ when $x = 16$, is

    A. 30 B. 33 C. 75 D. 105

14. Which one of the following characteristics is applicable to the equation $x + \frac{1}{x-1} = 1 + \frac{1}{x-1}$?

    A. It is equivalent to $x = 1$.
    B. It is equivalent to $x^2 - 2x + 1 = 0$.
    C. It has no roots.
    D. It has complex roots.

15. Since the period of a pendulum is proportional to the square root of its length, when the length of a pendulum is doubled, its period is

    A. doubled
    B. decreased between 50% and 60%
    C. increased between 40% and 50%
    D. quadrupled

16. The second term of the expansion of $(x+\frac{1}{x^3})^5$ is

    A. $5x^5$ B. $10x^5$ C. $5x^7$ D. $10x^7$

17. Which one of the following expresses the geometric mean (GM) CORRECTLY in terms of the arithmetic mean (AM) and the harmonic mean (HM)?

    A. $GM = \sqrt{AM \cdot HM^1}$
    B. $GM = \sqrt{AM \cdot HM}$
    C. $GM = AM \cdot HM$
    D. $GM = \overline{AM}^2 \, \overline{HM}^2$

18. If $\log_8 a = 2.5$ and $\log_2 b = 5$, then a, expressed in terms of b is

    A. $a = b^2$ B. $a = b^8$ C. $a = b^{\frac{3}{2}}$ D. $a = b^{\frac{5}{2}}$

19. Which one of the following statements concerning the method of interpolation by proportional parts is TRUE? It

    A. gives the exact value of the function
    B. assumes that the value of the function lies halfway between the two known values
    C. assumes that the curve between the two known points approximates closely the chord between these points
    D. is the process of estimating values of a function beyond the range of values of the variables actually plotted or calculated

20. Of the following, a representation of the product of three consecutive odd numbers where n is any positive integer is

    A. $n^3 - 4n$
    B. $n^3 - n$
    C. $n^3 + 6n^2 + 8n$
    D. $8n^3 + 3(4n^2-1) - 2n$

KEY (CORRECT ANSWERS)

1. C	6. B	11. A	16. A
2. C	7. B	12. C	17. B
3. B	8. A	13. A	18. C
4. D	9. B	14. C	19. C
5. A	10. C	15. C	20. C

SOLUTIONS TO PROBLEMS

1. Let x and 34-x be the two numbers whose mean is 17. Also, x:15 = 15:(34-x), which becomes $x^2 - 34x + 225 = 0$. (Ans. C)

2. $\frac{1}{x-1} + \frac{1}{x} + \frac{1}{x+1} = \frac{47}{60}$. $60x^2 + 60x + 60x^2 - 60 = 47x^3 - 47x$.
   This equation will simplify to $47x^3 - 180x^2 - 47x + 60 = 0$. (Ans. C)

3. A line perpendicular to $3x + 2y = 5$ has the general form of $2x - 3y = k$. Since this new line passes through (-3,0), k = -6. The desired equation is $2x - 3y + 6 = 0$. (Ans. B)

4. $\frac{t_1^2}{t_2^2} = \frac{d_1^3}{d_2^3}$. If $d_2 = 9 d_1$, then $d_1^3/d_1^3 = \frac{1}{729}$; since $t_1^2/t_2^2 = \frac{1}{729}$, $t_1/t_2 = \frac{1}{27}$. Thus, $t_2 = 27$ t. (Ans. D)

5. The set of rational numbers is denumerable, since each rational number can be placed in a one-to-one correspondence with the positive integers. The method is:

$$\frac{1}{1} \quad \frac{2}{1} \quad \frac{3}{1} \quad \frac{4}{1} \ldots$$

$$\frac{1}{2} \quad \frac{2}{2} \quad \frac{3}{2} \quad \frac{4}{2} \ldots$$

$$\frac{1}{3} \quad \frac{2}{3} \quad \frac{3}{3} \quad \frac{4}{3} \ldots$$

$$\frac{1}{4} \quad \frac{2}{4} \quad \frac{3}{4} \quad \frac{4}{4} \ldots$$

By counting in a diagonal fashion, each rational number will be accounted for. (Ans. A)

6. $y = x^2 + 1$ represents a function, since for each value of x, there is only one value of y. (Ans. B)

7. The intersection of (a, b, c) and (b, c, d) = (b, c), since the intersection consists only of elements common to both sets. (Ans. B)

8. C must contain the properties of both rhombi and rectangles, i.e., figures with four equal sides and four right angles. Only squares fulfill these conditions. (Ans. A)

9. The vector's length for $3 - \sqrt{2}i = \sqrt{3^2 + (\sqrt{2})^2} = \sqrt{11}$. (Ans. B)

10. $\sqrt[b]{x} + \sqrt[b]{y} \neq \sqrt[b]{x+y}$. This can be shown letting b = 2, x = 4, and y = 9.

    $\sqrt{4} + \sqrt{9} = 2 + 3 = 5 \neq \sqrt{13}$. (Ans. C)

11. $\dfrac{1}{x} - \dfrac{1}{y} = \dfrac{1}{z}$. Then, yz - xz = xy. Thus, z(y-x) = xy, and finally, z = xy/(y-x). (Ans. A)

12. $\sum_{x=1}^{n} 2x - 1 = 1 + 3 + 5 + ... + (2n - 1)$. Using the formula for an arithmetic progression,

    sum = $\dfrac{n}{2}(a + L)$ where a = 1st term, L = last term, sum = $\dfrac{n}{2}(1 + 2n - 1) = n^2$. (Ans. C)

13. $5 \cdot 16^0 + 3 \cdot 16^{\frac{3}{4}} + 4 \cdot 16^{-\frac{1}{2}} = (5)(1) + (3)(8) + 4(\dfrac{1}{4}) = 30$. (Ans. A)

14. Multiplying all terms by x-1, we get x(x-1) + 1 = x-1 + 1, which becomes $x^2 - 2x + 1 = 0$. The solution would be x = 1, but this value would make undefined. Thus, there exists no roots for the original equation. (Ans. C)

15. $P = K\sqrt{L}$ where P = period, K = constant, L = length. When L is doubled, This means that the period has been multiplied by $\sqrt{2}$ which represents an increase of about 41.4%. (Ans. C)

16. The second term $(5)(x^2)^4(\dfrac{1}{x^3}) = 5x^5$. (Ans. A)

17. Let $x_1, x_2, ..., x_n$ be the original n numbers. Then

    $AM = \dfrac{x_1 + ... + x_n}{n}$ $HM = n/(\dfrac{1}{x_1} + ... + \dfrac{1}{x_n})$. Now, $\sqrt{AM \cdot HM} = \sqrt{(x_1)(x_2)(...)(x_n)} = GM$

    (Ans. B)

18. $\log_8 a = 2.5$ means $a = 8^{2.5} = 2^{7.5} = 2^7\sqrt{2}$ or $128\sqrt{2}$ $\log_2 b = 5$ means $b = 2^5 = 32$. Since $a = 2^{7.5}$ and $b = 2^5$, $a = b^{\frac{3}{2}}$. (Ans. C)

19. Interpolation by proportional parts assumes the curve between two points can be approximated by the line segment joining these points. (Ans. C)

20. The three consecutive odd numbers are n, n+2, n+4. Then, $n(n+2)(n+4) = n^3 + 6n^2 + 8n$. (Ans. C)

TEST 4

DIRECTIONS: Each question or incomplete statement is followed by several suggested answers or completions. Select the one that BEST answers the question or completes the statement. *PRINT THE LETTER OF THE CORRECT ANSWER IN THE SPACE AT THE RIGHT.*

1. The fraction $\dfrac{a^2 + b^2 - c^2 + 2ab}{a^2 + c^2 - b^2 + 2ac}$ is (with suitable restrictions on the value of a, b, and c) reducible to which one of the following?

    A. $\dfrac{a+b+c}{a+b-c}$
    B. 1
    C. $\dfrac{a+b-c}{a-b+c}$
    D. None of these

2. Which one of the following choices represents the center and radius of the circle $x^2 + y^2 - 6x + 4y - 12 = 0$? Center

    A. (9, 4) radius 25
    B. (-3, 2) radius 5
    C. (3, -2) radius 5
    D. (-6, 4) radius 25

3. Which one of the following statements is TRUE concerning the graphs of the lines $5x + 4y = 3$ and $4x = 5y + 3$? They

    A. are parallel
    B. are identical
    C. intersect at right angles
    D. intersect at angles other than right angles

4. The number of distinct points common to the graphs of $x^2 + y^2 = 9$ and $y^2 = 9$ is

    A. zero
    B. one
    C. two
    D. four

5. Which one of the following choices gives the two asymptotes of $\dfrac{x^2}{25} - \dfrac{y^2}{9} = 1$?

    A. $-5x = 3y, 5x = -3y$
    B. $5x = 3y, 5x = -3y$
    C. $-3x = 5y, 3x = -5y$
    D. $3x = 5y, 3x = -5y$

6. Of the following, the quadratic equation whose roots are $(2+i)$ and $(2-i)$ is

    A. $x^2 - 4x + 5 = 0$
    B. $x^2 + 4x - 5 = 0$
    C. $2x^2 + 2x - 1 = 0$
    D. $2x^2 - 2x + 1 = 0$

7. Of the following, which one is a factor of $(x^{99} + 1)$?

    A. $(x+1)$
    B. $(x-1)$
    C. $(x+3)$
    D. $(x-3)$

8. Assume that an investment depreciates 20% of the original value during the first year, and then during the second year depreciates 80% of the value it had at the beginning of the second year.
   The uniform yearly rate of decrease that would have yielded the same resulting value at the end of two years is

   A. 40%   B. 47%   C. 50%   D. 60%

9. U represents the operation of the union of two sets. If A is the set of all numbers of the form 2n and B the set of all numbers of the form 2n+1, n being any integer, then A ∪ B is the set of all

   A. odd integers   B. even integers
   C. rational numbers   D. integers

10. Using a Venn diagram in which the circle A represents the set of rational numbers and B the set of non-terminating decimals, the section C represents the set of all

    A. transcendental numbers
    B. irrational numbers
    C. real numbers
    D. repeating decimals

11. The following *proof* was offered to show that 2=1. Suppose a and b are two names for the same number, then
    $a = b$
    $a^2 - b^2 = ab - b^2$
    $(a+b)(a-b) = b(a-b)$
    $a + b = b$
    $2b = b$
    $2 = 1$
    This *proof* is invalid because

    A. the commutative law does not hold for subtraction
    B. zero has no multiplicative inverse
    C. the commutative law does not hold for division
    D. the associative law does not hold for subtraction

12. Assume that for the first 90 miles of a 156 mile trip, a man averages 36 miles per hour. To achieve an average rate of 39 miles per hour for the entire trip, his average rate for the remainder of the trip, in miles per hour, must be

    A. 40   B. 42   C. 44   D. 48

13. A varies directly as the square of b and inversely as the cube of c. If b is tripled and c is doubled, the value of A is multiplied by

    A. 3/2   B. 6   C. 9/8   D. 2

14. $\dfrac{10}{\sqrt{3}} \times \dfrac{3\sqrt{2}}{\sqrt{5}}$ equals which one of the following?

    A. $2\sqrt{2}$ B. $10\sqrt{6}$ C. $6\sqrt{10}$ D. $2\sqrt{30}$

15. The root(s) of the equation $2\sqrt{x} = x - 3$ is (are)

    A. 9, 1   B. 9   C. -3, 1   D. 3, -1

16. Of the following, an equivalent sentence to
    $5(x+3) - 7 = 3x - 4(1+x)$ is

    A. $5x + 15 = 3x + 7 - 4 - 4x$
    B. $7x - 5x = 8 + 4$
    C. $5x + 3x - 4x = 7 - 15 - 4$
    D. $15 - 7 - 4 = 7x - 5x$

17. Of the following, the equation that expresses the relationship between the variables in the given table is

X	-1	2	3	-2
Y	-2	1	6	1

    is

    A. $y = 2x$
    C. $y = x + 3$
    B. $y - x^2 = -3$
    D. $y = x - 1$

18. If a certain wheel makes 100 revolutions in going a certain distance and a wheel a foot less in diameter makes 25 more revolutions in going the same distance, then the diameter of the larger wheel is _____ feet.

    A. 2   B. 2.5   C. 4   D. 5

19. If 4 quarts of a certain mixture of alcohol and water is at 50% strength, the number of quarts of water that must be added to make the alcohol strength of the new mixture 40% is

    A. 1   B. 2   C. 3   D. 10

20. When the price of a certain article increases from 20¢ to 25¢, the number of articles that can be purchased for d dollars decreases by

    A. $\dfrac{d}{100}$ B. $\dfrac{d}{20}$ C. $5b$ D. d

KEY (CORRECT ANSWERS)

1. C	6. A	11. B	16. A
2. C	7. A	12. C	17. B
3. C	8. D	13. C	18. B
4. C	9. D	14. D	19. A
5. D	10. D	15. B	20. D

SOLUTIONS TO PROBLEMS

1. Rewrite the fraction as $\dfrac{(a+b)^2 - c^2}{(a+c)^2 - b^2} = \dfrac{(a+b-c)(a+b+c)}{(a+c-b)(a+c+b)} = (a+b-c)/(a+c-b)$. (Ans. C)

2. Rewrite as $(x^2 - 6x + 9) + (y^2 + 4y + 4) - 9 - 4 - 12 = 0$, which becomes $(x-3)^2 + (y+2)^2 = 25$. The center is located at $(3,-2)$ and the radius is 5. (Ans. C)

3. The slopes of $5x+4y = 3$ and $4x = 5y+3$ are $-\dfrac{5}{4}$ and $\dfrac{4}{5}$. Since their slopes are negative reciprocals of each other, they intersect at right angles. (Ans. C)

4. The graphs of $x^2 + y^2 = 9$ and $y^2 = 9$ intersect at the two points $(0,3)$ and $(0,-3)$. (Ans. C)

5. Rewrite as $y = \pm \dfrac{3}{5}\sqrt{x^2 - 25}$. Then, the equations of the asymptotes are $y = \dfrac{3}{5}x$ and $y = -\dfrac{3}{5}x$. These can also be written as $3x = 5y$ and $3x = -5y$. (Ans. D)

6. The equation with roots $2 \pm i$ can be written as $[x-(2+i)][x-(2-i)] = 0$. This reduces to $x^2 - 4x + 5 = 0$. (Ans. A)

7. $x+1$ is a factor of $x^{99}+1$, since -1 is a root of $x^{99} + 1 = 0$. (Ans. A)

8. Let x = uniform yearly rate of decrease, expressed as a percent. Then,
$(1-\dfrac{x}{100})(1-\dfrac{x}{100}) = (.80)(.20) = .16$. Solving, we get $x = 60$. (Ans. D)

9. All integers can be represented by either $2n$ or $2n+1$, depending on whether the integer is even or odd. (Ans. D)

10. A repeating decimal is both non-terminating and rational. For example, $.\overline{6} = \dfrac{2}{3}$, which is rational. (Ans. D)

11. The fallacy of the argument occurs when one proceeds from line 3 to line 4. Dividing by $a-b$ means dividing by zero, but zero has no multiplicative inverse. (Ans. B)

12. Let x = average rate for the remaining 66 miles. Since total distance ÷ total time = average rate for entire trip, $156 \div (\dfrac{90}{36}+\dfrac{66}{x}) = 39$. This eqation could be simplified to $36x/(90x + 2376) = 39/156$. Solving, $x = 44$. (Ans. C)

6 (#4)

13. $A = kb^2/c^3$, where k = constant. Let b be replaced by 3b and c be replaced by 2c. Then, $A = k(3b)^2/(2c)^3$ or $A = \frac{9}{8}kb^2/c^3$. Thus, the new value of A has been obtained by multiplying the original A value by $\frac{9}{8}$.

14. $\frac{10}{\sqrt{3}} \cdot \frac{3\sqrt{2}}{\sqrt{5}} = \frac{30\sqrt{2}}{\sqrt{15}} = \frac{30\sqrt{2}}{\sqrt{15}} \cdot \frac{\sqrt{15}}{\sqrt{15}} = \frac{30\sqrt{30}}{15} = 2\sqrt{3}$. (Ans. D)

15. $2\sqrt{x} = x - 3$ Squaring both sides, $4x = x^2 - 6x + 9$. This becomes $x^2 - 10x + 9 = 0$, which factors as $(x-9)(x-1) = 0$. Only 9 is a root (1 does not check the original equation). (Ans. B)

16. $5(x+3) - 7 = 3x - 4(1+x)$ is equivalent to $5x + 15 - 7 = 3x - 4 - 4x$, which is equivalent to $5x + 15 = 3x + 7 - 4 - 4x$. (Ans. A)

17. Since 4 ordered pairs are given, let $y = Ax^3 + Bx^2 + Cx + D$. By substituting ordered pairs, we get the following: $-2 = -A + B - C + D$, $1 = 8A + 4B + 2C + D$. $6 = 27A + 9B + 3C + D$, and $1 = -8A + 4B - 2C + D$.
Solving, A = 0, B = 1, C = 0, and D = -3.
Thus, $y = x^2 - 3$ or $y - x^2 = -3$. (Ans. B)

18. Let D = diameter of larger wheel, D - .5 = diameter of smaller wheel. The respective circumferences are πD and $\pi D - .5\pi$. Then, $100\pi D = 125(\pi D - .5\pi)$. Solving, D = 2.5 ft. (Ans. B)

19. The original mixture has 2 quarts each of alcohol and water. Let x = amount of water added.
Then $\frac{2}{4+x} = .40$. Solving, x = 1 (Ans. A)

20. For d dollars, $\frac{100d}{20} = 5d$ articles can be bought, but when the price per article increases to 25¢, the purchasing power of d dollars is $\frac{100d}{25} = 4d$ articles. The actual decrease is d articles. (Ans. D)

EXAMINATION SECTION
TEST 1

DIRECTIONS: Each question or incomplete statement is followed by several suggested answers or completions. Select the one that BEST answers the question or completes the statement. *PRINT THE LETTER OF THE CORRECT ANSWER IN THE SPACE AT THE RIGHT.*

1. $\log(x^2-y^2)$ is equal to which one of the following?

   A. $2 \log x - 2 \log y$
   B. $\log(x+y) + \log(x-y)$
   C. $2 \log(x-y)$
   D. None of the above

2. If $\log x \geq \log 2 + 1/2 \log x$, then

   A. $x \geq 2$ B. $x \leq 2$ C. $x \leq 4$ D. $x \geq 4$

3. The graph of $y > x$ has points in quadrant(s)

   A. I *only*
   B. I and II *only*
   C. I, II, and III *only*
   D. I and III *only*

4. If $3x + 5 > x$ and n is a negative integer, an equivalent sentence is

   A. $n(3x+5) > nx$
   B. $3x+5+n < n+x$
   C. $n-(3x+5) > n-x$
   D. $\dfrac{3x+5}{n} < \dfrac{x}{n}$

5. The statement that is mathematically CORRECT is

   A. $\sin 2x = 2 \sin x \cos x$ for all values of x
   B. $x^0 = 1$ for all values of x
   C. $\sqrt{x^2} = x$ for all values of x
   D. $\dfrac{x^2-1}{x-1} = x+1$ for all values of x

6. If n is an integer, then $\left(-\dfrac{1}{\sqrt{-1}}\right)^{4n+5}$ is equal to

   A. 1   B. -1   C. i   D. -i

7. If $x + y = 2xy$, then $\dfrac{1}{x} + \dfrac{1}{y}$ equals

   A. 1
   B. 2
   C. 3
   D. none of the above

8. Two roots of the equation $x^3 + cx + d = 0$ are -1 and -2. The third root is

 A. 1 B. -3 C. 3 D. -7

9. A train makes a trip between two towns at the rate of a miles per hour and makes the return trip on the same track at the rate of b miles per hour.
The AVERAGE rate for the round trip is

 A. $\dfrac{2ab}{a+b}$ B. $\dfrac{a+b}{2}$ C. $\sqrt{ab}$ D. $\dfrac{2(a+b)}{ab}$

10. An automobile radiator contains 15 quarts of a 20% solution of antifreeze. How many quarts of the solution should be drained from the radiator and replaced with an equal amount of pure anti-freeze to raise the concentration to 50%?

 A. $4\dfrac{1}{2}$ B. $4\dfrac{3}{8}$ C. $5\dfrac{5}{8}$ D. $7\dfrac{1}{2}$

11. If f(x) and g(x) are two functions defined by $f(x) = 2x+1$ and $g(x) = x^2 - 2$, then g[f(x)] is

 A. $x^2 + 2x - 1$ B. $4x^2 + 4x - 1$
 C. $2x^2 - 3$ D. $4x^2 + 4x + 1$

12. If $\log 4x^5 - \log x^4 + \log 5 = 4$. the value of x is

 A. $\dfrac{1}{5}$ B. 5 C. 50 D. 500

13. The parabola whose equation is $(y-1)^2 = 4(x+2)$ has

 A. its vertex at (2, -1)
 B. its focus at (2, 1)
 C. a directrix whose equation is x = -3
 D. a relative minimum point

14. The equation $x^9 + 16x^3 + 64 = 0$ has _____ positive root(s), _____ negative root(s), and _____ imaginary roots.

 A. 2; 1; 6 B. 1; 0; 8 C. 0; 1; 8 D. 8; 1; 0

15. The coefficient of the fifth term of the expansion of $(x+1)^8$ is equal to

 A. 28 B. 56 C. $8C4$ D. $8C5$

16. One of the cube roots of -8i is

 A. -2i B. $\sqrt{3}+i$ C. $\sqrt{3}-i$ D. $-\sqrt{3}+i$

17. $\dfrac{x}{x^2-1} > 0$ if and only if

   A. $x > 1$ or $-1 < x < 0$ B. $x > 1$
   C. $|x| > 1$ D. $|x| < 1$

18. The domain of $f(x) = \dfrac{1}{\sqrt{9-x^2}}$, if $f(x)$ is real, is

   A. $x < 3$ B. $|x| < 3$
   C. $|x| < 3$ D. $|x| > 3$

19. The value of $(1+i)^4$ is

   A. $-4 + 8i$ B. $4 - 8i$ C. -4 D. 4

20. The sum of the reciprocals of the roots of the equation $ax^2 + bx + c = 0$ will be

   A. $-\dfrac{a}{b}$ B. $-\dfrac{b}{a}$ C. $-\dfrac{b}{c}$ D. $-\dfrac{c}{b}$

KEY (CORRECT ANSWERS)

1. B   11. B
2. A   12. D
3. C   13. C
4. D   14. C
5. A   15. C

6. C   16. C
7. B   17. A
8. C   18. B
9. A   19. C
10. C   20. C

SOLUTIONS TO PROBLEMS

1. $\text{Log}(x^2-y^2) = \text{Log}[(x+y)(x-y)] = \text{Log}(x+y) + \text{Log}(x-y)$.
   (Ans. B)

2. $\text{Log } 2 + \frac{1}{2}\text{Log } x = \text{Log } 2x^{\frac{1}{2}}$. Now, since $\text{Log } x \geq \text{Log } 2x^{1/2}$, $x \geq 2x^{1/2}$. This becomes $x^2 \geq 2x$ which is solved as $x \geq 2$.
   (Ans. A)

3. The dotted line represents $y = x$. The shaded area represents $y > x$ and it occupies parts of quadrants I, III, and all of quadrant II. (Ans. C)

4. If $3x + 5 > x$ and $n < 0$, then $\frac{3x+5}{n} < \frac{x}{n}$, since dividing by a negative number reverses the inequality. (Ans. D)

5. $x^0 = 1$ is NOT true if $x = 0$, since 0^0 is undefined. $\sqrt{x^2} = x$ only if $x \geq 0$, and if x is negative. $\frac{x^2-1}{x-1}$ is undefined if $x = 1$. However, $\sin 2x = 2 \sin x \cos x$ for all x. (Ans. A)

6. $\frac{1}{-\sqrt{-1}} = \frac{1}{-i} = \frac{1}{-i} \cdot \frac{i}{i} = \frac{i}{-i^2} = i$. Now, i runs in cycles of 4 as: i, $i^2 = -1$, $i^3 = -i$, $i^4 = 1$. If n is integral, then $4n+5$, when divided by 4, leaves a remainder of 1. This corresponds to i. (Ans. C)

7. $\frac{1}{x} + \frac{1}{y} = \frac{y+x}{xy} = \frac{2xy}{xy} = 2$. (Ans. B)

8. Since -1 is a root, $(-1)^3 + c(-1) + d = 0$. Also, since -2 is a root, $(-2)^3 + c(-2) + d = 0$. Solving, $c = -7$, $d = -6$. Now, $x^3 - 7x - 6 = (x+1)(x+2)(x-3)$; thus 3 is the last root. (Ans. C)

9. Let $x =$ distance each way. Time for first trip $= \frac{x}{a}$. Time for second trip $= \frac{x}{b}$. Average rate = total distance total time $= 2x \div (\frac{x}{a} + \frac{x}{b}) = 2x \div ([ax + bx]/ab) = 2ab/(a+b)$. (Ans. A)

10. Let x = amount of solution drained. At this point, there are 15-x quarts of the solution and 3-.20x quarts of antifreeze (recognize that for every quart of solution drained, only one-fifth of a quart of antifreeze is drained).
    Now add the x quarts of antifreeze, so that the solution again becomes 15 quarts and the amount of antifreeze = 3-.20x + x. Finally, 3-.20x + x = .50(15), whereby $x = 5\frac{5}{8}$.
    (Ans. C)

11. $g[f(x)] = g(2x+1) = (2x+1)^2 - 2 = 4x^2 + 4x + 1 - 2 = 4x^2 + 4x - 1$. (Ans. B)

12. $\text{Log } 4x^5 = \text{Log } 4 + 5 \text{ Log } x$ and $\text{Log } x^4 = 4 \text{ Log } x$.
    Thus, Log 4+5 Log x - 4 Log x + Log 5=4. Log x + Log 4 + Log 5=4, Log 20x = 4.
    This implies $10^4 = 20x$, x = 500. (Ans. D)

13. The parabola $(y-k)^2 = 4p(x-h)$ has a vertex at (h,k), directrix is x = h-p and focus of (h+p, k). For the equation $(y-1)^2 = 4(x+2)$, the vertex is (-2,1), directrix is the equation x = -3, and focus is (-1,1). (Ans. C)

14. Since all signs of the terms are positive, there can be no positive roots. Only choice C could be correct. (Ans. C)

15. Fifth coeff. $= \frac{8 \cdot 7 \cdot 6 \cdot 5}{1 \cdot 2 \cdot 3 \cdot 4} = 8 \text{ C } 4$. (Ans. C)

16. $(-8i)^{\frac{1}{3}} = [8(\cos 270° + i \sin 270°)]^{\frac{1}{3}} = 2(\cos 90° + i \sin 90°)$, $2(\cos 210° + i \sin 210°)$, and $2(\cos 330° + i \sin 330°)$. This leads to the three roots: $2i$, $-\sqrt{3} - i$, and $\sqrt{3} - i$. (Ans. C)

17. Case 1: Both x > 0 and $x^2-1 > 0$, satisfied by x > 1.
    Case 2: Both x < 0 and $x^2-1 < 0$, satisfied by -1 < x < 0. (Ans. A)

18. $\sqrt{9-x^2} > 0$, in order for f(x) to be real. Thus, $9-x^2 > 0$, solved by -3 < x < 3 or |x| < 3. (Ans. B)

19. $(1+i)^4 = 1 + 4i + 6i^2 + 4i^3 + i^4 = 1 + 4i - 6 - 4i + 1 = -4$. (Ans. C)

20. Let R_1, R_2 be the roots. Then, $\frac{1}{R_1} + \frac{1}{R_2} = \frac{R_2 + R_1}{R_1 R_2} = \frac{-\frac{b}{a}}{\frac{c}{a}} = -\frac{b}{c}$ (Ans. C)

TEST 2

DIRECTIONS: Each question or incomplete statement is followed by several suggested answers or completions. Select the one that BEST answers the question or completes the statement. *PRINT THE LETTER OF THE CORRECT ANSWER IN THE SPACE AT THE RIGHT.*

1. $\log 4 \div \log \frac{1}{4}$ is equal to

    A. -1   B. 0   C. 2 log 2   D. log 2

2. $(16)^{(-2)^{-2}}$ has the SAME value as

    A. $\frac{1}{16^4}$ B. $\frac{1}{2}$ C. 2   D. 16^4

3. Given the equation in determinant form $\begin{vmatrix} 2x & 1 \\ x & x \end{vmatrix} = 3$, the equation is satisfied for _____ values of x.

    A. two real   B. two imaginary
    C. no   D. all real

4. A purse contains one penny, one nickel, one dime, one quarter, and one half-dollar. How many different sums of money can be formed using one or more of these coins?

    A. 5   B. 16   C. 31   D. 32

5. The solution set of the equation $x^3 - 5x + 6 = 2x^2$ is

    A. {-1, 2, -3}   B. {1, -2, -3}   C. {-1, 1, -6}   D. {1, -2, 3}

6. The graph of $x^2 - 4y^2 = 0$ is a(n)

    A. hyperbola   B. parabola
    C. ellipse   D. pair of straight lines

7. The time required for one oscillation of a pendulum is given by the formula $t = 2\pi\sqrt{\frac{L}{G}}$, where L is the length and G is a constant.
   In order to DOUBLE the time for one oscillation, the length of the pendulum should be

    A. halved   B. doubled
    C. squared   D. quadrupled

8. The infinite repeating decimal $2.\overline{52}$ is equal to

    A. $2\frac{13}{25}$ B. $2\frac{14}{33}$ C. $2\frac{50}{99}$ D. $2\frac{52}{99}$

1.___

2.___

3.___

4.___

5.___

6.___

7.___

8.___

9. The distance travelled by a falling body is given by the formula $S = 16t^2$, where S is the distance, in feet, and t is the time in seconds.
   During the fifth second, a falling body will travel _____ feet.
   A. 80   B. 144   C. 256   D. 400

10. If $g = \dfrac{K}{d^2}$, then d varies

   A. *directly* as the square root of g
   B. *inversely* as the square of g
   C. *inversely* as the square root of g
   D. *directly* as the square of g

11. The set of values satisfying the inequality $\left|\dfrac{5-x}{3}\right| < 2$ is

   A. $1 < x < 11$
   B. $-1 < x < 11$
   C. $x < -1$ or $x > 11$
   D. $x < 1$ or $x > 11$

12. If $\log_{10}(x^2 - x - 2) = 1$, then x is equal to

   A. 4 or -3   B. -1 or 2   C. -4 or 3   D. 1 or -2

13. If the discriminant of the equation $ax^2 + 2bx + c = 0$ is equal to zero, then it is ALWAYS true that

   A. a, b, c form an arithmetic progression
   B. a, b, and c form a geometric progression
   C. b is always negative
   D. a and c are equal

14. If the square of a two digit number is DECREASED by the square of the number formed by reversing the digits, then the result is NOT ALWAYS divisible by

   A. 9
   B. the product of the digits
   C. the sum of the digits
   D. the difference of the digits

15. Fifteen girls left a mixed group of boys and girls. There remained two boys for each girl. After this, 45 boys leave the group, and there were 5 girls for each boy. The number of girls in the ORIGINAL group must have been

   A. 29   B. 40   C. 43   D. 50

16. The repeating decimal $0.\overline{247}$ may be represented by

   A. $\dfrac{2470}{9999}$
   B. $\dfrac{247247}{1,000,000}$
   C. $\dfrac{247}{999}$
   D. $\dfrac{247}{1000}$

17. Let x represent a positive real number. Consider the following statements:

    I. $\sqrt{-x} = -\sqrt{x}$

    II. $\sqrt[3]{-x} = -\sqrt[3]{x}$

    The CORRECT answer is:

    A. I and II are *false*
    B. I is *false* and II is *true*
    C. I is *true* and II is *false*
    D. I and II are *true*

18. If a and b are real numbers, then $\sqrt{a}\sqrt{b}$ is NOT equal to $\sqrt{ab}$ when

    A. a > 0 and b > 0
    B. a > 0 and b < 0
    C. a < 0 and b = 0
    D. a < 0 and b < 0

19. If $x^7 - 7x - 56$ is divided by x-2, the remainder is

    A. 28
    B. 58
    C. 86
    D. -170

20. Which of the following equations has 0 and 1+i as elements in its solution set?

    A. $x^2 - 2x + 2 = 0$
    B. $x^3 - 2x^2 + 2x = 0$
    C. $x^2 + 2x - 2 = 0$
    D. $x^3 + 2x^2 - 2x = 0$

KEY (CORRECT ANSWERS)

1. A
2. C
3. A
4. C
5. D

6. A
7. D
8. D
9. B
10. C

11. B
12. A
13. B
14. B
15. B

16. C
17. B
18. D
19. B
20. B

SOLUTIONS TO PROBLEMS

1. $\text{Log } 4 \div \text{Log } \frac{1}{4} = \text{Log } 4 \div [\text{Log } 1 - \text{Log } 4]$, and since $\text{Log } 1 = 0$, the result is $\text{Log } 4 \div -\text{Log } 4 = -1$. (Ans. A)

2. $(-2)^{-2} = \frac{1}{(-2)^2} = \frac{1}{4}$. Thus, $(16)^{(-2)^{-2}} = (16)^{(-2)^{-2}} = (16)^{\frac{1}{4}} = 2$ (Ans. C)

3. The value of the determinant $\begin{vmatrix} 2x & 1 \\ x & x \end{vmatrix}$ is $2x^2 - x$.

   Now, if $2x^2 - x = 3$, x can be -1 or $1\frac{1}{2}$, which are 2 real values. (Ans. A)

4. The number of different sums of money = $_5C_1 + {}_5C_2 + {}_5C_3 + {}_5C_4 + {}_5C_5 = 5 + 10 + 10 + 5 + 1 = 31$. Then, symbol $_nC_x$ means the number of combinations of n items taken x at a time. (Ans. C)

5. The expression $x^3 - 2x^2 - 5x + 6$ factors into $(x-1)(x+2)(x-3)$. Setting this product = to 0 gives roots of 1, -2, and 3. (Ans. D)

6. Any equation which can be written as $\frac{x^2}{a^2} - \frac{y^2}{b^2} = 1$ is a hyperbola. (a and b are constants.) Now, $x^2 - 4y^2 = 0$ can be written as $\frac{x^2}{4} - \frac{y^2}{1} = 0$, so that $a = 2$ and $b = 1$. (Ans. A)

7. Given $t = 2\pi \sqrt{\frac{L}{G}}$, in order to double the t value, the length L should be quadrupled. When L is replaced by 4L, the right side of the equation becomes. This is double the original t value. (Ans. D)

8. Let $N = .\overline{52}$. Then, and by subtraction $99N = 52$. Thus, $N = \frac{52}{99}$, and so $2.\overline{25} = 2 = \frac{52}{99}$. (Ans. D)

9. The distance traveled in 5 seconds = $16(5^2) = 400$ ft. The distance traveled in 4 seconds = $16(4^2) = 256$ ft.
   Thus, the distance traveled ONLY during the fifth second = $400 - 256 = 144$ ft. (Ans. B)

10. From $g = \frac{K}{d^2}$, we can get $d = \sqrt{\frac{K}{g}} = K'/\sqrt{g}$, where ($K, K'$ are constants.) This means that d varies inversely as the square root of g. (Ans. C)

11. Rewrite as $-2 < \dfrac{5-x}{3} < 2$, and the solution becomes $-1 < x < 11$ (Ans. B)

12. $\log_{10}(x^2-x-2) = 1$ implies $x^2 - x - 2 = 10$ or $(x-4)(x+3) = 0$. Solving, $x = 4$ or $x = -3$. (Ans. A)

13. Discriminant $= b^2 - 4ac$ in the equation $ax^2 + bx + c = 0$. Here, the discriminant $= 4b^2 - 4ac$. If this expression equals 0, $b^2 - ac = 0$. Thus, $b^2 = ac$ and so a, b, c form a geometric progression, since $\dfrac{c}{b} = \dfrac{b}{a}$. (Ans. B)

14. Let $10t+u$ be the original number. Then, $(10t+u)^2 - (10u+t)^2 = 99t^2 - 99u^2$, which is NOT necessarily divisible by the product of the digits, tu. Note that $99t^2 - 99u^2 = 99(t+u)(t-u)$ so that the quantities mentioned in selections A, B, and C are factors (can be divided into) of $99t^2 - 99u^2$. (Ans. B)

15. Let x = original number of girls. When 15 girls left, x-15 was the number of girls left, and 2(x-15) = the number of boys. When 45 boys then left, 2(x-15) - 45 = 2x - 75 = number of boys remaining. Since there were now five times as many girls as boys, we have x-15 = 5(2x-75). Solving, x = 40. (Ans. B)

16. Let $N = .\overline{247}$. Then, $1000N = 247.\overline{247}$. By subtraction, $999N = 247$ and so $N = 247/999$. (Ans. C)

17. As a numerical example, $\sqrt{-4} = 2i \neq -\sqrt{4}$, but $\sqrt[3]{-27} = -3 = -\sqrt[3]{27}$. (Ans. B)

18. $\sqrt{a} \cdot \sqrt{b} \neq \sqrt{ab}$ when both a and b are negative.
    Example: $\sqrt{-9} \cdot \sqrt{-25} = (3i)(5i) = 15i^2 = -15 \neq \sqrt{-9}\sqrt{-25} = \sqrt{225} = 15$. (Ans. D)

19. By the Remainder Theorem, the remainder is the value of $x^7 - 7x - 56$ when x is replaced by 2. This value is $2^7 - 7(2) - 56 = 58$. (Ans. B)

20. Since 1+i is one of the roots, 1-i must also be a root. Now, if 0, 1+i, and 1-i are the roots, then the equation with these roots can be written: $x(x-[1+i])(x-[1-i]) = 0$. This becomes $x^3 - 2x^2 + 2x = 0$. (Ans. B)

TEST 3

DIRECTIONS: Each question or incomplete statement is followed by several suggested answers or completions. Select the one that BEST answers the question or completes the statement. *PRINT THE LETTER OF THE CORRECT ANSWER IN THE SPACE AT THE RIGHT.*

1. The solution set for $x^2 - 2x - 3 < 0$ is

   A. $\{x \mid x < -1\}$
   B. $\{x \mid x > 3\}$
   C. $\{x \mid -1 < x < 3\}$
   D. $\{x \mid x < -1 \text{ or } x > 3\}$

2. If $\left|\dfrac{3(3x-5)}{2}\right| = 15$ then the solution set for x is

   A. $\{5\}$ B. $\{5, -5\}$ C. $\{-5, \dfrac{5}{3}\}$ D. $\{5, -\dfrac{5}{3}\}$

3. The graph of $\{(x,y) \mid ax^2 + by^2 = c\}$, where a, b, and c are real numbers, CANNOT be a(n)

   A. circle
   B. parabola
   C. ellipse
   D. hyperbola

4. An equation of the locus of a point whose distance from the origin is twice its distance from the point (3, 0) is

   A. $x^2 + y^2 + 8x + 12 = 0$
   B. $x^2 + y^2 - 8x + 12 = 0$
   C. $x^2 + y^2 + 12x + 18 = 0$
   D. $x^2 + y^2 - 12x + 18 = 0$

5. Which of the following expressions is equal to $\log_2 10$?

   A. $\dfrac{1}{\log_{10} 2}$ B. $\dfrac{10}{\log_{10} 2}$ C. $1 - \log_{10} 2$ D. $\log_{10} 2$

6. Consider the four relations:
   - I. $\{(x,y) \mid x+y = 6\}$
   - II. $\{(x,y) \mid x+y^2 = 6\}$
   - III. $\{(x,y) \mid x^2+y - 6\}$
   - IV. $\{(x,y) \mid x^2+y^2 = 6\}$

   Of the four relations, those which are also functions are

   A. I, II B. I, III C. I, IV D. II, III

7. If A represents the set of algebraic numbers and R represents the set of real numbers, then a number which belongs to $A \cap R$ is

   A. e B. π C. i D. $\sqrt{5}$

8. Let us define $a*b$ to mean $\dfrac{a - 2b}{3}$ where a and b represent integers. If $a = 15$, $b = 6$, and $c = 3$, then $a*(b*c)$ equals

45

A. 5   B. 0   C. $-\dfrac{5}{3}$ D. -2

9. The equations of two lines are, respectively, $a_1x + b_1y = c_1$ and $a_2x + b_2y = c$. The two lines are parallel IF and ONLY IF

   A. $a_1b_2 - a_2b_1 \neq 0$ and $c_1b_2 - c_2b_1 \neq 0$

   B. $c_1b_2 - c_2b_1 \neq 0$ and $c_1b_2 - c_2b_1 = 0$

   C. $c_1b_2 - c_2b_1 = 0$ and $c_1b_2 - c_2b_1 \neq 0$

   D. $a_1b_2 - a_2b_1 = 0$ and $c_1b_2 - c_2b_1 = 0$

10. Let r_1 and r_2 be the roots of the equation $x^2 - bx + c = 0$. If r_1^2 and r_2^2 are the roots of equation $x^2 - dx + e = 0$, then d equals

    A. $b^2 + c^2$ B. $b^2 + 2c$ C. $b^2 - 2c$ D. b^2

11. A trip from A to B was made at a speed of r km/hr. The return trip from B to A along the same route was made at a speed of 3r km/hr. The average speed, in km/hr, for the entire trip was

    A. $\dfrac{5}{4}r$ B. $\dfrac{3}{2}r$ C. $2r$ D. $\dfrac{5}{2}r$

12. In calculating an average, English and Social Studies are weighted at 3 each, Mathematics is weighted at 2, and Music is weighted at 1.
    If a student receives a grade of 82 in English, 85 in Mathematics, and 91 in Music, what grade MUST he achieve in Social Studies to attain an average of 85?

    A. 82   B. 84   C. 86   D. 87

13. The roots of the quadratic equation $4 = \dfrac{2}{x^2} + \dfrac{7}{x}$ are

    A. imaginary
    B. real, unequal, and rational
    C. real, unequal, and irrational
    D. real, equal, and rational

14. The arithmetic mean of two numbers is 17, and their geometric mean is 15. A quadratic equation of which the numbers are roots is

    A. $x^2 + 34x - 225 = 0$ B. $x^2 + 17x - 15 = 0$
    C. $x^2 - 34x + 225 = 0$ D. $x^2 - 17x + 15 = 0$

15. If $3x^4 - 3$ is factored completely, then the result is   15.____

    A. $3(x^2-1)(x2+1)$ B. $3(x+1)(x+1)(x-1)(x-1)$

    C. $(3x+3)(x-1)(x^2+1)$ D. $3(x^2+1)(x+1)(x-1)$

16. If then a solution for b would be   16.____

    A. $b = \dfrac{2S-2a}{m}$ B. $b = \dfrac{2m}{S} - a$ C. $b = \dfrac{2S-am}{m}$ D. $b = 2s-am$

17. The solution set of $x^2 = 2$ is NOT the empty set if the domain of x is either the   17.____

    A. real numbers or the rational numbers
    B. real numbers or the complex numbers
    C. irrational numbers or the rational numbers
    D. irrational numbers or the imaginary numbers

18. H varies directly as x and inversely as d^2.   18.____
If H = 20 when x = 2 and d = 3, find H when x = 4 and d = 6.

    A. 10   B. 20   C. 40   D. 90

19. Two of the roots of $x^3 + px + q = 0$ are 2 and 3.   19.____
The third root is

    A. 5   B. -5   C. 6   D. -6

20. If $\log_{10} 12 = a$ and $\log_{10} 2 = b$, then $\log_{10} 60$ equals   20.____

    A. a-b+1   B. 5a   C. 4a + 6b   D. $\dfrac{10a}{b}$

KEY (CORRECT ANSWERS)

1. C
2. D
3. B
4. B
5. A

6. B
7. D
8. A
9. C
10. C

11. B
12. C
13. B
14. C
15. D

16. C
17. B
18. A
19. B
20. A

SOLUTIONS TO PROBLEMS

1. $x^2 - 2x - 3 = (x-3)(x+1) < 0$
   Case 1: $x - 3 < 0$ and $x + 1 > 0$, which implies $-1 < x < 3$
   Case 2: $x - 3 > 0$ and $x + 1 < 0$, which is impossible Final answer: $-1 < x < 3$.
   (Ans. C)

2. Case 1: $3(3x-5)/2 = 15$, which yields $x = 5$
   Case 2: $3(3x-5)/2 = -15$, from which $x = -\frac{5}{3}$.
   (Answer: $\{5, -\frac{5}{3}\}$
   (Ans. D)

3. In the equation of a parabola, one variable is quadratic and the other variable must be linear. (Ans. B)

4. Let (x, y) be a general point. Then, $\sqrt{x^2+y^2} = 2\sqrt{(x-3)^2+y^2}$, which reduces to $x^2+y^2-8x+12=0$. (Ans. B)

5. Let $x = \log_2 10$. Then, $2^x = 10$, from which $x \log_{10} 2 = \log_{10} 10$ or $x \log_{10} 2 = 1$. Thus, $x = \frac{1}{\log_{10} 2}$. (Ans. A)

6. To be a function, each value of x must correspond to exactly one y. Only equations I and III are functions. (Ans. B)

7. Only $\sqrt{5} = 5^{\frac{1}{2}}$ is algebraic. Both e and π are transcendental. i is imaginary. (Ans. D)

8. $b*c = (b-2c)/3 = [6-2(3)]/3 = 0$. Now, $a*0 = [a-2(0)]/3 = (15-0)/3 = 5$. (Ans. A)

9. Slope of the first line $= -\frac{a_1}{b_1}$ Slope of the second line $= -\frac{a_2}{b_2}$.
   In order for the two lines to be parallel, $-\frac{a_1}{b_1} = -\frac{a_2}{b_2}$, which implies $a_1 b_2 - a_2 b_1 = 0$. Since the y intercepts must be different, $\frac{c_1}{b_1} \neq \frac{c_2}{b_2}$. This means $c_1 b_2 - c_2 b_1 \neq 0$. (Ans. C)

10. Since R_1, R_2 are roots of $x^2 - bx + c = 0$, we know that $R_1 + R_2 = b$ and $(R_1)(R_2) = c$. Likewise, we have R_1^2, R_2^2 are roots of $x^2 - dx + e = 0$; thus, $R_1^2 + R_2^2 = d$ and $(R_1^2)(R_2^2) = e$. Now, $R_1^2 + 2R_1R_2 + R_2^2 = (R_1 + R_2)^2 = b^2$ and since $2R_1R_2 = 2c$, we have $R_1^2 + 2C + R_2^2 = b^2$ or $R_1^2 + R_2^2 = b^2 - 2c$. This means $d = b^2 - 2c$. (Ans. C)

11. Average speed = total distance/total time $= (x+x)/(\frac{x}{r} + \frac{x}{3r}) = 2x/\frac{4x}{3r} = \frac{3}{2}r$. Here, x = distance from A to B. (Ans. B)

12. Let x = required score. Then, $\frac{(82)(3) + (x)(3) + (85)(2) + (91)(1)}{9} = 85$. Solving, $x = 86$. (Ans. C)

13. Convert the equation to $4x^2 - 7x - 2 = 0$, which becomes $(4x+1)(x-2) = 0$. The answers, 2 and $-\frac{1}{4}$, are real, unequal, and rational. (Ans. B)

14. Let x = 1st number, y = 2nd number. Then, $\frac{x+y}{2} = 17$ and $xy = 225$. By substitution of $y = 34-x$ from the first equation into the second equation, $x(34-x) = 225$. This becomes $x^2 - 34x + 225 = 0$. (Ans. C)

15. $3x^4 - 3 = 3(x^4 - 1) = 3(x^2 + 1)(x+1)(x-1)$. (Ans. D)

16. Dividing both sides by $\frac{1}{2}m$, $\frac{2S}{m} = a + b$, so $b = \frac{2S}{m} - a$ or, equivalently, $b = \frac{2S - am}{m}$. (Ans. C)

17. $x^2 = 2$ has roots $\pm\sqrt{2}$, provided the domain of x will include irrational numbers. (Ans. B)

18. $H = \frac{Kx}{d^2}$, where K is a constant. When $H = 20$, $x = 2$, $d = 3$, so $K = (20)(9)/2 = 90$. Thus, we can write $H = 90x/d^2$. Now, $H = (90)(4)/36 = 10$. (Ans. A)

19. Since 2, 3 are roots, $x-2$, $x-3$ are factors. Also, by the substitution of 2, 3 for x, we get $8 + 2p + q = 0$ and $27 + 3p + q = 0$. Solving, $p = -19$, $q = 30$. The equation becomes $x^3 - 19x + 30 = 0$. Let R = third root. Then, $(x-2)(x-3)(x-R) = x^3 - 19x + 30$. Thus, $R = -5$. (Ans. B)

20. $\log_{10} 60 = \log_{10}[(12)(10) \div 2] = \log_{10} 12 + \log_{10} 10 - \log_{10} 2 = a + 1 - b$ or $a - b + 1$. (Ans. A)

TEST 4

DIRECTIONS: Each question or incomplete statement is followed by several suggested answers or completions. Select the one that BEST answers the question or completes the statement. *PRINT THE LETTER OF THE CORRECT ANSWER IN THE SPACE AT THE RIGHT.*

1. The sum of the integers from 1 to 100, inclusive, is

    A. 5049 B. 5050 C. 5051 D. 5055

2. If $\sqrt{x+5} = 3$, then $(x+5)^2$ equals

    A. 9 B. 81 C. 3 D. 4

3. The solution set of $|5-2x| < 9$ is

    A. $\{x \mid x < -2\}$ B. $\{x \mid x > -2\}$
    C. $\{x \mid -2 < x < 7\}$ D. $\{x \mid x < -2 \text{ or } x > 7\}$

4. The solution set of the equation $\log x^2 = (\log x)^2$ is

    A. $\{0, 2\}$
    B. $\{1, 100\}$
    C. {all real values of x}
    D. {all real values of x > 0}

5. Simplify the following expression $\dfrac{(n+k+1)!}{(n+k-1)!}$

    A. $(n+k+1)(n+k)!$
    B. -1
    C. $(n+k+1)(n+k)$
    D. The expression cannot be simplified

6. The circle whose equation is $4x^2 + 4y^2 - 8x + 24y + 4 = 0$ has a radius whose length is

    A. 6 B. $\sqrt{6}$ C. 3 D. 9

7. If one root of a quadratic equation is $3+i$, then which of the following is a possible equation?

    A. $x^2 + 6x - 8 = 0$ B. $x^2 - 6x + 8 = 0$
    C. $x^2 + 6x - 10 = 0$ D. $x^2 - 6x + 10 = 0$

8. The graph of the equation is

    A. two straight lines B. an ellipse
    C. a straight line D. a hyperbola

9. How much pure hydrochloric acid should be added to 80 oz. of a 20% solution of hydrochloric acid to produce a solution which is 36% acid?

    A. 10 oz. B. 20 oz. C. 26.4 oz. D. 30 oz.

10. If f and g are functions such that f(x) = 3x+2 and f(g(x))= x, then g(x) =

   A. $\dfrac{x-2}{3}$ B. 2x+3   C. -3x+2   D. $\dfrac{x-3}{2}$

11. The lines whose equations are 2x + 3y = 7 and 3x - 4y = -15 intersect at the point P. What is the distance from P to the origin?

   A. $\dfrac{\sqrt{34}}{3}$ B. $\dfrac{\sqrt{85}}{4}$ C. $\sqrt{8}$ D. $\sqrt{10}$

12. The coefficient of the third term of the expansion of $(2x+\dfrac{1}{\sqrt{3x}})^6$ is

   A. $\dfrac{16}{3}$ B. 10   C. 15   D. 80

13. The infinite repeating decimal $0.\overline{04}$ (where 4 is repeated) is equal to

   A. $\dfrac{2}{45}$ B. $\dfrac{1}{25}$ C. $\dfrac{11}{225}$ D. $\dfrac{11}{250}$

14. Some properties that hold for equalities of real numbers are the
   I. reflexive property
   II. symmetric property
   III. transitive property

   Which of these properties hold true for the relation *greater than* applied to real numbers?

   A. III *only*   B. I, II, III
   C. II, III   D. I, III

15. The fraction $\dfrac{2}{1+2\sqrt{3}}$ is equivalent to

   A. $\dfrac{4\sqrt{3}+2}{13}$ B. $\dfrac{4\sqrt{3}-2}{11}$ C. $\dfrac{4\sqrt{3}+1}{13}$ D. $\dfrac{4\sqrt{3}-1}{11}$

16. If c represents a real number and $c \neq 0$, then the sum of the additive and multiplicative inverses of c is

   A. -1   B. 1-c   C. $\dfrac{(1+c)(1-c)}{c}$ D. $-\dfrac{1+c^2}{c}$

17. If A is the set of odd integers between 0 and 10 and B is a subset of integers such that B = {x|l < x < 6}, then the set $A \cap B$ is

   A. {3, 5}   B. {1, 3, 5}
   C. {1, 3, 5, 7, 9}   D. {1, 2, 3, 4, 5, 7, 9}

18. The sum of two numbers a and b is equal to their product. An equation which expresses this fact is:

    A. $b = \dfrac{a-1}{a}$
    B. $b = \dfrac{a}{a-1}$
    C. $b = \dfrac{a+1}{a}$
    D. $b = \dfrac{a}{a+1}$

    18.____

19. When $x^3 + 4x^2 + 3x - 10$ is divided by $x-1$, the remainder is

    A. -18
    B. -9
    C. -10
    D. -2

    19.____

20. If the roots of $x^2 + bx + c = 0$ are the negatives of the roots of $x^2 + 3x + 2 = 0$, then

    A. b = 3 and c = 2
    B. b = 3 and c = -2
    C. b = -3 and c = 2
    D. b = -3 and c = -2

    20.____

KEY (CORRECT ANSWERS)

1. B	11. D
2. B	12. D
3. C	13. A
4. B	14. A
5. C	15. B
6. C	16. C
7. D	17. A
8. D	18. B
9. B	19. D
10. A	20. C

SOLUTIONS TO PROBLEMS

1. Sum $= \frac{n}{2}(a+L)$ = number of numbers, a = first number, L = last number in an arithmetic progression. Thus, Sum $= \frac{100}{2}(1+100) = 5050$. (Ans. B)

2. $\sqrt{x+5} = 3$ means x = 4. Then, $(4+5)^2 = 81$. (Ans. B)

3. $|5-2x| < 9$ means $-9 < 5-2x < 9$, which implies $-2 < x < 7$. (Ans. C)

4. Log x^2 = 2Log x. Now, 2Log x = (Log x)^2. Factoring, we get Log x(2-Log x) = 0. If Log x = 0, x = 1. If 2- Log x = 0, then x = 100. The solution set is {1,100}. (Ans. B)

5. $\frac{(n+k+1)!}{(n+k-1)!} = \frac{(n+k+1)(n+k)(n+k-1)(...)(1)}{(n+k-1)(n+k-2)(...)(1)} = (n+k+1)(n+k)$ (Ans. C)

6. Transform the equation by first dividing by 4 to get $x^2 - 2x + y^2 + 6y = -1$. Then, $(x^2-2x+1)+(y^2+6y+9) = -1+1+9$ or $(x-1)^2+(y+3)^2 = 3^2$. The radius = 3. (Ans. C)

7. The other root must be 3-i. The sum of the roots is 6 and the product of the roots is 10. The equation must be $x^2 - 6x + 10 = 0$. (Ans. D)

8. $y = \frac{8}{x}$ becomes xy = 8. Any equation of the form xy = k, with k a constant, is a hyperbola. (Ans. D)

9. Let x = amount of acid added. Originally, there was (80)(.20) = 16 oz. of acid. Now, 16+x = .36(80+x). x = 20 oz. (Ans. B)

10. 3[g(x)] + 2 = x. Thus, $g(x) = \frac{x-2}{3}$. (Ans. A)

11. Solving 2x + 3y = 7 and 3x - 4y = -15, x = -1, y = 3. The point (-1, 3) is $\sqrt{(-1)^2 + (3)^2} = \sqrt{10}$ from the origin. (Ans. D)

12. Third term $= \frac{6 \cdot 5}{1 \cdot 2}(2x)^4(\frac{1}{\sqrt{3x}})^2 = 80x^4$, so the coefficient is 80. (Ans. D)

13. Let $N = .0\overline{4}$, so that $10N = .\overline{4}$. Now, by subtraction, 9N = .4 and $N = \frac{4}{90}$ or $\frac{2}{45}$ (Ans. A)

14. Only the transitive property holds, i.e.: if x > y and y > w, then x > w. (Ans. A)

15. $\dfrac{2}{1+2\sqrt{3}} \cdot \dfrac{1-2\sqrt{3}}{1-2\sqrt{3}} = \dfrac{2-4\sqrt{3}}{1-12} = \dfrac{4\sqrt{3}-2}{11}$. (Ans. B)

16. The additive inverse of c is $\dfrac{1}{c}$, and the multiplicative inverse of c is $\dfrac{1}{c}$. Now,

$-c + \dfrac{1}{c} = \dfrac{-c^2+1}{c} = \dfrac{(1+c)(1-c)}{c}$ (Ans. C)

17. A = {1, 3, 5, 7, 9}, B = {2, 3, 4, 5}, then $A \cap B = \{3, 5\}$. (Ans. A)

18. Since a + b = ab from the given information, a = ab-b or a = b(a-1), which becomes $b = \dfrac{a}{a-1}$. (Ans. B)

19. By the Remainder Theorem, when P(x) is divided by x-R, the remainder is P(R). In this example, the remainder is $P(1) = 1^3 + 4(1)^2 + 3(1) - 10 = -2$. (Ans. D)

20. The roots of $x^2 + 3x + 2 = 0$ are -1, -2. The negatives of these roots are 1, 2. Sum of roots $= -\dfrac{b}{1} = 3$, so b=-3. Product of roots $= \dfrac{c}{1} = 2$, so c = 2. (Ans. C)

EXAMINATION SECTION
TEST 1

DIRECTIONS: Each question or incomplete statement is followed by several suggested answers or completions. Select the one that BEST answers the question or completes the statement. *PRINT THE LETTER OF THE CORRECT ANSWER IN THE SPACE AT THE RIGHT.*

1. Let $b \in R$, the set of real numbers.
   The solution set of $b^2 > b$ is

   A. $\{b|b>1\}$
   B. $\{b|b<0 \text{ or } b>\}$
   C. $\{b|b<-1 \text{ or } b>1\}$
   D. R

2. If k represents a positive integer, $2^{k+1} + 2^k$ is equal to

   A. 4^{2k+1} B. 2^{2k+1} C. $3(2^{k+1})$ D. $3(2^k)$

3. A function, f(x), is defined as $f(x) = 2x^2 - 5$.
   The value of $f[f(2)]$ is

   A. 13   B. 22   C. 6   D. 9

4. If $\log_2 y = 5$, then y is equal to

   A. 7   B. 10   C. 25   D. 32

5. The graph of the equation $x^2 - 4x + y^2 = 12$ is a circle with radius _____, center _____.

   A. 4; (-2,0)   B. 4; (2,0)   C. 16, (-2,0)   D. 16; (2,0)

6. The TOTAL number of subsets of set {a,b,c,d} is

   A. 16   B. 15   C. 8   D. 4

7. If S represents the sum of the infinite geometric series
   $\frac{1}{4} + \frac{1}{8} + \frac{1}{16} + ...$, then

   A. $S = 1$ B. $S < 1$ C. $1 < S < 2$ D. $S > 2$

8. Let R represent the set of real numbers.
   If a*b is defined as $\frac{a+b}{2}$ where a and b represent any two elements in R, then

   A. a*1=a
   B. a*0=0
   C. a*(2b)=(2a)*b
   D. 2+(a*b) =(2+a)*(2+b)

9. A student observes that the same shaded part of a Venn diagram illustrates both sets $A \cap (B \cup C)$ and $(A \cap B) \cup (A \cap C)$. This suggests a property MOST closely resembling which property of real numbers?

   A. Commutative
   B. Distributive
   C. Associative
   D. Multiplicative inverse

10. If c represents a real number and $c \neq 0$, then the product of the additive and multiplicative inverses of c is

    A. 1 B. -c C. $\dfrac{1}{c}$ D. -1

11. For what value of k is 2 a root of the equation $2x^4 - 6x^3 + 4kx + 13 = 0$?

    A. $\dfrac{8}{3}$ B. $\dfrac{3}{8}$ C. $-\dfrac{3}{8}$ D. $-\dfrac{8}{3}$

12. The arithmetic mean between the roots of the equation $x^2 - 8x + 13 = 0$ is

    A. $-6\dfrac{1}{2}$ B. $6\dfrac{1}{2}$ C. -4 D. 4

13. The infinite repeating decimal of $0.0\overline{2}$ (where 2 is repeated) is equal to

    A. $\dfrac{2}{99}$ B. $\dfrac{11}{500}$ C. $\dfrac{1}{45}$ D. $\dfrac{22}{999}$

14. The relation between the Fahrenheit and Celsius readings may be stated $F = \dfrac{9}{5}C + 32$. The numerical readings on both scales are the same when the number of degrees is

    A. -8 B. -40 C. 8 D. 40

15. Which of the following pairs of equations represent parallel lines in a rectangular coordinate system?

    A. 3x-6y =9
       2x+4y = 6
    B. 3x-6y =9
       2x-4y = 6
    C. 3x-6y =9
       x-2y = 4
    D. 3x-6y = 9
       x+2y = 4

16. The graph below represents the solution set of which one of the following?

    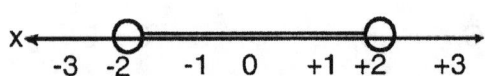

    A. $|x| < 2$ B. $|x| \leq 2$ C. $|x| = 2$ D. $|x| > 2$

17. Using the ordered pair (x,y) as an equivalent expression for $\dfrac{x}{y}$, the ordered pair representing the sum of (3, 8) and $\dfrac{x}{y}$ (2, 3) would be

    A. (1, 5) B. (5, 11) C. (25, 24) D. (25, 6)

18. Solve for x: $4^{x-2} = 1$

    A. $\dfrac{1}{4}$ B. 2 C. -2 D. $2\dfrac{1}{4}$

19. Twelve identical machines can finish a job in 8 days. The number of machines needed to finish the same job in 6 days would be   19.____

   A. 18   B. 16   C. 14   D. 9

20. The reciprocal of $\sqrt{3} - \sqrt{2}$ is equal to   20.____

   A. 1   B. $\sqrt{3} + \sqrt{2}$ C. $\dfrac{1}{\sqrt{3}} - \dfrac{1}{\sqrt{2}}$ D. $-\sqrt{3} + \sqrt{2}$

KEY (CORRECT ANSWERS)

1.	B	11.	B
2.	D	12.	D
3.	A	13.	C
4.	D	14.	B
5.	B	15.	C
6.	A	16.	A
7.	B	17.	C
8.	D	18.	B
9.	B	19.	B
10.	D	20.	B

SOLUTIONS TO PROBLEMS

1. $b^2 > b$ implies $b(b-1) > 0$. If seen $b > 0$ and $b-1 > 0$, then a solution is $\{b | b > 1\}$. If $b < 0$ and $b-1 < 0$, then a solution is $\{b | b < 0\}$. Final answer: $\{b | b < 0 \text{ or } b > 1\}$. (Ans. B)

2. $2^{k+1} + 2^k = 2^k(2+1) = 3(2^k)$. (Ans. D)

3. $f[f(2)] = f[2(2^2)-5] = f[3] = 2(3^2)-5 = 13$. (Ans. A)

4. $\log y_2 = 5$ implies $2^5 = y$, so $y = 32$. (Ans. D)

5. Rewrite as $x^2-4x+4+y^2=12+4$, which becomes $(x-2)^2 + (y-0)^2 = 4^2$. Thus, the radius is 4 and the center is $(2, 0)$. (Ans. B)

6. Given a set with n elements, the number of subsets $= 2^n$. In this example, $2^n = 2^4 = 16$. (Ans. A)

7. $S = \dfrac{a}{1-r}$, where a = first term, r = common ratio. Thus, $S = \dfrac{1}{4} \div (1-\dfrac{1}{2}) = \dfrac{1}{2}$. The only correct choice is $S < 1$. (Ans. B)

8. $2+(a*b) = 2+\dfrac{a+b}{2} = \dfrac{4+a+b}{2}$. Also, $(2+a)*(2+b) = \dfrac{2+a+2+b}{2} = \dfrac{4+a+b}{2}$. (Ans. D)

9. The distributive property would be apparent in an example like $5 \cdot (3+7) = (5 \cdot 3) + (5 \cdot 7)$. The $\cap$ symbol replaces $\cdot$ and the $\cup$ symbol replaces $+$. (Ans. B)

10. The additive, multiplicative inverses of c are $-c$ and $\dfrac{1}{c}$, respectively. Then, $(-c)(\dfrac{1}{c}) = -1$. (Ans. D)

11. $2(2^4) - 6(2^3) + 4k(2) + 13 = 0$. Solving, $k = \dfrac{3}{8}$. (Ans. B)

12. The sum of the roots $= 8$. Thus, their average $= 4$. It should be noted that in the equation $Ax^2 + Bx + C = 0$, the sum of the roots is. (Ans. D)

13. Let $N = .0\overline{2}$. Then, $10N = .\overline{2}$ and $9n = .2$. Thus $N = \dfrac{.2}{9} = \dfrac{2}{90} = \dfrac{1}{45}$. (Ans. C)

14. If $F = C$, then $C = \dfrac{9}{5}C + 32$. Solving, $C = -40$. (Ans. B)

15. Parallel lines have the same slope, but different y-intercepts. Both $3x-6y = 9$ and $x-2y = 4$ have slopes of $\dfrac{1}{2}$, but the y-intercepts are $-\dfrac{3}{2}$ and -2, respectively. (Ans. C)

16. The graph translates to -2 < x < 2, which becomes |x| < 2. (Ans. A)

17. $\dfrac{3}{8}+\dfrac{2}{3}=\dfrac{25}{24}$, which corresponds to (25, 24). (Ans. C)

18. $4^{x-2} = 1 = 4^0$. $x-2 = 0$. $x = 2$ (Ans. B)

19. Let x = number of required machines. Then, $\dfrac{12}{x}=\dfrac{6}{8}$. x = 16. (Ans. B)

20. $\dfrac{1}{\sqrt{3}-\sqrt{2}} = \dfrac{1}{\sqrt{3}-\sqrt{2}} \cdot \dfrac{\sqrt{3}+\sqrt{2}}{\sqrt{3}+\sqrt{2}} = \dfrac{\sqrt{3}+\sqrt{2}}{1} = \sqrt{3}+\sqrt{2}$ (Ans. B)

TEST 2

DIRECTIONS: Each question or incomplete statement is followed by several suggested answers or completions. Select the one that BEST answers the question or completes the statement. *PRINT THE LETTER OF THE CORRECT ANSWER IN THE SPACE AT THE RIGHT.*

1. The graph of the equation $\dfrac{x^2}{9} - \dfrac{y^2}{16} = 1$ is a(n)

    A. parabola   B. circle   C. ellipse   D. hyperbola

2. If $_{18}C_5 = {}_{18}C_{r+2}$ and $r \neq 3$, then $_rC_5 =$

    A. 18   B. 462   C. 7   D. 13860

3. If universal set U contains subsets A, B, and C, as shown in the accompanying Venn diagram below, then the shaded area may be represented by

    A. $A \cap B \cap C$
    B. $(A \cap C) \cup (B \cap C)$
    C. $(A \cup C) \cap (B \cup C)$
    D. $(A \cap C) \cup C$

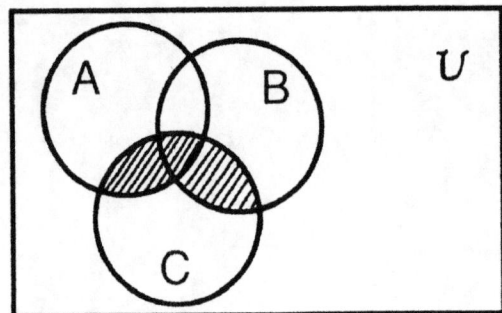

4. The repeating decimal $0.\overline{314}$ may be represented by

    A. $\dfrac{.314314}{1000000}$ B. $\dfrac{314}{1000}$ C. $\dfrac{314}{990}$ D. $\dfrac{314}{999}$

5. An article was sold for m dollars at a gain of 15% on the cost. The cost, in dollars, of the article was

    A. $\dfrac{m}{.15}$ B. $\dfrac{m}{1.15}$ C. .15m   D. 1.15m

6. A student takes six class tests during the term. If his arithmetic average was p for the first three tests and q for the next two tests, what mark on the sixth test will give him an average of 80 for all the tests?

    A. 480 - (3p+2q)
    C. 480 - (p+q)
    B. 80 - (3p+2q)
    D. 80 - (p+q)

7. The sum of a number, x, and its reciprocal is equal to the product of the same number and its reciprocal.
Which of the following equations can be used to find this number?

A. $x^2 + x + 1 = 0$ B. $x^2 + x - 1 = 0$
   C. $x^2 - x + 1 = 0$ D. $x^2 - x - 1 = 0$

8. Two lines have equations $ax + by + c = 0$ and $dx + ey + f = 0$.
   The graphs of these lines will be perpendicular to each other if and *only* if

   A. $ae - bd = 0$ B. $ad - be = 0$
   C. $ad + be = 0$ D. $ae + bd = 0$

9. A certain printing press can print an edition of a newspaper in 4 hours. After this press has been at work for 1 hour, a second press also starts to print the same edition. Working together, both presses require one more hour to finish the job.
   How many hours would it have taken the second press to print the edition if it had worked alone?

   A. 5   B. 2   C. 3   D. 4

10. The sum of the squares of the roots of the equation $x^2 - 6x + 4 = 0$ is

    A. 28   B. 10   C. 18   D. 23

11. The fraction, $\dfrac{x^{-1} + y^{-1}}{x^{-1}}$ is equivalent to

    A. $\dfrac{x}{x+y}$ B. $\dfrac{x+y}{x}$ C. $1 + \dfrac{1}{y}$ D. $1 + \dfrac{x}{y}$

12. When $x^{29} - 3x^{21} + 2$ is divided by $x-1$, the remainder is

    A. -2 B. 0   C. 3   D. 4

13. If * is an associative binary operation such that $a*b = c$, $c*d = e$, and $b*d = f$, then $a*f$ equals

    A. b   B. c   C. d   D. e

14. Which of the following functions has an inverse relation which is NOT a function?

    A. $f(x) = \dfrac{1}{2}x - 2$ B. $f(x) = x^2 + 3$
    C. $f(x) = \log_{10} x$ D. $f(x) = \text{Arc sin } x$

15. On the curve $y = x^2$, two points P and Q are chosen having abscissas a and b, respectively.
    The slope of $\overleftrightarrow{PQ}$ is

    A. $a+b$ B. $a-b$ C. $b-a$ D. $\dfrac{a-b}{a+b}$

16. A can 3 inches in diameter contains 12 fluid ounces of water. A can filled to the same height but 4 inches in diameter contains _____ fluid ounces.

    A. 16   B. 18   C. $21\frac{1}{3}$ D. $28\frac{4}{9}$

17. The solution set of $x^2 < x$, where x is a real number, is

    A. $\{x|x < 0\}$ B. $\{x|0 < x < 1\}$
    C. $\{x|x > 0\}$ D. $\{x|x < 1\}$

18. If $\log V = t \log E + \log K$, then

    A. $V = (KE)^t$ B. $V = E^t + K$
    C. $V = KE^t$ D. $V = tE + K$

19. The number of distinct chords which can be drawn connecting 5 points on a circle is

    A. 20   B. 15   C. 10   D. 5

20. The equation of the axis of symmetry for the curve $y^2 = x - 6y$ is

    A. $y - 6 = 0$ B. $2x = 3y$
    C. $x - 3 = 0$ D. $y + 3 = 0$

KEY (CORRECT ANSWERS)

1. D
2. B
3. B
4. D
5. B

6. A
7. C
8. C
9. B
10. A

11. D
12. B
13. D
14. B
15. A

16. C
17. B
18. C
19. C
20. D

SOLUTIONS TO PROBLEMS

1. Any equation in the form, $\dfrac{x^2}{a^2} - \dfrac{y^2}{b^2} = 1$ is a hyperbola. Here, a, b are constants. (Ans. D)

2. $_{18}C_5 = \dfrac{18!}{5!\,13!}$ which $= \dfrac{18!}{13!\,5!} = {_{18}C_{13}}$

   Since r + 2 = 13, r = 11.
   Now, $_{11}C_5 = (11!)/[5!\cdot 6!] = 462$. (Ans. B)

3. Recognize that the shaded area can be illustrated as

   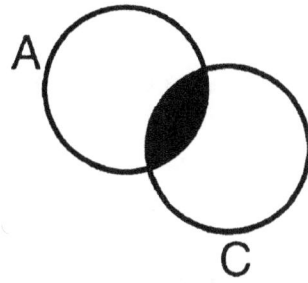 +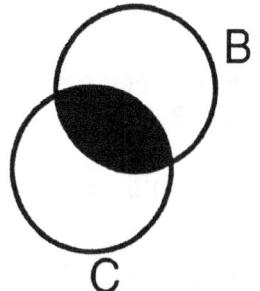

   = (A ∩ C + (B ∩ C) = (A ∩ C) ∪ (B ∩ C) (Ans. B)

4. Let $N = 0.\overline{314}$. Then, $1000N = 314.\overline{314}$ and by subtraction $999N = 314$. Thus, $N = 314/999$. (Ans. D)

5. Let C = cost. Then, m = C + .15C = 1.15C. Finally, C = m/1.15. (Ans. B)

6. An average of p for the first three tests implies a total of 3p. Likewise, an average of q for the next two tests implies a total of 2q. Let x = score on sixth test.

   Now, $\dfrac{3p + 2q + x}{6} = 80$, which means x = 480 - 3p - 2q. (Ans. A)

7. We have x + 1/x = (x)(1/x), which implies $(x^2+1)/x = 1$. This equation can be rewritten as $x^2 - x + 1 = 0$. (Ans. C)

8. The slope of the first line is $-\dfrac{a}{b}$, and the slope of the second line is $-\dfrac{d}{e}$. In order for the two lines to be perpendicular to each other, the slope of one line must equal the negative reciprocal of the other line. Thus, $-\dfrac{a}{b} = -1/-\dfrac{d}{e}$ which implies that ad + be = 0. (Ans. C)

9. Let x = number of hours the second press would need if it were to work alone. In performing the present job, the first press will have worked 2 hours and the second press will have worked 1 hour. The sum of the fractions representing the respective parts of the job done by each press equals 1. Thus, $2/4 + 1/x = 1$. Consequently, x = 2 hours. (Ans. B)

10. Let R_1, R_2 = the two roots. $R_1 + R_2 = 6$ and $R_1 R_2 = 4$.

    So, $(R_1+R_2)^2 = R_1^2 + 2R_1R_2 + R_2^2 = 36$. Since $2R_1R_2 = 8$, this means $R_1^2 + R_2^2 = 28$. (Ans. A)

11. Rewrite the expression as $(\frac{1}{x}+\frac{1}{y})/\frac{1}{x} = \frac{1}{x}/\frac{1}{x}+\frac{1}{y}/\frac{1}{x} = 1+\frac{x}{y}$ (Ans. D)

12. By the Remainder Theorem, the remainder is the value of $x^{29} - 3x^{21} + 2$ when x = 1. Value = $x^{29} - 3(1)^{21} + 2 = 0$. (Ans. B)

13. $a*f = a*(b*d) = (a*b)*d = c*d = e$ (Ans. D)

14. The inverse of $f(x) = x^2 + 3$ is $g(x) = \pm\sqrt{x-3}$, and thus g(x) is NOT a function. (Ans. B)

15. The coordinates of P: (a, a^2) and the coordinates of Q (b, b^2). The slope of $\overleftrightarrow{PQ} = (b^2-a^2)/(b-a) = b+a = a+b$. (Ans. A)

16. Volume of first can $= (\pi)(\frac{3}{2})^2(H) = 27\pi H$ cubic inches.

    The volume of the second can = cubic inches. Thus, the ratio of volumes of the first can to the second Let x = number of fluid ounces in the second can. Then,

    $\frac{12}{x} = \frac{9}{16}$ and $x = 21\frac{1}{3}$. (Ans. C)

17. $x^2 < x$ becomes $x^2 - x < 0$. Then, $x(x-1) < 0$.
    Case 1: x < 0 and x-1 > 0 simultaneously. This is impossible
    Case 2: x > 0 and x-1 < 0 simultaneously. This implies 0 < x < 1. (Ans. B)

18. Rewrite the right side of the equation as Log E^t + Log K = Log $(E^t)(K)$. Now, Log V = Log $(E^t)(K)$, so $V = KE^t$.

19. The problem resolves into $_5C_2 = 5 \cdot 4/2 = 10$. (Ans. C)

20. Rewrite the equation as $x = y^2 + 6y$, which becomes $x = (y^2+6y+9) - 9$ which can be written as $x = (y+3)^2 - 9$. Axis of symmetry is y = -3 or y+3 = 0. (Ans. D)

TEST 3

DIRECTIONS: Each question or incomplete statement is followed by several suggested answers or completions. Select the one that BEST answers the question or completes the statement. *PRINT THE LETTER OF THE CORRECT ANSWER IN THE SPACE AT THE RIGHT.*

1. The series represented by the expression $\sum_{k=1}^{n}(2k-1)$ is equal to

   A. $\dfrac{n(n+1)}{2}$ B. n^2 C. $(n+1)^2$ D. $n(n+1)$

2. The graph of $|x|+|y|=4$ is

   A. a square
   B. two intersecting lines
   C. two parallel lines
   D. one line

3. If $x<b<0$ means that x and b are numbers such that x is less than b and b is less than zero, then

   A. $x^2 > bx > b^2$
   B. $x^2 < b^5 < 0$
   C. $x^2 > bx$ but $bx<0$
   D. $x^2 > b^2$ but $b^2 < 0$

4. If x is positive and log log x, then

   A. x has no minimum or maximum value
   B. the maximum value of x is 1
   C. the maximum value of x is 4
   D. the minimum value of x is 4

5. If the third term of a geometric progression is $\dfrac{1}{6}$ and the seventh term is $\dfrac{1}{6}$, the first, term is

   A. $\dfrac{1}{81}$ B. $\dfrac{1}{72}$ C. $\dfrac{1}{54}$ D. $\dfrac{1}{48}$

6. Which values of x will satisfy the equation $3^{x^2-7x} = \left(\dfrac{1}{3}\right)^{4x+1}$

   A. $x = \dfrac{4 \pm \sqrt{5}}{2}$ B. $x = \dfrac{3 \pm \sqrt{3}}{2}$ C. $x = \dfrac{3 \pm \sqrt{5}}{2}$ D. $x = \dfrac{2 \pm \sqrt{3}}{2}$

7. Which values of x satisfy the following equation involving a determinant?
$$\begin{vmatrix} x & 2 & 1 \\ -1 & 1 & -1 \\ 3 & 2 & 3x \end{vmatrix} = 0$$

1. ____
2. ____
3. ____
4. ____
5. ____
6. ____
7. ____

A. $x = -\frac{11}{3}, x = 1$ B. $x = \frac{3}{4}, x = -1$

C. $x = -\frac{7}{8}, x = 2$ D. $x = 4, x = 3$

8. Which of the following expresses $x^3 - 2x^2 - 5x + 6$ as the product of three linear factors?

    A. $(x-1)(x-2)(x-3)$ B. $(x-1)(x+2)(x+3)$
    C. $(x-1)(x-2)(x+3)$ D. $(x-1)(x+2)(x-3)$

9. If $f(x) = 3^x$, then $f(x) + f(x+1) =$

    A. 4   B. $f(x)$ C. $3f(x)$ D. $4f(x)$

10. The number of distinct points of intersection of the relations $x^2 + 9y^2 = 1$ and $x^2 + 9y^2 = 9$ is

    A. 1   B. 2   C. 3   D. 0

11. Simplify the product $(256)^{.16} (256)^{.09}$

    A. 4   B. 16   C. 64   D. 256.25

12. The sixth term of the expansion of $(\frac{2}{x\sqrt{3}} + \frac{x^2}{2})^9$ is

    A. $7x^6$ B. $10x^6$ C. $63x^7$ D. $18x^7$

13. A man has five close friends.
    In how many ways may he invite one or more of them to accompany him on a hunting trip?

    A. 5   B. 10   C. 31   D. 32

14. When $x^2 + 3x^2 + cx + 5$ is divided by $x-2$, the remainder is 13. The value of c is

    A. -6   B. -2   C. 2   D. 6

15. The real values of x and y that satisfy the equation $3x + 2y + xi = 11 + 1 - 2yi$ may be described as follows:

    A. $x > 0$ and $y > 0$ B. $x > 0$ and $y < 0$
    C. $x < 0$ and $y < 0$ D. $x < 0$ and $y > 0$

16. The equation of the tangent to the curve $y = x^3 - x^2 + x - 1$ at the point on the curve where $x = 1$ is

    A. $y = 0$ B. $2y + x = 1$
    C. $y = 2x + 2$ D. $y = 2x - 2$

17. A group of boys and girls have an average (arithmetic mean) weight of 40 kg. If the average weight of the girls is 35 kg and the average weight of the boys is 50 kg, then the ratio of boys to girls is

   A. 2:3 B. 1:2 C. 3:2 D. 2:1

17.____

18. The value of the product $(\log_a b)(\log_b a)$, where $(a>1, b>1)$ is

   A. 1 B. 0 C. ab D. a+b

18.____

19. If $f(x) = 2x - 3$ and $g(x) = x^2 - 4$, find $f[g(x)] - g[f(x)]$.

   A. $-2(x^2-6x+8)$
   B. $-x^2 + 2x + 1$
   C. $x^2 - 2x - 1$
   D. $-2(x^2+6x+3)$

19.____

20. A plane makes the trip from City A to City B, traveling at an average rate of 380 miles per hour. On the return trip, the plane flies at an average of 420 miles per hour. The average rate of the plane for the roundtrip, in miles per hour, is

   A. 398 B. 401 C. 400 D. 399

20.____

KEY (CORRECT ANSWERS)

1. B
2. A
3. A
4. D
5. C

6. C
7. A
8. D
9. D
10. D

11. A
12. A
13. C
14. A
15. B

16. D
17. B
18. A
19. A
20. D

SOLUTIONS TO PROBLEMS

1. This summation is $1+3+5+ \ldots + 2n-1$, which is an arithmetic progression whose sum can be written as $\frac{n}{2}[1+(2n-1)] = n^2$. (Ans. B)

2. The graph appears as: (Ans. A)

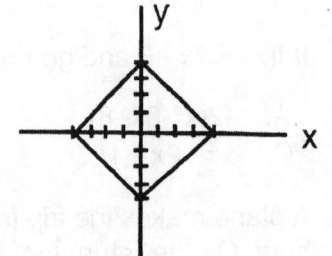

3. Since $x < b < 0$, both x and b are negative numbers. Using $x < b$, if both terms are multiplied by x, the order of inequality changes; thus, $x^2 > bx$. Now, if both terms are multiplied by b (from $x < b$), then $bx > b^2$. Thus, $x^2 > bx > b^2$. Note that b^2, x^2, bx are all greater than 0. (Ans. A)

4. $\text{Log } 2 + \frac{1}{2}\text{Log } x = \text{Log } 2 + \text{Log}\sqrt{x} = \text{Log } 2\sqrt{x}$. Since $x > 0$ and $\text{Log } x \geq \text{Log } 2\sqrt{x}$, we get $x \geq 2\sqrt{x}$. This implies $x^2 \geq 4x$, which would yield (normally) $x \geq 4$ or $x \leq -4$; BUT since x is positive, the only acceptable answer is $x \geq 4$. Thus, 4 is the minimum value of x. (Ans. D)

5. $t_n = ar^{n-1}$, where t_n = nth term, a = first term, r = ratio of each term to preceding term and n = number of terms. $\frac{1}{6} = ar^2$ and $\frac{27}{2} = ar^6$. Divide the second equation by the first equation to get $r^4 = 81$. Thus, $r = 3$ or -3, with either value of r, $a = \frac{1}{54}$. (Ans. C)

6. Rewrite as $3^{x^2-7x} = (3^{-1})^{4x+1} = 3^{-4x-1}$. Equating exponents, we get $x^2 - 7x = -4x - 1$ or $x^2 - 3x + 1 = 0$. Using the quadratic formula, $x = (3 \pm \sqrt{5})/2$. (Ans. C)

7. $\begin{vmatrix} x & 2 & 1 \\ -1 & 1 & -1 \\ 3 & 2 & 3x \end{vmatrix} = 3x^2 - 6 - 2 - (3 - 2x - 6x) = 3x^2 + 8x - 11$

Now solving $3x^2 + 8x - 11 = 0$ to get $(3x+11)(x-1) = 0$. Thus, $x = 1$ and $-\frac{11}{3}$. (Ans. A)

5 (#3)

8. Since -2 is a solution of $x^3 - 2x^2 - 5x + 6 = 0$, $x+2$ is a factor. Likewise, the numbers 1 and 3 are solutions of $x^3 - 2x^2 - 5x + 6$; so $(x-1)$ and $(x-3)$ are factors. The three factors are $(x-1)$, $(x+2)$, $(x-3)$. (Ans. D)

9. $f(x) + f(x+1) = 3^x + 3^{x+1} = 3x(1+3^1) = 4(3^x) = 4f(x)$. (Ans. D)

10. Substitute $x^2 = 1 - 9y^2$ into the second equation $(1-9y^2) + 9y^2 = 9$. This leads to $0y^2 = 8$. Thus, no solution. (Ans. D)

11. $(256)^{.16}(256)^{.09} = 256^{.25} = \sqrt[4]{256} = 4$. (Ans. A)

12. sixth term $= (_9C_5)(\frac{2}{x\sqrt{3}})^4(\frac{x^2}{2})^5 = (126)(\frac{2^4}{9x^4})(\frac{x^{10}}{2^5}) = 7x^6$. (Ans. A)

13. $_5C_1 + {}_5C_2 + {}_5C_3 + {}_5C_4 + {}_5C_5 = 5 + 10 + 10 + 5 + 1 = 31$, where $_aC_b$ means combinations of a items taken b at a time. (Ans. C)

14. The polynomial $x^3 + 3x^2 + cx + 5$ must have a value of 13 when 2 is substituted for x. (Remainder Theorem). Thus, $8 + 12 + 2c + 5 = 13$. Then, $c = -6$. (Ans. A)

15. If $a + bi = c + di$, then $a = c$ and $b = d$. Thus, $3x + 2y = 12$ and $x = -2y$. Then, $x = 6$, $y = -3$. Choice B is CORRECT. (Ans. B)

16. Determine $\frac{dy}{dx} = 3x^2 - 2x + 1$. Evaluate $3x^2 - 2x + 1$ at $x = 1$ to get 2. Thus, the tangent has a slope of 2 and passes through $(\frac{1}{3}, 0)$. Note that the 0 y-value was obtained by evaluating $x^3 - x^2 + x - 1$ at $x = 1$. Finally, the equation of the tangent is $y = 2x - 2$. (Ans. D)

17. Let x = number of boys, y = number of girls. Realize that the total weight of the entire group of boys and girls can be expressed as either the total number of boys and girls times their average weight or the total weight of boys plus the total weight of the girls. Thus, $(x+y)(40) = 50x + 35y$. This reduces to $10x = 5y$ or $x:y = 1:2$. (Ans. B)

18. Let $\log_a b = x$ so that $a^x = b$. Let $\log_b a = y$ so that $b^y = a$. By substitution, $a^x = (b^y)^x = b$. This implies that $xy = 1$. (Ans. A)

19. $f[g(x)] = f(x^2-4) = 2(x^2-4) - 3 = 2x^2 - 11$
    $g[f(x)] = g(2x-3) = (2x-3)^2 - 4 = 4x^2 - 12x + 5$
    Now, $f[g(x)] - g[f(x)] = -2x^2 + 12x - 16 = -2(x^2-6x+8)$. (Ans. A)

20. Let distance from A to B be x miles. Average rate = total distance divided by total time = $= (x+x) \div (\frac{x}{380} + \frac{x}{420}) = 2x \div [(x)(800)/159{,}600] = 399$ mph. (Ans. D)

TEST 4

DIRECTIONS: Each question or incomplete statement is followed by several suggested answers or completions. Select the one that BEST answers the question or completes the statement. *PRINT THE LETTER OF THE CORRECT ANSWER IN THE SPACE AT THE RIGHT.*

1. The values of x that satisfy the equation |3x-4| = |5-4x| may be described as follows: 1.___

    A. 2 values of x < 0
    B. 2 values of x > 0
    C. 1 value of x > 0, 1 value of x < 0
    D. 2 values of x > 0, 2 values of x < 0

2. Two of the roots of the equation $2x^3 - 12x^2 + px + q = 0$ are 2 and 3. The third root is   2.___

    A. 1   B. 2   C. -1   D. -7

3. An equation with real coefficients has 2+i, 3, and 4 among its roots. The LOWEST possible degree of the equation is   3.___

    A. 5   B. 6   C. 3   D. 4

4. In the complex number system $\frac{1}{i} + \frac{1}{i^2} + \frac{1}{i^3}$ equals   4.___

    A. 1   B. -1   C. 2i   D. 1-i

5. The value of $[1-2(2-3)^{-1}]^{-1}$ is   5.___

    A. -1   B. 2   C. $\frac{1}{3}$ D. $-\frac{1}{3}$

6. An eleventh year mathematics class studying complex numbers was asked to express the quotient $\frac{\sqrt{36}}{\sqrt{-9}}$ in terms of i.   6.___

    Student A wrote $\frac{\sqrt{36}}{\sqrt{-9}} = \sqrt{\frac{36}{-9}} = \sqrt{-4} = 2i$

    Student B wrote $\frac{\sqrt{36}}{\sqrt{-9}} = \frac{6}{3i} = \frac{2}{i}$

    Student C wrote $\frac{\sqrt{36}}{\sqrt{-9}} = \frac{6}{3i} = \frac{2}{i} \cdot \frac{i}{i} = \frac{2i}{i^2} = \frac{2i}{-1} = -2i$

    The students who expressed this CORRECTLY were

    A. A and B *only*   B. A and C *only*
    C. B and C *only*   D. all three

7. The expression $\dfrac{1}{a^{-1}+b^{-1}}$ equals

   A. $a+b$ B. $\dfrac{1}{-a-b}$ C. $(a+b)^1$ D. $\dfrac{ab}{a+b}$

8. If $f(x) = 2^x$, where x is real, and if f^{-1} denotes the inverse function of f, then when $a > 1$ and $b > 1$, $\dfrac{f^{-1}(a)}{f^{-1}(b)} =$

   A. $\dfrac{2^b}{2^a}$ B. $\log_2 a - \log_2 b$ C. $\dfrac{\log_2 a}{\log_2 b}$ D. $\dfrac{b}{2^a}$

9. The x-intercept(s) of the graph $y = x^3 - 6x^2 + 12x - 8$ is(are)

   A. 1 and 2   B. 2   C. -8 and 2   D. -8

10. The third term in the expansion of $(x-2y)^8$ is

    A. $112x^6y^2$ B. $-112x^6y^2$ C. $28x^5y^3$ D. $-28x^5y^3$

11. How many hours does it take a train, traveling at an average rate of 30 mph between stops, to travel m miles if it makes s stops of t minutes each?

    A. $\dfrac{2m+st}{60}$ B. $\dfrac{m+st}{60}$ C. $30m + st$ D. $\dfrac{m}{30}+st$

12. When a positive integer x is divided by a positive integer y, the quotient is w and the remainder is z where w and z are integers.
    The remainder when x+3wy is divided by y is

    A. z   B. w   C. 3w   D. 0

13. A train takes 12 seconds to pass through the entrance of a tunnel. Fifteen seconds later, the train is completely out of the tunnel. Assuming that the speed of the train remains constant and the tunnel is 435 yards long, the length of the train is _____ yards.

    A. 348   B. 360   C. 372   D. 384

14. The area of the circle whose equation is $x^2 + y^2 + 4x - 1 = 0$ is

    A. π B. 5π C. 16π D. 25π

15. The solution set of $|x+2| \le 6$ is

    A. $-8 \le x \le 4$ B. $x \le -8$ or $x \ge 4$
    C. $-4 \le x \le 8$ D. $x \le -4$ or $x \ge 8$

16. In a class, three times as many students passed a test as failed. The arithmetic mean of grades on the test for the entire class was double the arithmetic mean of all failures on the test.
    If the arithmetic mean of all the passing grades was 84, then the arithmetic mean of all failing grades was

    A. 32 B. 36 C. 42 D. 46

17. The measure of a side of a square is 10. The radius of the circle circumscribed around the square is CLOSEST to

    A. 5 B. 6 C. 7 D. 9

18. Which of the following represents the solution set for x in the equation $\log_8(x-1) + \log_8(x+1) = 1$?

    A. {3, -3} B. {-3} C. {3} D. {8}

19. The expression in SIMPLEST form is

    A. $\dfrac{\sqrt{x}}{2}$ B. $\dfrac{\sqrt{x}+1}{3}$ C. $\dfrac{\sqrt{x}+2}{4}$ D. $\dfrac{2\sqrt{x}-1}{x-1}$

20. A person makes a deposit in a bank which gives 6.4% simple interest per year. After 270 days, his money has grown to 1,310 dollars from the interest.
    Assuming that the bank's interest is based on a year of 360 days, the amount that the person *initially* deposited was

    A. $1150 B. $1175 C. $1225 D. $1250

KEY (CORRECT ANSWERS)

1.	B		11.	A
2.	A		12.	A
3.	D		13.	A
4.	B		14.	B
5.	C		15.	A
6.	C		16.	B
7.	D		17.	C
8.	C		18.	C
9.	B		19.	A
10.	A		20.	D

SOLUTIONS TO PROBLEMS

1. Either $3x-4 = 5-4x$ or $3x-4 = -(5-4x)$. The solution becomes: $x = \frac{9}{7}$ and $x = 1$. Thus, we have 2 values of $x > 0$. (Ans, B)

2. Since 2 is a root, $16 - 48 + 2p + q = 0$. Since 3 is also a root, $54 - 108 + 3p + q = 0$. Solving, $p = 22$, $q = -12$. Now, $2x^3 - 12x^2 + 22x - 12 = 0$, which equals $x^3 - 6x^2 + 11x - 6 = 0$ can be written as $(x-2)(x-3)(x-R) = 0$. Solving, $R = 1$. Thus, 1 is the third root. (Ans. A)

3. If $2+i$ is a root, then so is $2-i$. Thus, there are at least 4 roots, and 4 must be the lowest possible degree. (Ans. D)

4. This expression can be written as is $\frac{i^2 + i + 1}{i^3} = \frac{i}{i^3} = \frac{i}{-i} = -1$

5. $[1 - 2(2-3)^{-1}]^{-1} = [1 - 2(\frac{1}{-1})]^{-1} = 3^{-1} = \frac{1}{3}$ (Ans. C)

6. Only students B and C CORRECTLY changed to $3i$ first. It should be noted that student C is expressing the answer in preferred form over the form that student B is submitting. (Ans. C)

7. $\frac{1}{a^{-1} + b^{-1}} = \frac{1}{\frac{1}{a} + \frac{1}{b}} = \frac{1}{\frac{b+a}{ab}} = \frac{ab}{b+a}$ or $\frac{ab}{a+b}$ (Ans. D)

8. To find $f^{-1}(x)$, interchange x and y and solve for y.
Let $y = 2^x$. Change to $x = 2y$, which is equivalent to $y = \log_2 x$. Thus, $f^{-1}(x) = \log_2 x$.
Now, $\frac{f^{-1}(a)}{f^{-1}(b)} = \frac{\log_2 a}{\log_2 b}$. (Ans. C)

9. The x-intercept(s) are found by setting $y = x^3 - 6x^2 + 12x - 8 = 0$. But, $x^3 - 6x^2 + 12x - 8 = (x-2)^3$. The solution of $(x-2)^3 = 0$ is 2. (Ans. B)

10. The third term is $(\frac{8 \cdot 7}{1 \cdot 2}) x^6 (-2y)^2 = 112 x^6 y^2$. (Ans. A)

11. Total time = time to travel m miles with no stops + time to (in hours) make s stops of t minutes each $\frac{m}{30} + \frac{st}{60} = \frac{2m + st}{60}$ (Ans. A)

12. $\dfrac{x}{y} = w + \dfrac{z}{y}$ from the given information. Now,

    $(x+3wy) \div y = \dfrac{x}{y} + 3w = (w + \dfrac{z}{y}) + 3w = 4w + \dfrac{z}{y}$. Thus, z is the remainder. (Ans. A)

13. The speed of the train is x/12, where the length of the train is x yards. Then, 435 ÷ (x/12) = 15, and thus x = 348. Note that in the 12 seconds required to pass through the tunnel's entrance, the train is traveling the distance of its own length. (Ans. A)

14. Rewrite as $(x+2)^2 + y^2 = 5$, which implies that the radius SQUARED equals 5. Thus, area $= 5\pi$. (Ans. B)

15. |x+2| ≤ 6 is equivalent to -6 ≤ x+2 ≤ 6, which yields -8 ≤ x ≤ 4. (Ans. A)

16. Let x = number of students who failed, 3x = number of students who passed, and y = mean of all failing grades. Now, 4x students took the test, and the mean for all 4x students is found as follows: $[(84)(3x) + (y)(x)] / 4x = 63 + \dfrac{y}{4}$. Since this value is double the mean of all failures, we get: $63 + \dfrac{y}{4} = 2y$. Thus, y = 36. (Ans. B)

17. The radius of the circumscribed circle = $(\dfrac{1}{2})$ (diagonal of the square) =

    $= (\dfrac{1}{2})(10\sqrt{2}) = 5\sqrt{2} \approx 7.07$. The closest answer is 7. (Ans. C)

18. $\text{Log}_8(x-1) + \text{Log}_8(x+1) = \text{Log}_8(x^2-1)$. Now, $\text{Log}_8(x^2-1) = 1$ $x^2-1 = 81$. This leads to 3 and -3 as values of x. But Log (negative number) is undefined. Thus, x = 3 only. (Ans. C)

19. Simplifying the numerator

    $\sqrt{x^2 + 2x\sqrt{x} + x} = \sqrt{x(x + 2\sqrt{x} + 1)} = \sqrt{x(\sqrt{x}+1)(\sqrt{x}+1)} = (\sqrt{x}+1)\sqrt{x}$. Now, the problem becomes $\dfrac{(\sqrt{x}+1)(\sqrt{x})}{2(\sqrt{x}+1)} = \dfrac{\sqrt{x}}{2}$. (Ans. A)

20. D = initial deposit. 6.4% for a year = (6.4) $(\dfrac{270}{360})$ % = 4.8% for 270 days. Thus, D + .048D = 1310. D = 1250. (Ans. D)

EXAMINATION SECTION
TEST 1

DIRECTIONS: Each question or incomplete statement is followed by several suggested answers or completions. Select the one that BEST answers the question or completes the statement. *PRINT THE LETTER OF THE CORRECT ANSWER IN THE SPACE AT THE RIGHT.*

1. If a*b is defined as a + 2b, where a and b are real numbers, then 1._____

   A. the operation * is commutative
   B. the operation * is associative
   C. the operation * has the closure property
   D. a*1 = a

2. If x is a real number, the solution set of $\{x \mid -x^2 + 3x - 2 < 0\}$ may be described in which one of the following ways? 2._____

   A. $\{x \mid x < 1 \text{ or } x > 2\}$ B. $\{x \mid x < -2 \text{ or } x > -1\}$
   C. $\{x \mid -2 < x < -1\}$ D. $\{x \mid 1 < x < 2\}$

3. If a car travels two equal distances with a different speed for each distance, then its average speed for the entire trip is (with consistent units) which one of the following? The _____ mean of the speeds involved. 3._____

   A. geometric   B. arithmetic
   C. reciprocal of the arithmetic   D. harmonic

4. If $\log_4 x + \log_4 1/3 = -5/2$, then x equals 4._____

   A. $\frac{3}{32}$ B. $\frac{5}{8}$ C. $\frac{3}{4}$ D. 4

5. If r and s are the roots of $x^2 - px + q = 0$, then $r^2 + s^2$ equals 5._____

   A. $p^2 + 2q$ B. $p^2 - 2q$ C. $p^2 + q^2$ D. $p^2 - q^2$

6. The number of terms in the simplified expansion of $[(x+2y)^2(x-2y)^2]^3$ is which one of the following? 6._____

   A. 6   B. 7   C. 12   D. 13

7. If $0.3^x = 6$, log 2 = .3010, and log 3 = .4771, then the value of x to the nearest tenth is 7._____

   A. -1.6   B. -1.5   C. -.5   D. -.3

8. The sum of the roots of the equation $|x|^2 + |x| - 6 = 0$ is 8._____

   A. -6   B. -1   C. 0   D. 1

9. If the complex number a + bi is represented by the ordered pair (a,b), then the multiplicative inverse of the complex number (1,-1) may be represented by which one of the following? 9._____

   A. (-1,1)   B. (1,-1)   C. $(\frac{1}{2},\frac{1}{2})$ D. $(\frac{1}{2},-\frac{1}{2})$

77

10. If x and y are real numbers, the area of the region containing the points defined by $\{(x,y) | (x^2+4y^2 < 16) \cap (2y \geq x-2) \cap (x \geq 0) \cap y \leq 0\}$ is

    A. 1 B. 2 C. 4 D. 6

11. If line AB passes through points (6,0) and (2,3) and intersects the Y-axis at point P, then the line which is perpendicular to AB and passes through point P has a slope and Y-intercept, respectively, equal to

    A. $-\frac{3}{4}$ and $4\frac{1}{2}$
    B. $\frac{3}{4}$ and $4\frac{1}{2}$
    C. $\frac{4}{3}$ and -8
    D. $\frac{4}{3}$ and $4\frac{1}{2}$

12. If a plane parallel to the base of a cone divides the altitude into two segments from vertex to base in the ratio a:b, then which one of the following is the ratio of the volumes of the two parts into which this cone is divided?

    A. $a^3:b^3$
    B. $a^3:b(3a^2+3ab+b^2)$
    C. $a^3:(a+b)^3$
    D. $b^3:a(a^2+3ab+3b^2)$

13. Of the following, the equation of a circle which passes through (2,0) and (6,0) and is tangent to the Y-axis is

    A. $(x-4)^2 + (y-\sqrt{12})^2 = 4$
    B. $(x-\sqrt{12})^2 + (y-3)^2 = 8$
    C. $(x-4)^2 + (y-\sqrt{12})^2 = 16$
    D. $x^2 + (y-12)^2 = 16$

14. Which one of the following lines is NOT an asymptote of the graph of the equation $xy^2 - y^2 - 4x + 1 = 0$?

    A. $x = 1$ B. $x = -1$ C. $y = 2$ D. $y = -2$

15. The SHORTEST distance from the point (-8,2) to the curve $x^2 + y^2 - 8x - 14y + 40 = 0$ is

    A. 5 B. 8 C. 12 D. 13

16. The equation of the ellipse, the length of whose minor axis is 8 and whose foci are at the points in which the circle $x^2 + y^2 = 9$ intercepts the x-axis, is which one of the following?

    A. $\frac{x^2}{9} + \frac{y^2}{16} = 1$
    B. $\frac{x^2}{16} + \frac{y^2}{9} = 1$
    C. $\frac{x^2}{16} + \frac{y^2}{25} = 1$
    D. $\frac{x^2}{25} + \frac{y^2}{16} = 1$

17. The equation of the directrix of the parabola $y^2 - 4x - 6y + 9 = 0$ is

    A. $x = -2$ B. $x = -1$ C. $x = 1$ D. $x = 2$

18. The solution set of $2x^2 + 7x - 4 < 0$ consists of all real values of x, such that 18.____

    A. x>4 or x<1/2
    B. x < -4 or x > 1/2
    C. -4 < x < -1/2
    D. -4 < x < 1/2

19. The repeating decimal, .152525.., is equivalent to which one of the following fractions? 19.____

    A. $\dfrac{146}{957}$
    B. $\dfrac{151}{990}$
    C. $\dfrac{6,101}{40,000}$
    D. $\dfrac{610,101}{4,000,000}$

20. If $3x^3 - 9x^2 + kx - 12$ is exactly divisible by x - 3, then it is also exactly divisible by which one of the following 20.____

    A. $3x^2 - x + 4$
    B. $3x^2 - 4$
    C. $3x^2 + 4$
    D. x - 4

KEY (CORRECT ANSWERS)

1.	C	11.	D
2.	A	12.	C
3.	D	13.	C
4.	A	14.	B
5.	B	15.	B
6.	B	16.	D
7.	B	17.	B
8.	C	18.	D
9.	C	19.	B
10.	A	20.	C

SOLUTIONS TO PROBLEMS

1. $a*b = a+2b$, which is still a real number when a,b are reals. Note: $a*b \neq b*a$ since $a+2b \neq b+2a$ and that neither the associative property nor the statement $a*1 = a$ hold.
   (Ans. C)

2. $-x^2 + 3x - 2 < 0$ means $x^2 - 3x + 2 > 0$, which implies $(x-2)(x-1) > 0$. Case 1: both $(x-2)$ and $(x-1) > 0$, which implies $x > 2$. Case 2: both $(x-2)$ and $(x-1) < 0$, which implies $x < 1$.
   The final answer is $x > 2$ or $x < 1$. (Ans. A)

3. Let D = common distance. Let x_1 = 1st speed, x_2 = 2nd speed. Average speed = total distance total time = $(D+D) \div (\frac{D}{x_1} + \frac{D}{x_2}) = (2x_1 x_2)/(x_1 + x_2)$. The harmonic mean of two numbers $x_1, x_2 = 1/(\frac{1}{x_1} + \frac{1}{x_2}) \div 2$, which can be shown to be equivalent to $(2x_1 x_2)/(x_1 + x_2)$.
   (Ans. D)

4. $\log_4 x + \log_4 \frac{1}{3} = \log_4 \frac{1}{3}x$ by a rule of logs. Now, $\log_4 \frac{1}{3}x = \frac{5}{2}$ means $\frac{1}{3}x = 4^{-\frac{5}{2}} = \frac{1}{32}$.
   Thus, $x = \frac{3}{32}$ (Ans. A)

5. $rs = q$ and $r + s = p$, since this follows as properties as the roots of a quadratic equation. $(r+s)^2 = r^2 + 2rs + s^2 = p^2$. Since $rs = q$, we have $r^2 + 2q + s^2 = p^2$. Now, $r^2 + s^2$ must be $p^2 - 2q$. (Ans. B)

6. $[(x+2y)^2 (x-2y)^2]^3 = \{[(x+2y)(x-2y)]^2\}^3 = (x^2-4y^2)^6$.
   This last expression has seven different terms. (Ans. B)

7. $.3^x = 6$ means $(x)(\log .3) = \log 6$. Then, $(x)[(\log 3) + \log .1] = [\log 3 + \log 2]$. $x(.4771 - 1) = .4771 + .3010$. Solving, $x = -1.488$ or approx. -1.5. (Ans. B)

8. If x is positive, this equation reads $x^2 + x - 6$ and if x is negative, the equation reads $x^2 - x - 6$. For x positive, the sum of the two roots; $= -1$, and for x negative, the sum of the two roots $= 1$. Thus, the sum of all four roots = 0. (Ans. C)

9. $(1,-1)$ means $1-i$. The multiplicative inverse is $\frac{1}{1-i}$ which $= (\frac{1}{1-i})(\frac{1+i}{1+i}) = \frac{1+i}{2} = \frac{1}{2} + \frac{1}{2i}$. This is represented by $(\frac{1}{2}, \frac{1}{2})$. (Ans. C)

10.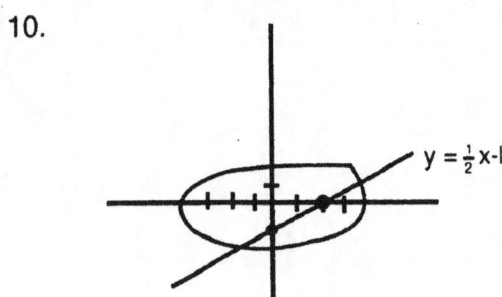
    $x^2 + 4y^2 < 16$ becomes $\frac{x^2}{4^2} + \frac{y^2}{2^2} < 1$, which represents the inside of an ellipse shown here.
    Shaded area = $(\frac{1}{2})(1)(2) = 1$. (Ans. A)

11.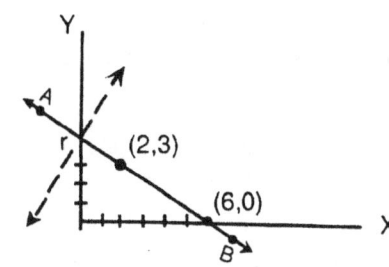

The equation of $\overleftrightarrow{AB}$ is $y = -\frac{3}{4}X + \frac{9}{2}$ r

Then, P is located at $(0, \frac{9}{2})$. Now, slope of dotted line $= \frac{4}{3}$. (Ans. D)

12.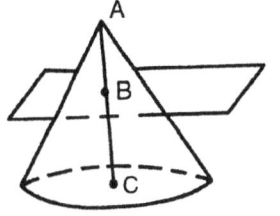

Let AB = a, BC = b, r = radius of circular base of small cone, R = radius of base of large cone. Note: a:a+b = r:R Volume of small cone =

$\frac{1}{3}\pi r^2 a$ Volume of large cone $= \frac{1}{3}\pi R^2(a+b)$

Ratio of volumes $= r^2 a/R^2(a+b) = a^3/(a+b)^3$ (Ans. C)

13.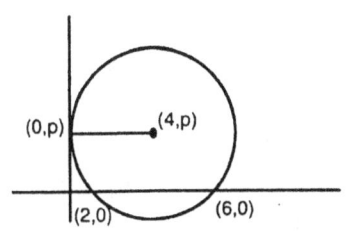

Let point of tangency be (0,p). Since a radius drawn to p must be parallel to the x-axis, the y coordinate of the center is p. Also, the x coordinate is 4 because the center must be equidistant from (2,0) and (6,0). Now, distance from (0,p) to (4,p) = 4 = distance from (4,p) to (2,0) = $\sqrt{p^4 + 4}$. Solving, $4 = \sqrt{p^4 + 4}$, $p = \sqrt{12}$ A circle with center at $(4, \sqrt{12})$ and radius of 4 has equation $(x-4)^2 + (y-\sqrt{12})^2 = 16$. (Ans. C)

14. x = -1 is NOT an asymptote since by substitution, $-y^2 - y^2 + 4 + 1 = 0$ and $y = \pm\sqrt{2.5}$. For the other choices, an unsolvable equation appears. (Ans. B)

15.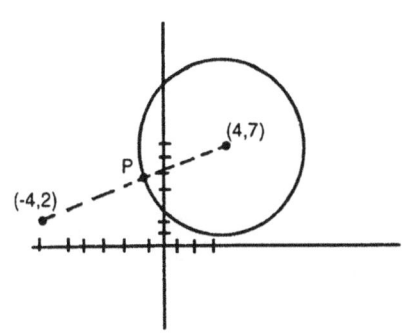

Rewrite $x^2 + y^2 - 8x - 14y + 40 = 0$ as $(x-4)^2 + (y-7)^2 = 2$. This is a circle with center at (4,7) and radius = 5. The shortest distance will be the distance from (-8,2) and p. The equation of the dotted line is $y = \frac{5}{2}x + \frac{64}{12}$ and p lies at the intersection of this dotted line and the circle, which is 5 units from (4,7). Since the distance from (-8,2) to (4,7) is 13, the distance from (-8,2) to p must be 8. (Ans. B)

16. 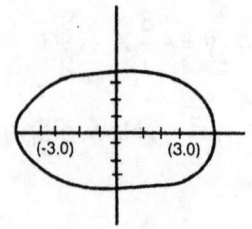 Foci are at ($\pm 3,0$), a = 5, b = 4, so the equation is $x^2/25 + y^2/16 = 1$. Here, a = 1/2 · length of major axis and b = 1/2 · length of minor axis. (Ans. D)

17. If the equation of a parabola is given by $(y-k)^2 = 4p(x-h)$ and the equation of the directrix is $x = h-p$. Transform $y^2 - 4x - 6y + 9 = 0$ to $(y-3)^2 = 4(x-0)$. Thus, p = 1, h = 0. The equation of the directrix is x = -1. (Ans. B)

18. By factoring, $(2x-1)(x+4) < 0$, which is solved by:

    Case 1: $2x-1 < 0$ and $x+4 > 0$, which implies $-4 < x < \frac{1}{2}$.

    Case 2: $2x-1 > 0$ and $x+4 < 0$,
    which has no answer. Final answer: $-4 < x < 4\frac{1}{2}$. (Ans. D)

19. Let N = .152525.., then 100N = 15.2525. Now, 99N = 15.1.

    Thus, N = $\frac{151}{990}$. (Ans. B)

20. 3 must be a solution of $3x^3 - 9x^2 + kx - 12 = 0$ if x-3 is a factor.
    $3(3)^3 - 9(3)^2 + k(3) - 12 = 0$. Then, k = 4. Since $3x^3 - 9x^2 + 4x - 12 = (x-3)(3x^2+4)$, then $3x^2 + 4$ must also divide evenly into $3x^3 - 9x^2 + 4x - 12$. (Ans. C)

TEST 2

DIRECTIONS: Each question or incomplete statement is followed by several suggested answers or completions. Select the one that BEST answers the question or completes the statement. *PRINT THE LETTER OF THE CORRECT ANSWER IN THE SPACE AT THE RIGHT.*

1. A, B, and C are the vertices of an equilateral triangle. A man traveled along its perimeter with the following average speeds: from A to B at r feet per minute, from B to C at s feet per minute, and from C to A at t feet per minute.
His average speed for the entire trip, in feet per minute, was

   A. $1/3(r+s+t)$
   B. $1/3(1/r+1/s+1/t)$
   C. $\dfrac{3rst}{rs+rt+st}$
   D. none of the above

   1.____

2. Given the three sets of coplanar points represented by: $3x + 4y \leq 24$, $x \geq 1$, and $y \geq 2$, then the area of the polygon common to the three sets of points is

   A. 2 B. $\dfrac{169}{24}$ C. 14 D. $\dfrac{169}{12}$

   2.____

3. Other things being equal, the electrical resistance of a wire varies directly as its length and inversely as the square of its diameter.
If a wire 400 feet long and 2.5 mm in diameter has a resistance of 1.1 ohms, then the resistance of a wire of the same material whose length is 300 feet and whose diameter is 2 mm is, to the NEAREST tenth of an ohm,

   A. .5
   B. 1.0
   C. 1.3
   D. none of the above

   3.____

4. Consider the following sets of numbers: positive irrational numbers, complex numbers, positive real numbers, positive rational numbers, positive integers, positive even integers. These sets can be arranged in a nest of sets and subsets, with the exception of one of them.
The one which does NOT fit in such a nest is

   A. positive even integers
   B. complex numbers
   C. positive irrational numbers
   D. positive rational numbers

   4.____

5. If p, r, s, and t are non-negative real numbers; p, r, and s are in arithmetic progression; and r, s, and t are in geometric progression, which one of the following statements is NOT true?

   A. If $p \neq r$, then $s \neq t$
   B. $rt = (2r-p)^2$
   C. $rs = pt$
   D. If $p = 0, t = 4r$

   5.____

6. Of the following, the equation which represents the set of points such that the distance of each from the point (5,3) is twice its distance from the x axis is

   A. $x^2 - 3y^2 - 10x - 6y + 34 = 0$
   B. $x^2 - y^2 - 10x - 6y + 34 = 0$
   C. $x^2 - 3y^2 - 34 = 0$
   D. $x^2 - 3y^2 - 8x + 34 = 0$

   6.____

7. In the hyperbola $9x^2 - y^2 - 36 = 0$, the eccentricity is

   A. $2\sqrt{5}$ B. $\sqrt{10}$ C. $2\sqrt{10}$ D. 12

8. Which one of the following statements is TRUE concerning the graph of $xy - 2y = x$? It is

   A. continuous
   B. asymptotic only to the line $x = 2$
   C. asymptotic only to the line $y = 1$
   D. asymptotic to both lines $x = 2$ and $y = 1$

9. Given $\log 2 = 0.3010$, $\log 3 = 0.4771$, and $\log 7 = 0.8451$. Using these values, find $\log 46\ 2/3$.

   A. .6690   B. 1.6690   C. 1.6232   D. .6232

10. $x^2 - 6x + 8 > 0$ is TRUE for all values of x where

    A. $2 < x < 4$
    C. $x < 4$
    B. $x < 2$ or $x > 4$
    D. $x > 2$

11. The graph of $|x| + |y| = 8$ consists of

    A. one straight line
    C. the sides of a square
    B. a pair of straight lines
    D. a circle

12. The expansion of the determinant:

    $$\begin{vmatrix} x+a & x+2a & x+3a \\ x+2a & x+3a & x+4a \\ x+3a & x+4a & x+5a \end{vmatrix}$$

    is, when simplified,

    A. equal to 0
    B. a third degree expression in x
    C. a linear expression in x
    D. an expression that contains x, but does not contain x

13. The fraction $\dfrac{6}{x^2 - x}$ is equal to the sum of two other fractions whose denominators are x and x-1, respectively, and whose numerators are integers.
    Of the following, which one is one of the two fractions?

    A. $\dfrac{-6}{x-1}$ B. $\dfrac{-3}{x-1}$ C. $\dfrac{6}{x-1}$ D. $\dfrac{3}{x-1}$

14. A certain number is represented by $1+\dfrac{1}{x^2}$, with x a real number.

    If the sum of this number and its reciprocal is 2 1/6, then x MUST be either

    A. $\sqrt{-3} - \sqrt{-3}$
    B. $\sqrt{3}$ or $-\sqrt{3}$
    C. 2 or -2
    D. $\sqrt{2}$ or $-\sqrt{2}$

15. The solution of the inequality $4^{2-2x} < 8x^2$ is

    A. x < -2
    B. x > 2/3
    C. x > 2/3 or x < -2
    D. x > 2/3 and x < -2

16. If the annual percent increase in population of a given community is known to have been constant, and if the population in 1990 was a, and in 2000 was b, then the expression below that represents the population for 1995 was

    A. $\dfrac{a+b}{2}$
    B. $\sqrt{ab}$
    C. $\dfrac{2ab}{a+b}$
    D. $\dfrac{ab}{a+b}$

17. The set of values satisfying the inequality $\left|\dfrac{10-x}{3}\right| < 2$ is

    A. 4 < x < 16
    B. 4 > x > -16
    C. -4 > x > -16
    D. x < 16

18. If the radius of a sphere is doubled, the percent increase in volume is

    A. 200
    B. 400
    C. 700
    D. 800

19. The sum of the reciprocals of the roots of the equation $x^2 + px + q = 0$ is

    A. $-\dfrac{p}{q}$
    B. $\dfrac{q}{p}$
    C. $\dfrac{p}{q}$
    D. $-\dfrac{q}{p}$

20. If $n \neq 0$, the expression $n\sqrt{\dfrac{20}{4^{n+2} + 2^{2n+2}}}$ is equal to

    A. $\dfrac{1}{4}$
    B. $\dfrac{1}{2}n\sqrt{10}$
    C. $\dfrac{1}{4}n\sqrt{5}$
    D. $\dfrac{4}{n}$

KEY (CORRECT ANSWERS)

1. C
2. B
3. C
4. C
5. C

6. A
7. B
8. D
9. B
10. B

16. C
17. A
18. C
19. D
20. C

21. B
22. A
23. D
24. A
25. A

SOLUTIONS TO PROBLEMS

1. Let d = distance of each side. The times required to travel from A to B, B to C, and C to A are d/r, d/s, and d/t, respectively. Average speed = total distance ÷ total time = 3d/(d/r+d/s+d/t) = 3rst/(rs+rt+st). (Ans. C)

2. The vertices of A, B, C are $(1, 5\frac{1}{4})$, $(1,2)$ and $(5\frac{1}{3}, 2)$, respectively.

   Area = $(\frac{1}{2})$ (BC)(AB) = $(\frac{1}{2})(4\frac{1}{3})(3\frac{1}{4})$ = 169/24. (Ans. B)

3. $R = KL/D^2$, where R = resistance, L = length, D = diameter, K = constant.
   1.1 = (K)(400)/6.25, so that K = .0172. Now, R = (.0172)(300)/4 = about 1.3. (Ans. C)

4. The positive irrational numbers don't fit in the nest. From the smallest to largest set, we have: positive even integers, positive integers, positive rational numbers, positive real numbers, complex numbers. (Ans. C)

5. Let p = 1, r = 3, s = 5, t = $\frac{25}{3}$. Then, rs = 15 ≠ pt = $\frac{25}{3}$
   Algebraically, we must have r = (p+s)/2 and r/s = s/t. (Ans. C)

6. Let (x,y) be any point of the required equation. The distance from (x,y) to the x-axis is y. The distance from (x,y) to (5,3) is $\sqrt{(x-5)^2 - (y-3)^2}$. Now, 2y = $\sqrt{x^2 - 10x + 25 + y^2 - 6y + 9}$, which becomes $x^2 - 3y^2 - 10x - 6y + 34 = 0$. (Ans. A)

7. Rewrite as $\frac{x^2}{4} \cdot \frac{y^2}{36} = 1$, so that a = 2, b = 6, c = $\sqrt{40}$ or $2\sqrt{10}$

   Eccentricity = $\frac{c}{a} = \frac{2\sqrt{10}}{2} = \sqrt{10}$. (Ans. B)

8.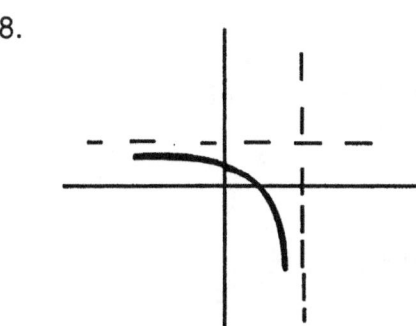

   xy - 2y = x would be asymptotic to x = 2 (since 2y-2y ≠ 2) and to y = 1 (since x-2 ≠ x). (Ans. D)

9. $\text{Log } 46\tfrac{2}{3} = \text{Log } \dfrac{140}{3} = \text{Log } 140 - \text{Log } 3 = (\text{Log } 10 + \text{Log } 7 + \text{Log } 2) - \text{Log } 3 = 1.6690$. (Ans. B)

10. Factor into $(x-4)(x-2) > 0$.
    Case 1: Both factors are > 0, so that $x > 4$.
    Case 2: Both factors are < 0, so that $x < 2$.
    Final answer is $x < 2$ or $x > 4$. (Ans. B)

11. 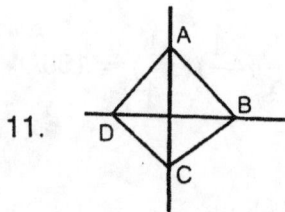 The vertices are: $A(0,8)$, $B(8,0)$, $C(0,-8)$, and $D(-8,0)$.
    The graph is actually a combination of 4 segments: $x+y = 8$, $y-x = 8$, $x+y = -8$, $y-x = -8$.
    This represents a square.
    (Ans. C)

12. This determinant can be reduced to $\begin{vmatrix} 1 & 2 & 3 \\ 2 & 3 & 4 \\ 3 & 4 & 5 \end{vmatrix}$
    The value becomes $(1)(3)(5) + (2)(4)(3) + (3)(4)(2) - (3)(3)(3) - (2)(2)(5) - (1)(4)(4) = 0$.
    (Ans. A).

13. Writing $\dfrac{6}{x^2 - x} = \dfrac{-6}{x} + \dfrac{6}{x-1}$ one of the fractions is $\dfrac{6}{x-1}$ (Ans. C)

14. The reciprocal of $1 + \dfrac{1}{x^2}$ is $\dfrac{x^2}{x^2 + 1}$. The sum of these two expressions is, which is equal to.
    This is equivalent to $6x^4 + 12x^2 + 6 + 6x^4 = 13x^4 + 13x^2$.
    Solving, $x = \pm\sqrt{2}$ and $\pm 3i$. Thus, only choice D is correct since $\pm 3i$ are imaginary numbers. (Ans. D)

15. $4^{2-2x} < 8^{x^2}$ can be rewritten as $2^{4-4x} < 2^{3x^2}$, which becomes $4 - 4x < 3x^2$. Now, $(3x-2)(x+2) > 0$, which leads to $x > \dfrac{2}{3}$ or $x < -2$. (Ans. C)

16. Let k = annual percent increase. Then, $a(1 + \dfrac{k}{100})^{10} = b$
    Thus, $k = \sqrt[10]{b/a} - 1$. Now, in 1995, the population can be denoted as
    $a(1 + \sqrt[10]{b/a} - 1)^5 = a \cdot \sqrt{b/a} = \sqrt{ab}$. (Ans. B)

17. $\left| \dfrac{10-x}{3} \right| < 2$ means $-2 < \dfrac{10-x}{3} < 2$, which is satisfied by $4 < x < 16$.
    (Ans. A)

18. Volume = $\frac{4}{3}\pi R^3$. If 2R replaces R, new volume = $\frac{32}{3}\pi^2 R^3$

    $2^3 = 8$. The percent increase is 800%. (Ans. D)

19. Let R_1, R_2 be the two roots. We require $\frac{1}{R_1} + \frac{1}{R_2}$, which equals $(R_2+R_1)/(R_1)(R_2)$ = Sum of roots/Product of roots = $-p/q$. (Ans. A)

20. $\sqrt[n]{\dfrac{20}{4^{n+2} + 2^{2n+2}}} = \sqrt[n]{\dfrac{2^2 \cdot 5}{2^{2n+4} + 2^{2n+2}}} = \sqrt[n]{\dfrac{2^2 \cdot 5}{2^{2n+2}(2^2+1)}} = \sqrt[n]{\dfrac{1}{2^{2n}}} = \dfrac{1}{4}$ (Ans. A)

TEST 3

DIRECTIONS: Each question or incomplete statement is followed by several suggested answers or completions. Select the one that BEST answers the question or completes the statement. *PRINT THE LETTER OF THE CORRECT ANSWER IN THE SPACE AT THE RIGHT.*

1. If log 2 = .301, log 3 = .477, and log 7 = .845, then log 14.4 =

    A. 1.158   B. 1.447   C. 2.158   D. 2.447

2. If $\dfrac{A}{x^2-1} + \dfrac{B}{x^2+2} = \dfrac{2x^2+3}{(x^2-1)(x^2+2)}$, the value of (A+B) is

    A. -2   B. $\dfrac{2}{3}$ C. $\dfrac{4}{3}$ D. 2

3. The product of $(1-1/6)(1-1/7)(1-1/8)\ldots(1-\dfrac{1}{n+4})(1-\dfrac{1}{n+5})$ is

    A. $\dfrac{3}{(n+4)(n+5)}$ B. $\dfrac{5}{n+4}$ C. $\dfrac{5}{n+5}$ D. ∞

4. The 8th term of $(\dfrac{2a}{3} - \dfrac{3}{2a})^{12}$ is

    A. $\dfrac{1782}{a^2}$ B. $-1782a^2$ C. $\dfrac{-1782}{a^2}$ D. $1782a^2$

5. If $f(x) = \dfrac{x}{x-1}$, then $f(x+1) =$

    A. $\dfrac{1}{f(x)}$ B. $\dfrac{1}{f(x)} + 2$ C. $\dfrac{1}{f(x)} + \dfrac{2}{x}$ D. $f(x) + 2$

6. A 25-foot ladder is placed against a vertical wall so that the foot of the ladder is 7 feet from the bottom of the wall.
   If the top of the ladder slips 4 feet, then how many feet will the foot of the ladder slide?

    A. 4   B. 5   C. 8   D. 9

7. A regular octagon is formed by cutting off each corner of a square whose side is 6. The length of one side of the octagon is

    A. 2   B. $2\sqrt{2}$ C. $2\sqrt{2} - 2$ D. $6\sqrt{2} - 6$

8. The solution set for $x^2 - x - 2 > 0$ may be represented by which one of the following?

    A. $\{x|x>-1\} \cup \{x|x<2\}$ B. $\{x|x>-1\} \cap \{x|x<2\}$
    C. $\{x|x<-1\} \cup \{x|x>2\}$ D. $\{x|x<-1\} \cap \{x|x>2\}$

9. The figure below is the graph of which one of the following sentences?

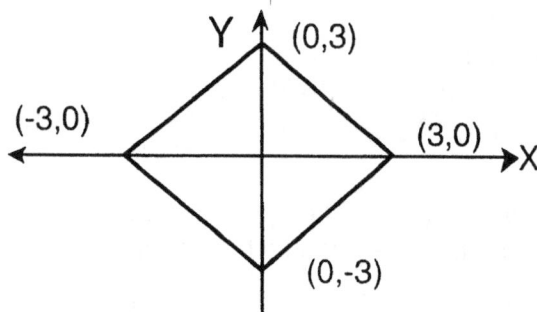

A. $x^2+y^2=9$
B. $|x|=3$ and $|y|=3$
C. $|x+y|=3$
D. $|x| + |y|=3$

10. If the operation * is defined as follows: a*b = 2a + 3b, and all other numerical operational rules hold as always, then the value of 1*(3*2) is equal to

A. 13
B. 22
C. 28
D. 38

11. If f = {(1,3), (2,5), (3,5)}, which one of the following statements is FALSE?

A. The domain of f is {1,2,3}
B. f(f[1]) = 5
C. f is a function
D. The inverse of f is a function

12. The integers, modulo 7, form a group under *multiplication* x. The inverse of 4 x 6 is

A. 1
B. 3
C. 5
D. 6

13. If X and Y are subsets of the set I, and X^1 and Y^1 are the complements of X and Y, respectively, with respect to I, then the complement of X ∩ Y is

A. $X^1 \cap Y$
B. $X \cup Y^1$
C. $X^1 \cap Y^1$
D. $X^1 \cup Y^1$

14. An Abelian group is a group whose elements satisfy

A. the commutative law but not the associative law
B. the associative law but not the commutative law
C. both the commutative and the associative laws
D. neither the commutative nor the associative laws

15. The shaded portion below is

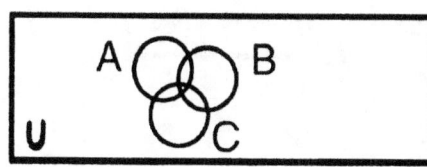

A. $C \cap (A \cup B)^1$
B. $C \cap (A \cup B)$
C. $C \cup (A \cup B)^1$
D. $C \cup (A \cup B)$

16. The equations of the asymptotes of $2x + 3y + 1 = xy$ are

   A. $x - 3 = 0$ and $y - 2 = 0$
   B. $x - 3 = 0$ and $3y + 1 = 0$
   C. $2x + 1 = 0$ and $y - 2 = 0$
   D. $2x + 1 = 0$ and $3y + 1 = 0$

17. The distance between point A(1,2,-1) and point B (x,-2,4) is $5\sqrt{2}$.
    Which one of the following pairs represents the possible values of x?

   A. 1 and 2   B. 1 and -2   C. 4 and 2   D. 4 and -2

18. Find the coordinates of the center of a circle whose equation is $x^2 + y^2 - 4x - 2y - 75 = 0$.

   A. (4,1)   B. (1,4)   C. (2,1)   D. (1,2)

19. The endpoints of a diameter of a circle are (-6,4) and (8,6).
    If A and B are the y-intercept points of the circle, then the length of AB is

   A. $5\sqrt{2}$ B. 10   C. 14   D. $10\sqrt{2}$

20. The equation $r = \dfrac{3}{1 - \cos\theta}$ represents a(n)

   A. circle   B. ellipse   C. hyperbola   D. parabola

KEY (CORRECT ANSWERS)

1.	A	11.	D
2.	D	12.	C
3.	C	13.	D
4.	C	14.	C
5.	C	15.	A
6.	C	16.	A
7.	D	17.	D
8.	C	18.	C
9.	D	19.	C
10.	D	20.	D

SOLUTIONS TO PROBLEMS

1. $\text{Log } 14.4 = \text{Log } \dfrac{144}{10} = \text{Log } 144 - \text{Log } 10 = \text{Log } 2^4 + \text{Log } 3^2 - \text{Log } 10 = (4)(.301) + (2)(.477) - 1 = 1.158$. (Ans. A)

2. $\dfrac{A}{x^2-1} + \dfrac{B}{x^2+2} = \dfrac{A(x^2+2) + B(x^2-1)}{(x^2-1)(x^2+2)}$
   Thus, since $Ax^2 + Bx^2 = 2x^2$, $A + B = 2$. (Ans. D)

3. This product can be rewritten as $(\dfrac{5}{6})(\dfrac{6}{7})(...)(\dfrac{n+3}{n+4})(\dfrac{n+4}{n+5})$.
   Through multiple cancellations, this becomes $\dfrac{5}{n+5}$. (Ans. C)

4. The eighth term $= -(_{12}C_7)(\dfrac{2a}{3})^5(\dfrac{3}{2a})^7 = (-792)(\dfrac{9}{4a^2}) = -\dfrac{1782}{a^2}$
   This procedure is known as the binomial expansion. (Ans. C)

5. $f(x+1) = \dfrac{x+1}{x+1-1} = \dfrac{x+1}{x} = \dfrac{x-1}{x} + \dfrac{2}{x} = \dfrac{1}{f(x)} + \dfrac{2}{x}$ (Ans. C)

6. Using the Pythagorean Theorem, the top of the ladder is $\sqrt{25^2 - 7^2} = 24$ feet above the ground. If it slips 4 feet, the distance from the base of the ladder to the wall is $\sqrt{25^2 - 20^2} = 15$ feet. Thus, the ladder will have slid $15 - 7 = 8$ feet. (Ans. C)

7.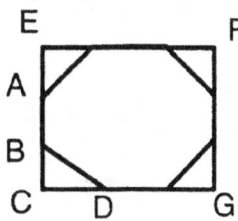
   Let C,E,F,G be vertices of the square. Let $BC = CD = EA = x$.
   Then, $BD = \sqrt{x^2 + x^2} = x\sqrt{2}$.
   Now, $AB = x\sqrt{2}$. Since $EC = 6 = EA + AB + BC = x + x\sqrt{2} + x$.
   Solving, $x = 6 - 3\sqrt{2}$.
   Thus, $AB = (6 - 3\sqrt{2})(\sqrt{2}) = 6\sqrt{2} - 6$ (Ans. D)

8. $x^2 - x - 2 > 0$ becomes $(x-2)(x+1) > 0$.
   Case 1: $x-2 > 0$ and $x+1 > 0$, which yields $x > 2$
   Case 2: $x-2 < 0$ and $x+1 < 0$, which yields $x < -1$
   Thus, either $x > 2$ or $x < -1$; i.e., $\{x|x<-1\} \cup \{x|x>2\}$ (Ans. C)

9. The four sides can be represented by $x+y = 3$, $y = x-3$, $y = -x-3$, and $y = x+3$. Condensing, this is equivalent to $|x| + |y| = 3$. (Ans. D)

10. 1 * (3*2) = 1 * [(2)(3)+(3)(2)] = 1 * 12 = 2(1)+3(12) = 38 (Ans. D)

11. Inverse of f = {(3,1),(5,2),(5,3)}, which is NOT a function. (Ans. D)

12. 4 x 6 = 24, which is 3(mod 7). The inverse n is such that 3 x n = 1. By trying different numbers, we find n = 5. (Ans. C)

13. 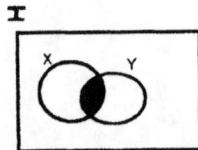 Complement of X ∩ Y is everything in I which is NOT shaded = $X^1 \cup Y^1$. (Ans. D)

14. A group must have the property of associativity. If it is an Abelian group, the commutativity property must also exist. (Ans. C)

15. 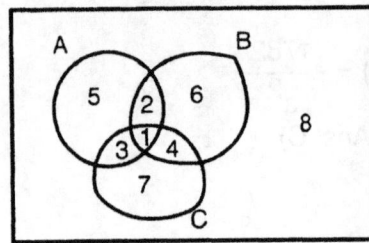 By numbering the regions, we seek region 7.
C = regions 1,3,4,7 and A ∪ B = regions 1,2,3,4,5,6.
Thus, $(A \cup B)^1$ = regions 7,8.
Now, C K $(A \cup B)^1$ = region 7. (Ans. A)

16. If x = 3, 2x+3y+1 = xy becomes 6+3y+1 = 3y (no value for y).
If y = 2, the above equation becomes 2x+6+1 = 2x (no value for x) (Ans. A)

17. Distance = $\sqrt{(1-x)^2 + (2-[-2])^2 + (-1-4)^2} = 5\sqrt{2}$
This reduces to $x^2 - 2x - 9 = 0$. Solving, x = 4 and x = -2. (Ans. D)

18. Rewrite as $x^2 - 4x + 4 + y^2 - 2y + 1 = 75 + 4 + 1$, which becomes $(x-2)^2 + (y-1)^2 = 80$. The center is located at (2,1). (Ans. C)

19. 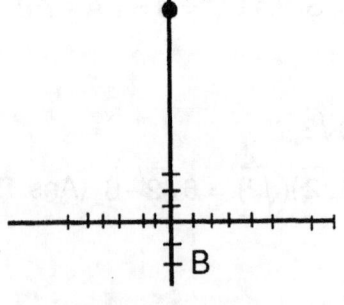 The center of the circle is $(\frac{-6+8}{2}, \frac{4+6}{2}) = (1,5)$
The radius is of length $\sqrt{(8-1)^2 + (6-5)^2} = \sqrt{50}$
Thus, the equation of the circle can be written as $(x-1)^2 + (y-5)^2 = 50$. The y-intercepts would be solutions to $(0-1)^2 + (y-5)^2 = 50$. So, the y-intercepts are 12 and -2. Length of AB = 14. (Ans. C)

20. Convert the equation to r - r cos θ = 3, which becomes
$\sqrt{x^2+y^2} - x = 3$. This simplifies to $y^2 = 6x+9$, which is a parabola. (Ans. D)

TEST 4

DIRECTIONS: Each question or incomplete statement is followed by several suggested answers or completions. Select the one that BEST answers the question or completes the statement. *PRINT THE LETTER OF THE CORRECT ANSWER IN THE SPACE AT THE RIGHT.*

1. What is the equation of the perpendicular bisector of the line segment whose end points are (2,6) and (-4,3)?

    A. $4x + 2y - 5 = 0$
    B. $x - 2y + 10 = 0$
    C. $4x - 2y + 13 = 0$
    D. $x + 2y - 8 = 0$

    1.____

2. Which one of the following principles involving exponents that are natural numbers MOST directly suggests the definition that $x = 1$?

    A. $x^a \div x^b = x^{a-b}, x \neq 0, a \geq b$
    B. $(x^a)^b = x^{ab}$
    C. $x^a y^a = (xy)^a$
    D. $x^a \div y^a = (\frac{x}{y})^a, y \neq 0$

    2.____

3. The first and second terms of a geometric series are x^{-4} and x^t, and $(x \neq 0)$, respectively. If x^{52} is the eighth term of the series, t is equal to

    A. 5/2   B. 24/7   C. 4   D. 16/3

    3.____

4. The resistance of a wire is directly proportional to the length and inversely proportional to the cross-sectional area. A 100-foot roll of a given size wire has a resistance of 4 ohms. A 250-foot roll of wire, whose diameter is one-third that of the wire on the first roll, will have a resistance, in ohms, of

    A. 3 1/3   B. 30   C. 54   D. 90

    4.____

5. The multiplicative inverse of $1 + \sqrt{2}$ is which one of the following?

    A. $1 + \sqrt{2}$ B. $-1 + \sqrt{2}$ C. $-1 - \sqrt{2}$ D. $1 - \sqrt{2}$

    5.____

6. Which one of the following describes the roots of the equation $x^2 - 2ix - 1 = 0$ (where $i = \sqrt{-1}$)?

    A. Imaginary and equal
    B. Imaginary and unequal
    C. Rational and equal
    D. Rational and unequal

    6.____

7. Eliminating t from a parametric equations, $x = 1 - e^t$ and $y = 1 + e^{-t}$, yields

    A. $y = \frac{1}{x-1}$
    B. $y = \frac{x-2}{x-1}$
    C. $y = \frac{2-x}{x-1}$
    D. $y = \frac{x}{x-1}$

    7.____

8. If $|2x+3| < 7$, then

    A. $-5 < x < -2$
    B. $-2 < x < 5$
    C. $2 < x < 5$
    D. $-5 < x < 2$

    8.____

95

9. The solution set of $7x - 3 > (x+1)^2$ is which one of the following?

   A. $\{x|x < 1\} \cap \{x|x > 4\}$
   B. $\{x|x < 1\} \cup \{x|x > 4\}$
   C. $\{x|x > 1\} \cap \{x|x < 4\}$
   D. $\{x|x > 1\} \cup \{x|x < 4\}$

10. Two roots of the equation $x^3 + px + q = 0$ are -1 and 3. The third root is

    A. 1   B. -1   C. 2   D. -2

11. The ratio of $\log_2 15$ to $\log_8 225$ is

    A. 1/2   B. 2/1   C. 3/2   D. 2/3

12. If the logarithms in the equation $2 \log_{10} x - \log_{10}(30-2x) = 1$ are real numbers, then the solution set of this equation is which one of the following?

    A. $\{10, -30\}$ B. $\{10\}$ C. $\{-30\}$ D. $\{\ \}$

13. The determinant $\begin{vmatrix} a & 3 & 2 \\ 1 & 0 & 2 \\ 3 & 1 & -1 \end{vmatrix}$ has the value 19.

    The value of $\underline{a}$ is

    A. -19   B. -19/2   C. -2   D. 2

14. The line segment joining the points (-4,1) and (8,-8) is cut by the y-axis to form two line segments in the ratio

    A. 1:3   B. 1:2   C. 2:3   D. 2:5

15. If the lines whose equations are $2x + 3y = 7$ and $3x + ay = 12$ intersect at an angle of 90, then the value of a is

    A. $-\dfrac{9}{2}$ B. $+\dfrac{9}{2}$ C. -2   D. +2

16. In the figure at the right, line AB is perpendicular to line BC. Line segment XY slides into different positions so that X is always on AB, and Y is always on BC. If Z is the midpoint of XY, then the locus of Z is

    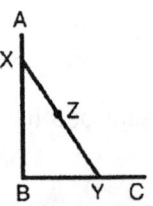

    A. a line
    B. an arc of a circle
    C. one branch of a hyperbola
    D. an arc of an ellipse

17. The area of the triangle, bounded by the lines whose equations are $5y = 4x - 5$ and $2x + 5y = 25$, respectively, and the y-axis, is

    A. 10   B. 15   C. 18   D. 20

18. The coordinates of the vertex of the parabola $y = x^2 + 8x - 3$ are   18._____

    A. (-8,-3)   B. (8,125)   C. (4,45)   D. (-4,-19)

19. If k is real and $ax + by + c = 0$ and $dx + ey + f = 0$ are the equations of two intersecting   19._____
    lines, then the equation of a system of lines passing through their intersection

    A. $(ax+by+c) + k(dx+ey+f) = 0$
    B. $k(ax+by+c)(dx+ey+f) = 0$
    C. $(ax+by+c) + (dx+ey+f) = k$
    D. $K(\dfrac{ax+by+c}{dx+ey+f}) = 0$

20. The graph of $|x| + |y| \geq 1$ includes points in quadrant(s)   20._____

    A. I but no other quadrants
    B. I and II but no other quadrants
    C. I, II, and III but no other quadrants
    D. I, II, III, and IV

KEY (CORRECT ANSWERS)

1.	A	11.	C
2.	A	12.	D
3.	C	13.	D
4.	D	14.	B
5.	B	15.	C
6.	A	16.	B
7.	B	17.	B
8.	D	18.	D
9.	C	19.	A
10.	D	20.	D

SOLUTIONS TO PROBLEMS

1.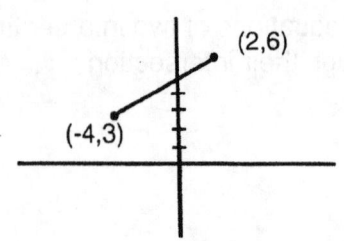
   The midpoint of the line segment is (-1,4.5). Since the slope of this segment is 4, the slope of the perpendicular bisector is -2. The equation of the perpendicular bisector is $y - 4.5 = -2(x+1)$, which becomes $4x + 2y - 5 = 0$. (Ans. A)

2. Since $x^a \div x^b = x^{a-b}$. Letting $a = b$, this can be written as $x^a \div x^a = x^0$ and $x^a \div x^a$ must be 1. Thus, $x^0 = 1$. Note: the correction in selection A from a > b to a ^ b. (Ans. A)

3. $x^t \div x^{-4} = x^{t+4}$ and this must be the common ratio of the geometric series. x^{52} = eighth term $(x^{-4})(x^{t+4})$ Now, $52 = 7t+24$ and so $t = 4$. (Ans. C)

4. $R = KL/A$, where R = resistance, K = constant of proportionality, L = length, A = area. Let 9 = cross-sectional area of the first wire. Since the second wire has a diameter only 1/3 that of the first wire, its area would be $\frac{1}{9}(9) = 1$. $4 = (K)(100)/9$ and $K = .36$. Now, resistant of second wire = $(.36)(250)/1 = 90$ ohms. (Ans. D)

5. $(1+\sqrt{2})(M) = 1$, where M = multiplicative inverse.
   $M = 1/(1+\sqrt{2}) = [1/(1+\sqrt{2})][(1-\sqrt{2})/(1-\sqrt{2})] = -1 + \sqrt{2}$ (Ans. B)

6. The roots of $x^2 - 2ix - 1 = 0$ are $[2i \pm \sqrt{(2i)^2 - 4(1)(-1)}]/2 = (2i\pm)/2 = i$ (double root). This is an imaginary root. (Ans. A)

7. Since $e^t = 1 - x$, $e^{-t} = \dfrac{1}{1-x}$ = So, $y = 1 + e^{-t} = 1 + \dfrac{1}{1-x} = \dfrac{2-X}{1-X} = \dfrac{X-2}{X-1}$ (Ans. B)

8. $|2x+3| < 7$ means $-7 < 2x + 3 < 7$, which yields $-5 < x < 2$. (Ans. D)

9. $7x - 3 > (x+1)^2$ simplifies to $x^2 - 5x + 4 < 0$ or $(x-4)(x-1) < 0$. The solution is $1 < x < 4$, which means $\{x|x > 1\} \cap \{x|x < 4\}$. (Ans. C)

10. $(-1)^3 + p(-1) + q = 0$ and $(3)^3 + p(3) + q = 0$. Solving these two equations yields $p = -7$ and $q = -6$. The original equation becomes $x^3 - 7x - 6 = 0$. Since $x^3 - 7x - 6 = (x+1)(x-3)(x+2)$, the third root is -2. (Ans. D)

11. $\log_2 15 = x$ means $2^x = 15$. $\log_8 225 = y$ means $8^y = 225$ or $(2^3)^y = 15^2$. This implies $2^{\frac{3}{2}y} = 15$ and so $x = \frac{3}{2}y$. Thus, the ratio of $\log_2 15$ to $\log_8 225 = x/y = 3/2$. (Ans. C)

12. $2\log_{10} x = \log_{10} x^2$. $2\log_{10} x - \log_{10}(30-2x) = \log_{10}(\frac{x^2}{30-2x})$. Now, if $\log_{10}(\frac{x^2}{30-2x}) = 120$, $\frac{x^2}{30-2x} = 10$. Thus, the solution becomes none of the given real numbers. In fact, because $30-2x$ must be > 0, this would force $x < 15$. Final answer is $\{\}$. (Ans. D)

13. The value of the determinant is gotten by: $(a)(0)(-1) + (3)(2)(3) + (2)(1)(1) - (2)(0)(3) - (3)(1)(-1)-(a)(1)(2)$ and this $= 19$ Thus, $18 + 2 + 3 - 2a = 19$, and so $a = 2$. (Ans. D)

14.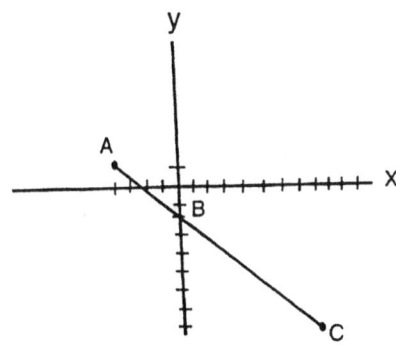

Slope of $\overline{AC} = \frac{-8-1}{8-(-4)} = -\frac{3}{4}$ B is located at $(0,-2)$. $AB = \sqrt{4^2+3^2} = 5$ and $BC = \sqrt{8^2+6^2} = 10$. $5:10 = 1:2$ (Ans. B)

15. Two lines which intersect at 90 will have slopes which are negative inverses of each other. The slope of $2x + 3y = 7$ is $-\frac{2}{3}$, and so the slope of $3x + ay = 12$ must be $\frac{3}{2}$. Thus, $-\frac{3}{a} = \frac{3}{2}$ and $a = -2$. (Ans. C)

16.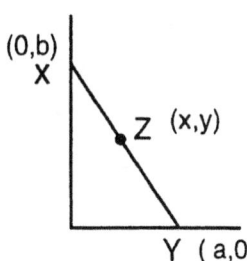

Z = midpoint, distance of XY = constant. Thus, $\sqrt{a^2+b^2}$ is a constant. Now, distance of XZ = distance of YZ.

$\sqrt{x^2+(y-b)^2} = \sqrt{(x-z)^2+y^2}$.

Simplifying, $x^2+y^2-2by+b^2 = x^2-2ax+a^2+y^2$. (Ans. B)

17.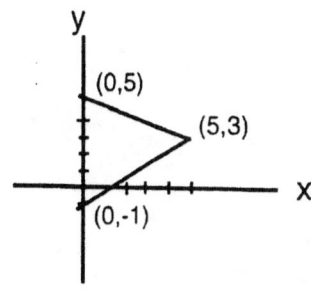

Using the segment connecting $(0,-1)$ and $(0,5)$ as the base, the height would extend from $(5,3)$ to $(0,3)$. Area $= (\frac{1}{2})(\text{base})(\text{height}) = (\frac{1}{2})(6)(5) = 15$. (Ans. B)

18. Rewrite $y = x^2 + 8x - 3$ as $y = (x+4)^2 - 19$. The vertex is $(-4,-19)$, and this represents the lowest point of the parabola. (Ans. D)

19. Since $ax + by + c = 0$ and $dx + ey + f = 0$, the sum of these two equations would also be zero. Also, $k(dx+ey+f) = 0$. Thus, $(ax+by+c) + k(dx+ey+f) = 0$. (Ans. A)

20. 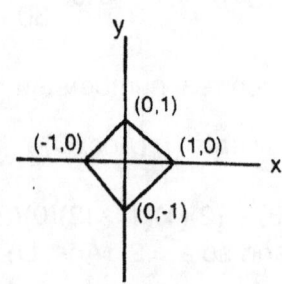 The square on the left is identifiec by: $|x| + |y| = 1$. The graph of $|x| + |y| \geq 1$ would also include everything exterior to the square, and so would include points in all four quadrants. (Ans. D)

EXAMINATION SECTION
TEST 1

DIRECTIONS: Each question or incomplete statement is followed by several suggested answers or completions. Select the one that BEST answers the question or completes the statement. *PRINT THE LETTER OF THE CORRECT ANSWER IN THE SPACE AT THE RIGHT.*

1. If the projections of the legs of a right triangle on the hypotenuse are in the ratio of 1:2, then the ratio of the smaller leg to the larger leg is

    A. 1:2   B. 1:3   C. $1:\sqrt{2}$ D. $1:\sqrt{3}$

    1.____

2. Which one of the following is equivalent to $\tan\frac{\theta}{2} + \cot\frac{\theta}{2}$?

    A. $2\sin\theta$ B. $2\sec\theta$ C. $2\csc\theta$ D. $2\cos\theta$

    2.____

3. In triangle ACD, angle D is a right angle and B is a point on AD between A and D. If angle CBD is represented by x, angle CAD by y, AB by d, and CD by h, then which one of the following is equal to h?

    A. $\dfrac{d}{\cot y - \cot x}$ B. $\dfrac{d}{\cot x - \cot y}$

    C. $\dfrac{d}{\tan x - \tan y}$ D. $\dfrac{d}{\cot x + \cot y}$

    3.____

4. Among the following, the one that is the polar graph of $r = 2\cos\theta$ is a

    A. straight line through (2, 0°)
    B. circle centered at (1, 0°) with radius = 1
    C. straight line through the pole
    D. circle centered at the pole, with radius = 1

    4.____

5. If the bisector of the right angle of a certain right triangle divides the hypotenuse into segments in the ratio 3:5, then the ratio of the longer segment of the hypotenuse to the longer leg of the triangle is

    A. $\sqrt{34}:8$
    B. $\sqrt{17}:2$
    C. 3:5
    D. not determinable from the given data

    5.____

6. In triangle ABC, C = 90°, BC = 3, AC = 4; point D lies on $\overline{AB}$. Angle DCB = 30°; the length of CD is

    A. $\dfrac{5}{4-\sqrt{3}}$ B. $\dfrac{24}{3+4\sqrt{3}}$ C. $\dfrac{24}{4+3\sqrt{3}}$ D. $\dfrac{3\sqrt{3}}{2}$

    6.____

7. If the sides of a triangle are 3, 4, and x, which one of the following will represent only those values of x for which the triangle will be acute?

   A. $1 < x < \sqrt{7}$
   B. $1 < x < 5$
   C. $\sqrt{7} < x < 5$
   D. $\sqrt{7} < x < 7$

8. The number of elements in the solution set of sin x + cos 2x = 1, if the domain of x is $0 \leq x < 2\pi$, is

   A. 2
   B. 3
   C. 4
   D. 5

9. All of the points which are both on the line 3x + 5y = 15 and equidistant from the coordinate axes lie in quadrant(s)

   A. I only
   B. I and II only
   C. I, II, III only
   D. I, II, III, IV

10. Which one of the following is an element of the solution set of $2 \sin^2 x - 3 \sin x - 2 = 0$ if $0 \leq x \leq 2$?

    A. 2/3
    B. 5/6
    C. 7/6
    D. none of these

11. If the greatest common factor of two numbers x and y is c, c being composite, and X is the set of prime factors of x, while Y is the set of prime factors of y, then the set of prime factors of c is

    A. equal to $X \cup Y$
    B. a proper subset of $X \cup Y$
    C. equal to $X \cap Y$
    D. a proper subset of $X \cap Y$

12. In making up a blend containing 45% cotton, 35% dacron, and 20% wool, the formula needed to determine the weight C of cotton needed to mix with D pounds of dacron and W pounds of wool is

    A. $C = \dfrac{.45(W+D)}{.55}$
    B. $C = \dfrac{.55(W+D)}{.45}$
    C. $C = \dfrac{.35D + .20W}{.45}$
    D. $C = .45(.35D + .20W)$

13. A piece of wire 6 1/4 yards long is to be cut into two pieces such that the longer piece is one and one-half as long as the shorter piece.
    The length, in inches, of the SHORTER piece must be

    A. 90
    B. 100
    C. 135
    D. 150

14. The number of cc of water that must be added to 75 cc of a 60% solution of alcohol and water to change it to a 50% solution is CLOSEST to

    A. 10
    B. 15
    C. 20
    D. 30

15. A rectangular picture measuring x inches by y inches is surrounded by a frame of uniform width z inches.
    The number of square inches in the area of the frame is

    A. $2xz + 2yz + 4z^2$
    B. $xy + 2xz + 2yz + 4z^2$
    C. $2xz + 2yz + 2z^2$
    D. $2xy + 2xz + 2yz$

16. When $x^3 + 4x^2 + 3x - 10$ is divided by x-2, the remainder is

    A. 20   B. 8   C. -8   D. -10

17. Which one of the following subsets of the set of integers is closed under addition and multiplication?

    A. {0, 1, 2, 3}   B. {0, 1, 2}   C. {0, 1}   D. {0}

18. The total number of subsets of set {a, b, c} is

    A. 6   B. 7   C. 3   D. 8

19. A small hose can fill a tank with water in two hours while a larger hose can fill the same tank in one hour. The number of minutes it will take for the tank to be filled if both hoses are used at the same time is

    A. 30   B. 40   C. 45   D. 90

20. The volume of an average atom is about 10^{-23} cubic centimeters. The volume of one gene in a human body is about 10^{-17} cubic centimeters.
    Using these figures, we can conclude that the ratio of the volume of a gene to that of an atom is about

    A. 60 to 1   B. 1 to 10^6 C. 10^{-6} to 1   D. 10^6 to 1

21. The solution set of the equation $\frac{x}{x-3} - \frac{1}{x+2} = \frac{15}{x^2-x-6}$ is

    A. ∅   B. {3, -4}   C. {3}   D. {-4}

22. If the graphs of y = 2 log x and y = log 2x are drawn on the same set of axes, these graphs will

    A. not intersect
    B. intersect at one point only
    C. intersect at two points only
    D. coincide

23. A gear with 48 teeth drives a 64 tooth idler gear which, in turn, is engaged to a gear with 32 teeth.
    If the first gear rotates at 1200 rpm, then the last gear rotates, in rpm, at

    A. 800   B. 900   C. 1600   D. 1800

24. The power used in an electric circuit is proportional to the square of the current flow. If the power used in a circuit is 630 watts when the current is 3 amperes, then the power in watts when the current is 4 amperes will be

    A. 354 3/8   B. 472 1/2   C. 840   D. 1120

25. The intensity of illumination, I, on the page of a book varies inversely as the square of the distance, d, between the book and the source of light.
    If I = 6 when d = 4, then the value of I when d = 8 is

    A. 24   B. 8   C. 4.5   D. 1.5

26. Find the solution set of cos 2A + 3 cos A = -2 where $0° \leq A \leq 360°$

    A. {0°, 60°, 300°}   B. {60°, 180°, 300°}
    C. {120°, 180°, 240°}   D. {0°, 120°, 240°}

27. The algebraic statement $x^2 + y^2 = (x+y)^2$ is

    A. true for all values of x and y
    B. never true
    C. true only if x and/or y equals zero
    D. true only if x equals y

28. If the formula $a = \dfrac{V-v}{t}$ is solved for v, the expression equivalent to v is

    A. at - V   B. V - at   C. $-\dfrac{at}{V}$ D. $\dfrac{V}{at}$

29. If $\log_4 y = 3$, then y is equal to

    A. 81   B. 64   C. 12   D. 7

30. The distance between the two parallel lines 3x - 4y = 7 and 9x - 12y = 5 is

    A. 1/3   B. 16/15   C. 7/5   D. 26/15

KEY (CORRECT ANSWERS)

1.	C	16.	A
2.	C	17.	D
3.	A	18.	D
4.	B	19.	B
5.	A	20.	D
6.	B	21.	D
7.	C	22.	B
8.	C	23.	D
9.	B	24.	D
10.	D	25.	D
11.	C	26.	C
12.	A	27.	C
13.	A	28.	B
14.	B	29.	B
15.	A	30.	B

SOLUTIONS TO PROBLEMS

1. 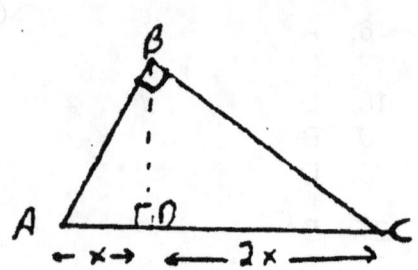 The altitude BD is the geometric mean of AD and DC. So, BD = $x\sqrt{2}$. Using the Pythagorean Theorem twice, we get AB = $x\sqrt{3}$ and BC = $x\sqrt{6}$. Now, AB/BC = $x\sqrt{3}/x\sqrt{6}$, which reduces to $1:\sqrt{2}$. (Ans. C)

2. $\tan\dfrac{\theta}{2} + \cot\dfrac{\theta}{2} = \dfrac{\sin\dfrac{\theta}{2}}{\cos\dfrac{\theta}{2}} + \dfrac{\cos\dfrac{\theta}{2}}{\sin\dfrac{\theta}{2}} = \dfrac{1}{(\cos\dfrac{\theta}{2})(\sin\dfrac{\theta}{2})} = \dfrac{1}{\sqrt{\dfrac{1+\cos\theta}{2}}\sqrt{\dfrac{1-\cos\theta}{2}}}$

   $= \dfrac{2}{\sin\theta} = 2\csc\theta$. (Ans. C)

3.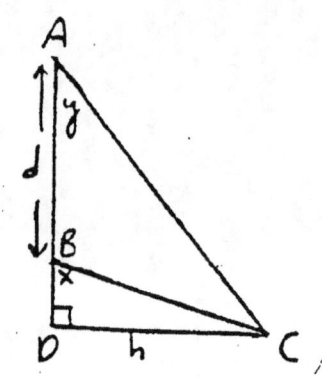
   tan x = h/BD or BD = h cot x
   tan y = h/(d+h cot x)
   d tan y + h(tan y cot x) = h
   h = d tan y/(1-tan y cot x) = d/(cot y - cot x).
   (Ans. A)

4. The graph of any equation in the form r = 2a cos θ is a circle centered at (a, 0). Since a = 1 in this example, the graph is a circle centered at (1, 0°) with radius = 1. (Ans. B)

5. 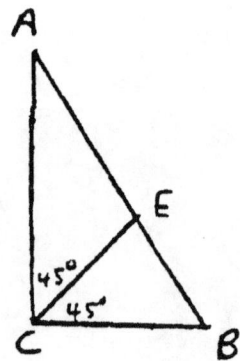 Let EB = 3, AE = 5. Using the Law of sines for triangles ACB and EAC and letting ∠B = k°, AB/sin 90° = AC/sin k° and AE/sin 45° = AC/sin ∠AEC. Now, and by solving the two equations involving AC and k, we get k = 59.036° and AC = 6.86.
   Finally, AE/AC = 5/6.86 = .7289, which is $\sqrt{34}/8$. (Ans. A)

6.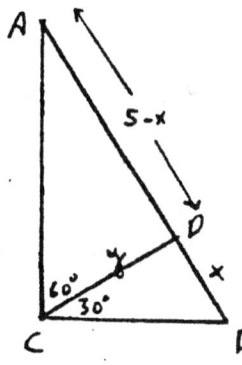

$\angle ACB = 90°$, $AB^2 = 3^2 + 4^2$, so $AB = 5$.

$\tan \angle B = \dfrac{4}{3}$, thus $\angle B = 53°$. Now, $\angle A = 37°$.

Using Law of Sines,

$\dfrac{\sin 53°}{y} = \dfrac{\sin 60°}{x}$ and $\dfrac{\sin 47°}{y} = \dfrac{\sin 60°}{5-x}$.

Solving these two equations,

$CD = y = \dfrac{24}{3 + 4\sqrt{3}}$. (Ans. B)

7. <u>Case 1:</u> The angle opposite x is largest (if x = largest side). Call this $\angle A$. By the Law of Cosines, $x^2 = 3^2 + 4^2 - (2)(3)(4)\cos \angle A$, which becomes $\dfrac{x^2 - 25}{-24} = \cos \angle A$.

In order for to be acute, $\dfrac{x^2 - 25}{-24} > 0$. Solving, $x < 5$.

<u>Case 2:</u> The angle opposite 4 is largest (x is not the largest side). Call this $\angle B$.
$4^2 = 3^2 + x^2 - (2)(3)(x) \cos \angle B$.

$16 = 9 + x^2 - 6x \cos \angle B$, which becomes $\dfrac{7 - x^2}{-6x} = \cos \angle B$.

Now, for $\angle B$ to be acute, we must have $\dfrac{7-x^2}{-6x} > 0$.

Solving, $x > \sqrt{7}$. Thus, $\sqrt{7} < x < 5$. (Ans. C)

8. $\sin x + \cos 2x = 1$ can be written as $\sin x - 2\sin^2 x + 1 = 1$, which is $\sin x (1 - 2\sin x) = 0$. Solving, $\sin x = 0$ gives 0, π. Solving $1 - 2\sin x = 0$ gives $\pi/6$, $5\pi/6$. Thus, there are four answers. (Ans. C)

9. The two points which are equidistant from both the coordinate axes and which lie on the line $3x + 5y = 15$ are found by identifying the intersection of $3x + 5y = 15$ with both $y = x$ and $y = -x$. Thus, the two points are $(15/8, 15/8)$ and $(-15/2, 15/2)$.
These points are in quadrants I and II, respectively. (Ans. B)

10. Factor as $(2\sin x + 1)(\sin x - 2) = 0$. Then, $\sin x = -1/2$ and $\sin x = 2$. From $\sin x = -1/2$, we get $x = 210°$ or $7\pi/6$ radians. Since $7\pi/6 \approx 3.67$, none of the first three selections is correct. Note that $\sin x = 2$ has no solution. (Ans. D)

11. Let $c = p_1 \cdot p_2 \cdot p_3$, where p_1, p_2, p_3 are primes. Then, $x = (p_1 \cdot p_2 \cdot p_3)$ (other primes) and $y = p_1 \cdot p_2 \cdot p_3)$ (other primes) different than those contained in x).
Now, $X \cap Y = \{p_1, p_2, p_3\} = \{$prime factors of c$\}$. (Ans. C)

12. Since D = .35(Total Wt) and W = .20(Total Wt), D + W = .55(Total Wt) or Total Wt = (D+W)/.55. Now, C = .45(Total Wt), which by substitution becomes C = .45(D+W)/.55. (Ans. A)

13. Use x for the shorter piece, 1.5x for the longer piece, x + 1.5x = 6.25. x = 2.5 yds. = 90 in. Note the correction in the wording. (Ans. A)

14. Let x be required number. The original amount of water = (.40)(75) = 30 cc. The new solution will have (30+x) cc of water and (75+x) cc of alcohol and water. Then, we have (30+x)/(75+x) = 50% = .50. Solving, x = 15. (Ans. B)

15. 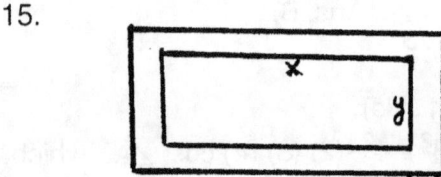 Area of frame = area of larger rectangle - area of smaller rectangle = $(x+2z)(y+2z) - xy$
   = $2xz + 2yz + 4z^2$. (Ans. A)

16. The remainder is the value of $x^3 + 4x^2 + 3x - 10$ when x = 2.
    Thus, $2^3 + 4(2^2) + 3(2) - 10 = 20$. (Ans. A)

17. Only {0} is closed under addition and multiplication {0, 1, 2, 3} and {0, 1, 2} are open under both operations, and {0, 1} is open under addition. (Ans. D)

18. If a set has n elements, 2^n = number of subsets.
    Here, n = 3, so $2^3 = 8$. (Ans. D)

19. Let x = required time operating together (in minutes)
    $\frac{x}{120} + \frac{x}{60} = 1$, which yields x = 40. Note that $\frac{x}{120}$ represents the fraction of the tank that will be filled by the small hose. (Ans. B)

20. $10^{-17}/10^{-23} = 10^6$ or 10^6 to 1. (Ans. D)

21. Multiplying the equation by (x-3)(x+2): x(x+2) - (x-3) = 15. Then, $x^2 + 2x - x + 3 = 15$, whereby (x+4)(x-3) = 0, leading to x = -4 and x = 3. However, a value of x = 3 causes two denominators to be zero, and so must be rejected. Only x = -4 can be accepted. (Ans. D)

22. To find out if there is any intersection, set 2 Log x = Log 2x. Since 2 Log x = Log x^2, we get $x^2 = 2x$. This statement leads to x = 0 and x = 2. However, x = 0 is rejected since Log 0 does not exist. Thus, only x = 2 is a point of intersection. (Ans. B)

23. Let x = speed of 64 tooth idler. By inverse proportion, 1200/x = 64/48 and x = 900. Likewise, if y = speed of last gear, 900/y = 32/64. y = 1800 rpm. (Ans. D)

24. $P = KC^2$ where P = power, C = current. $630 = (K)(3^2)$ and K = 70. Now, $P = 70C^2$. When C = 4, $P = (70)(4^2) = 1120$. (Ans. D)

25. $I = k/d^2$, k a constant. $6 = k/16$, so $k = 96$.
    Now, $I = 96/d^2$. If $d = 8$, $I = 96/64 = 1.5$. (Ans. D)

26. Since $\cos 2A = 2\cos^2 A - 1$, the given equation becomes:
    $2\cos^2 A - 1 + 3\cos A = -2$, which will transform to:
    $2\cos^2 A + 3\cos A + 1 = 0$ or $(2\cos A + 1)(\cos A + 1) = 0$.
    From $2\cos A + 1 = 0$, $A = 120°, 240°$ and from $\cos A + 1 = 0$, $A = 180°$.
    Final answer is $\{120°, 180°, 240°\}$. (Ans. C)

27. Since $(x + y)^2 = x^2 + 2xy + y^2$, this expression can $= x^2 + y^2$ only if $2xy = 0$. This means either x or y or both $x, y = 0$. (Ans. C)

28. $a = \dfrac{V-v}{t}$ implies $at = V - v$. Then, $v = V - at$. (Ans. B)

29. $\log_4 y = 3$ means $y = 4^3 = 64$. (Ans. B)

30. Transforming both equations to slope-intercept form, $y = \dfrac{3}{4}x - \dfrac{7}{4}$ and $y = \dfrac{3}{4}x - \dfrac{5}{12}$. The equation of any line perpendicular to these two lines has the form $y = -\dfrac{4}{3}x + k$, k a constant.

    Let $k = 0$. Then, $y = -\dfrac{4}{3}x$ intersects $y = \dfrac{3}{4}x - \dfrac{7}{4}$. Converting to decimals, we get $(.84, -1.12)$ and $(-.2, -.27)$. Distance between these points =
    $\sqrt{(.84-.2)^2 + (-1.12+.27)^2} = 1.064 \approx \dfrac{16}{15}$. (Ans. B)

BOOLEAN ALGEBRA

CONTENTS

	Page
CLASSES AND ELEMENTS	1
VENN DIAGRAMS	1
BASIC EXPRESSIONS	3
APPLICATIONS TO SWITCHING CIRCUITS	4
The "AND" Operation	4
The "OR" Operation	6
The "NOT" Operation	7
The "NOR" Operation	8
The "NAND" Operation	9
OUTPUT USED AS INPUT	10
Problems	12
Answers	13
DEDUCING INPUTS FROM OUTPUTS	13
Problems	14
Answers	14
POSTULATES AND THEOREMS	15
Law of Identity	15
Commutative Law	15
Associative Law	16
Idempotent Law	16
Law of Double Negation	17
Complementary Law	17
Law of Intersection	17
Law of Union	18
Law of Dualization (De Morgan's Theorem)	18
Distributive Law	19
Law of Absorption	20

BOOLEAN ALGEBRA

The father of Boolean algebra was George Boole, who was an English logician and mathematician. In the spring of 1847, he wrote a pamphlet on symbolic logic. Later he wrote a much larger text on which are founded the mathematical theories of logic. He did not regard logic as a branch of mathematics, but he did point out that a close analogy between symbols of algebra and those symbols which he devised to represent logical forms does exist.

Boolean algebra lay almost dormant until 1937 when Boole's algebra was used to write symbolic analyses of relay and switching circuits. Boolean algebra has now become an important subject to be learned in order to understand electronic computer circuits.

CLASSES AND ELEMENTS

We have previously determined that in our universe we can logically visualize two divisions; all things of interest in any discussion are in one division, and all other things not of interest are in the other division. These two divisions comprise a set or class called the *universal class*. All objects contained in the universal class are called *elements*. We also identify a set or class containing no elements; this class is called the *null class*.

If we group some elements of the universal class together to form the combinations which are possible in a particular discussion, we call each of these combinations a class. In Boolean logic, these combinations called classes should not be confused with the null class or universal class. Actually, these classes are subclasses of the universal class. It should also be noted that the elements and classes in Boolean algebra are the sets and subsets previously discussed.

Each class is dependent upon its elements and the possible states (stable, nonstable, or both) that the elements can take.

Boolean algebra is that algebra which is based on Boolean logic and concerned with all elements having only two possible stable states and no unstable states.

To determine the number of classes or combinations of elements in Boolean algebra, we solve for the numerical value of 2^n where n equals the number of elements. If we have two elements (each element has two possible states), then we have 2^n or 2^2 possible classes. If we let the elements be A and B, then A may be true or false and B may be true or false. The classes which could be formed are as follows:

    A true and B false
    A true and B true
    A false and B true
    A. false and B false

where we use the connective word "and." We could also form classes by use of the connective word "or" which would result in a different form of classes.

VENN DIAGRAMS

Since the Venn diagram is a topographical picture of logic, composed of the universal class divided into classes depending on the n number of elements, we show this logic as follows.

We may consider the universal class as containing submarines and atomic powered sound sources. Let A equal submarines and B equal atomic powered sound sources. Therefore, we have four classes which are:

1. Submarines and not atomic
2. Submarines and atomic
3. Atomic and not submarines
4. Not submarines and not atomic

A diagram of these classes is

We may show these classes separately by

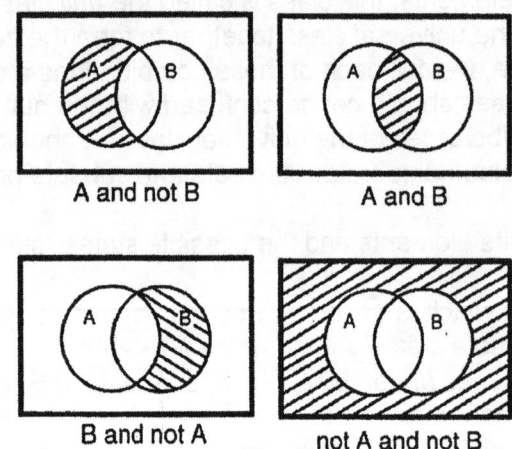

These four classes are called minterms because they represent the four minimum classes. The opposite of the minterms are called maxterms and are shown by

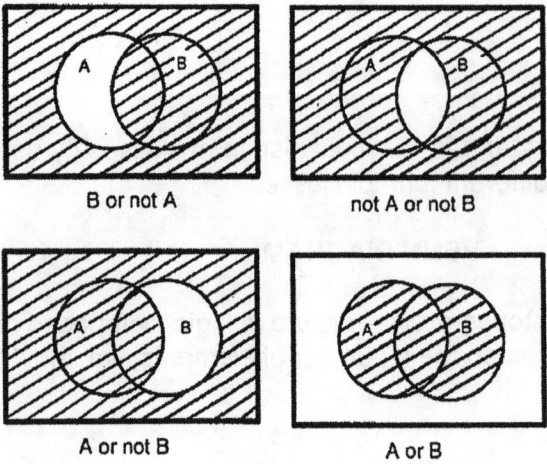

We will discuss minterms and maxterms in more detail later in the chapter.

BASIC EXPRESSIONS

It has been seen that the Venn diagram may be used to represent a picture of logic. The logic previously used was written in longhand, and used the words "and," "or," and "not." We used these words as a basis for combining elements to form classes in Boolean algebra logic descriptions. The symbols from sets and subsets are $\cap$ for "and," $\cup$ for "or," and $-$ for "not." The relationships of symbols are given by the following:

Sets and Subsets	Words	Boolean Algebra
$\cap$	and	$\bullet$
$\cup$	or	+
-	not	-

The following are examples of these relationships:
1. A•B reads A and B
2. A+B reads A or B
3. $\overline{A}$ reads not A

Relationships to the previously indicated classes, about submarines and atomic powered sound are:
1. A and not B = A•$\overline{B}$
2. A and B - A•B
3. B and not A = B•$\overline{A}$
4. not A and not B = $\overline{A}$•$\overline{B}$

Also,
1. B or not A = B + $\overline{A}$
2. not A or not B = $\overline{A}$ + $\overline{B}$
3. A or not B = A+$\overline{B}$
4. A or B = A+B

Notice that
    A•$\overline{B}$
    A•B
    B•$\overline{A}$
    $\overline{A}$•$\overline{B}$

are called minterms. As related to algebra, there is a minimum number of terms in each; that is, one. Notice also that
    B+$\overline{A}$
    $\overline{A}$+$\overline{B}$
    A+$\overline{B}$
    A+B

are called maxterms. As related to algebra, there is a maximum number of terms in each. That is, two.

A further relationship may be made to sets and subsets as follows:
$$A \bullet \overline{B} = A \cap B$$
$$A \bullet B = a \cap B$$
$$B \bullet \overline{A} = B \cap A$$
$$\overline{A} \bullet \overline{B} = A \cap B$$

If we take any of these minterms, such as A•B, and find its component, we have, according to DeMorgan's Theorem

$$\overline{A \bullet B} = \overline{(A \cap B)}$$
$$= \overline{A} \cup \overline{B}$$
$$= \overline{A} + \overline{B}$$

which is a maxterm; therefore, the complement of a minterm is a maxterm.

APPLICATIONS TO SWITCHING CIRCUITS

Since Boolean algebra is based upon elements having two possible stable states, it becomes very useful in representing switching circuits. The reason for this is that a switching circuit can be in only one of two possible states. That is, it is either open or it is closed. We may represent these two states as 0 and 1, respectively. Since the binary number system consists of only the symbols 0 and I, we employ these symbols in Boolean algebra and call this "binary Boolean algebra."

THE "AND" OPERATION

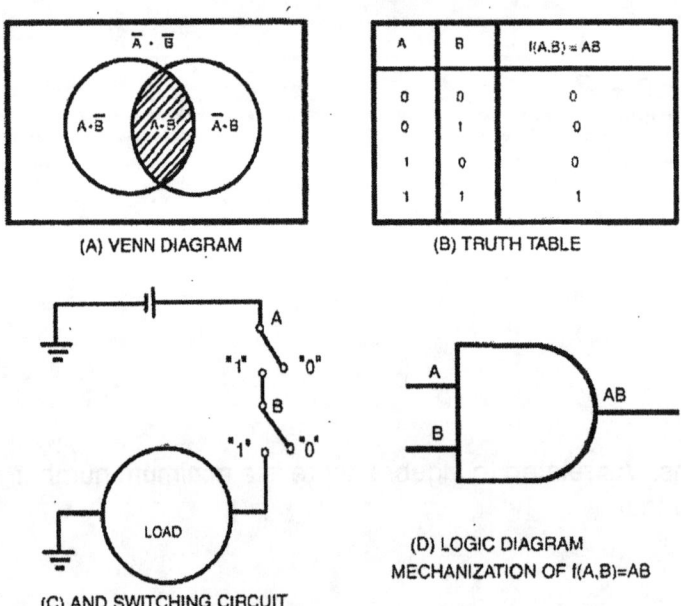

Figure 1 - The AND Operation

Let us consider the Venn diagram in Figure 1(A). Its classes are labeled using the basic expressions of Boolean algebra. Note that there are two elements, or variables, A and B. The shaded area represents the class of elements that are A•B in Boolean notation and is expressed as: f(A,B) = A•B.

The other three classes are also indicated in Figure 1(A). This expression is called an AND operation because it represents one of the four minterms previously discussed. Recall that AND indicates class intersection and both A and B must be considered simultaneously.

We can conclude then that a minterm of n variables with each variable present in either its noncomplemented o its complemented form, and is considered an AND operation.

For any Boolean function, there is a corresponding truth table which shows, in tabular form, the true conditions of the function for each way in which conditions can be assigned its variables. In Boolean algebra, 0 and 1 are the symbols assigned to the variables of any function. Figure 1(B) shows the AND operation function of two variables and its corresponding truth table.

This function can be seen to be true if one thinks of the logic involved: AB is equal to A and B which is the function f(A,B). Thus, if either A or B takes the condition of 0, or both take this condition, then the function f(A,B) equal AB is equal to 0. But if both A and B take the condition of 1, then the AND operation function has the condition of 1.

Figure 1(C) shows a switching circuit for the function f(A,B) equal AB in that there will be an output only if both A and B are closed. An output in this case equals 1. If either switch is open, 0 condition, then there will be no output or 0.

In any digital computer equipment, there will be many circuits like the one shown in Figure 1(C). In order to analyze circuit operation, it is necessary to refer frequently to these circuits without looking at their switch arrangements. This is done by logic diagram mechanization as shown in Figure 1(D). This indicates that there are two inputs, A and B, into an AND operation circuit producing the function in Boolean algebra form of AB. These diagrams simplify equipment circuit diagrams by indicating operations without drawing all the circuit details.

It should be understood that while the previous discussion concerning the AND operation dealt with only two variables that any number of variables will fit the discussion. For example, in Figure 2 three variables are shown along with their Venn diagram, truth table, switching circuit, and logic diagram mechanization.

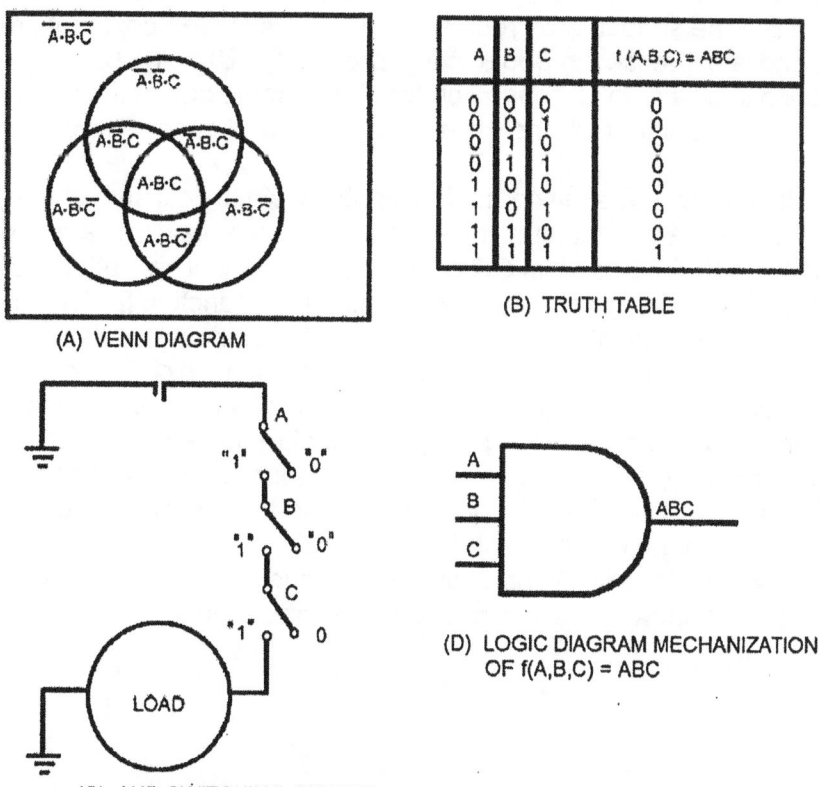

Figure 2 - The AND Operation (Three Variables)

THE "OR" OPERATION

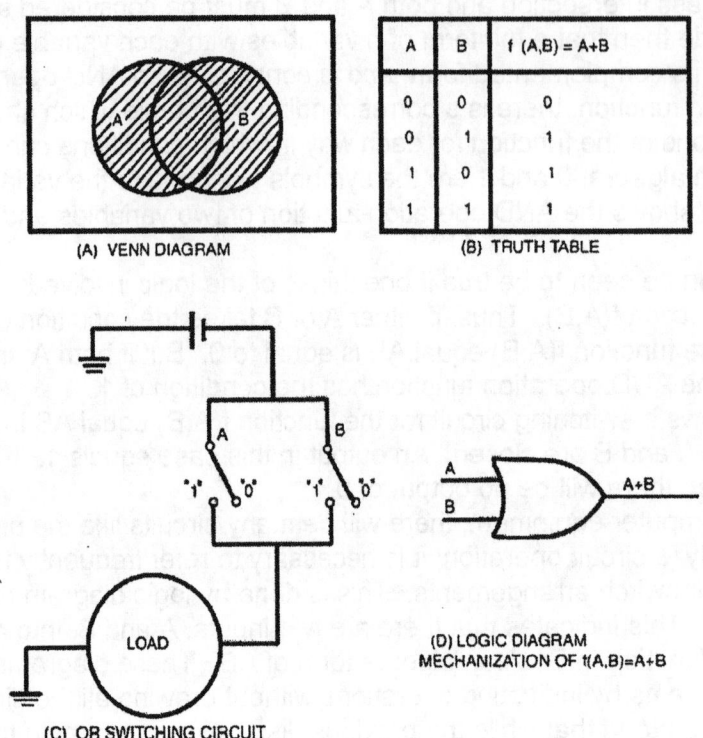

Figure 3 - The OR Operation

We will now consider the Venn diagram in Figure 3(A). Note that there are two elements, or variables, A and B. The shaded area represents the class of elements that are A+B in Boolean notation and is expressed in Boolean algebra as: $f(A,B) = A + B$.

This expression is called an OR operation for it represents one of the four maxterms previously discussed. Recall that OR indicates class union and either A or B or both must be considered.

We can conclude then that a maxterm of n variables is a logical sum of these n variables where each variable is present in either its noncomplemented or its complemented form.

In Figure 3(B), the truth table of an OR operation is shown. This truth table can be seen to be true if one thinks of A+B being equal to A or B which is the function f(A,B). Thus, if A or B takes the value 1, then f(A,B) must equal 1. If not, then the function equals zero.

Figure 3(C) shows a switching circuit for the OR operation which is two or more switches in parallel. It is apparent that the circuit will transmit if either A or B is in a closed position; that is, equal to 1. If, and only if, both A and B are open, equal to 0, the circuit will not transmit.

The logic diagram for the OR operation is given in Figure 3(D). This means that there are two inputs, A and B, into an OR operation circuit producing the function in Boolean form of A+B. Note the difference in the diagram from that of Figure 2(D).

As in the discussion of the AND operation, the OR operation may also be used with more than two inputs. Figure 4 shows the OR operation with three inputs.

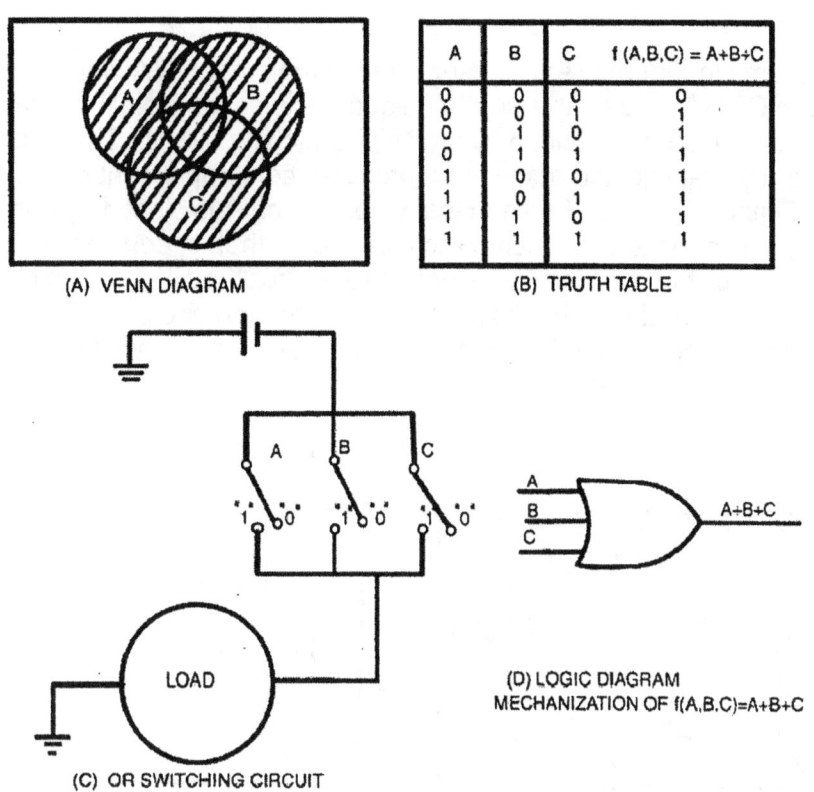

Figure 4 - The OR Operation (Three Variables)

THE "NOT" OPERATION

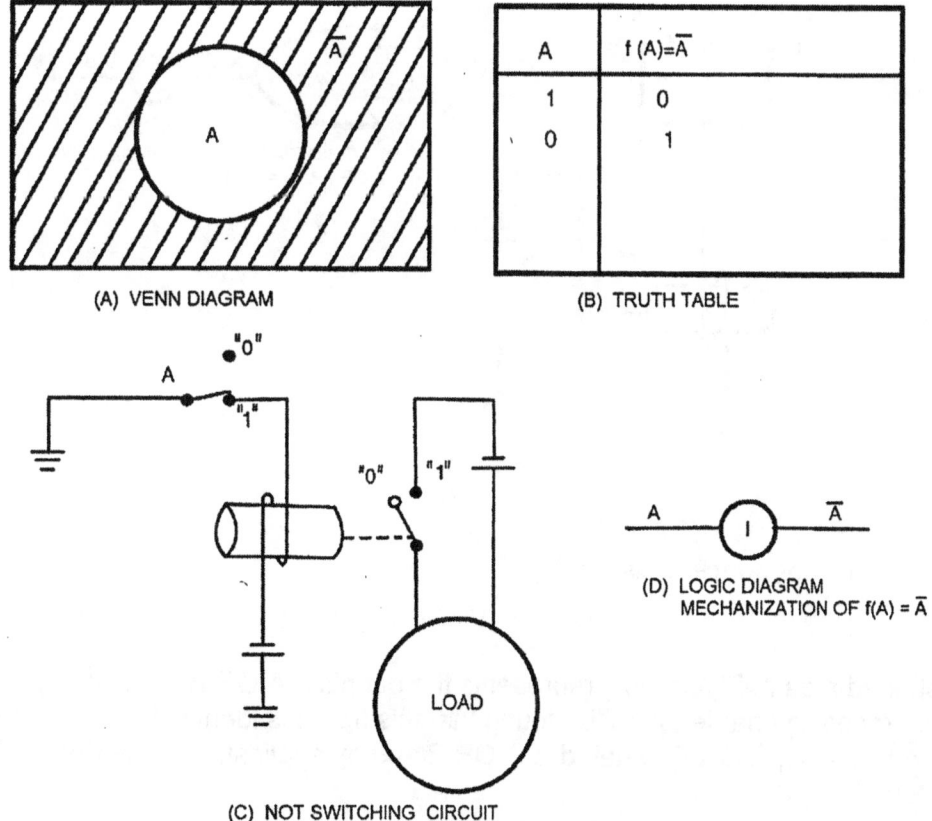

Figure 5 - The NOT Operation

The shaded area in Figure 5(A) represents the complement of A which in Boolean algebra is A and read as "NOT A." The expression f(A) equals A is called a NOT operation. The truth table for the NOT operation is explained by the NOT switching circuit. The requirement of a NOT circuit is that a signal injected at the input produce the complement of this signal at the output. Thus, in Figure 5(C) it can be seen that when switch A is closed, that is, equal to 1, the relay opens the circuit to the load. When switch A is open, that is, equal to 0, the relay completes a closed circuit to the load. The logic diagram for the NOT operation is given in Figure 5(D). This means that A is the input to a NOT operation circuit and gives an output of $\overline{A}$. The NOT operation may be applied to any operation circuit such as AND or OR. This is discussed in the following section.

THE "NOR" OPERATION

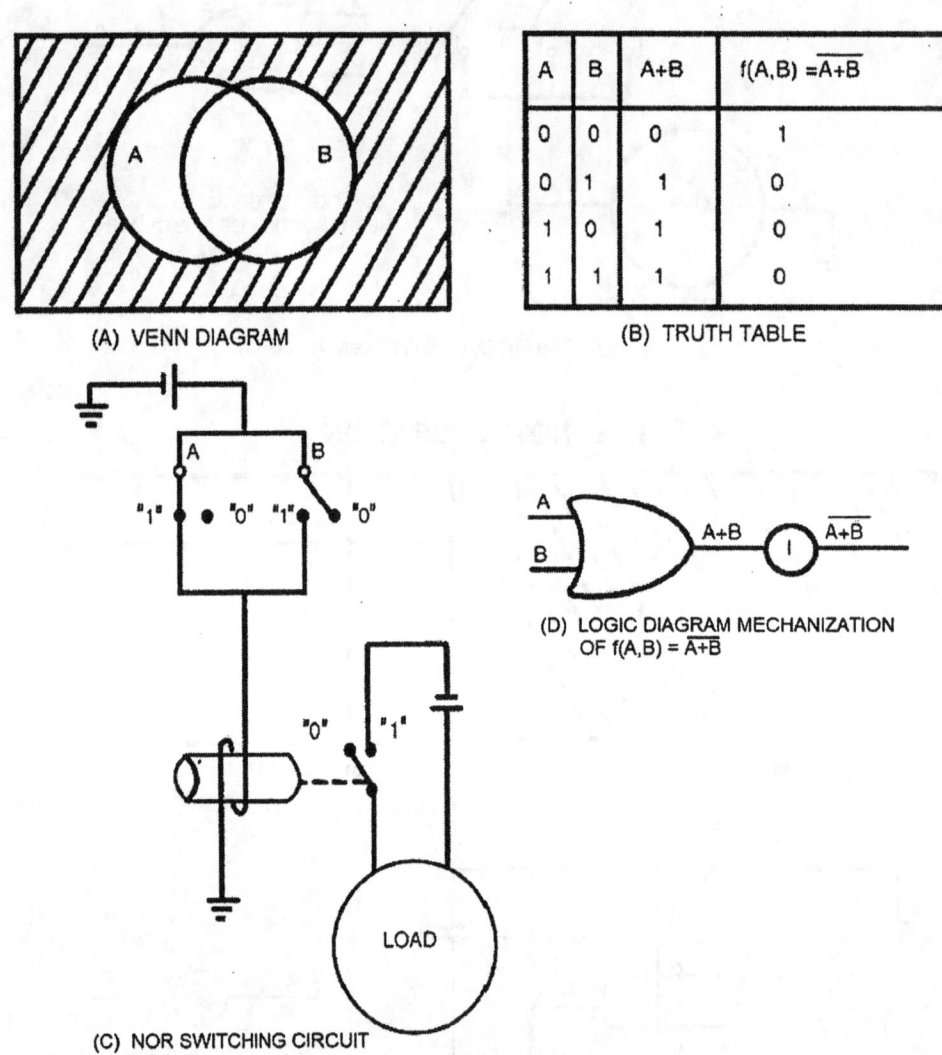

Figure 6 - The NOR Operation

The shaded area in Figure 6(A) represents the quantity, A OR B, negated. If reference is made to the preceding chapter, it will be found that this figure is identical to the minterm expression $\overline{A}\,\overline{B}$; that is, A OR B negated is A OR B and by application of DeMorgan's Theorem is equal to $\overline{A}\,B$.

The truth table for the NOR operation is shown in Figure 6(B). The table shows that if either A or B is equal to 1, then f(A,B) is equal to 0. Furthermore, if A and B equal 0, then f(A,B) equals 1.

The NOR operation is a combination of the OR operation and the NOT operation. The NOR switching circuit in Figure 6(C) is the OR circuit placed in series with the NOT circuit. If either switch A, switch, or both are in the closed position, equal to 1, then there is no transmission to the load. If both switches A and B are open, equal to 0, then current is transmitted to the load.

The logic diagram mechanization of f(A,B) equal A + B (NOR operation) is shown in Figure 6(D). It uses both the OR logic diagrams and the NOT logic diagrams. The NOR logic diagram mechanization shows there are two inputs, A and B, into an OR circuit producing the function in Boolean form of A + B. This function is the input to the NOT (inverter) which gives the output, in Boolean form, of $\overline{A+B}$. Note that the whole quantity of A + B is complemented and not the separate variables.

THE "NAND" OPERATION

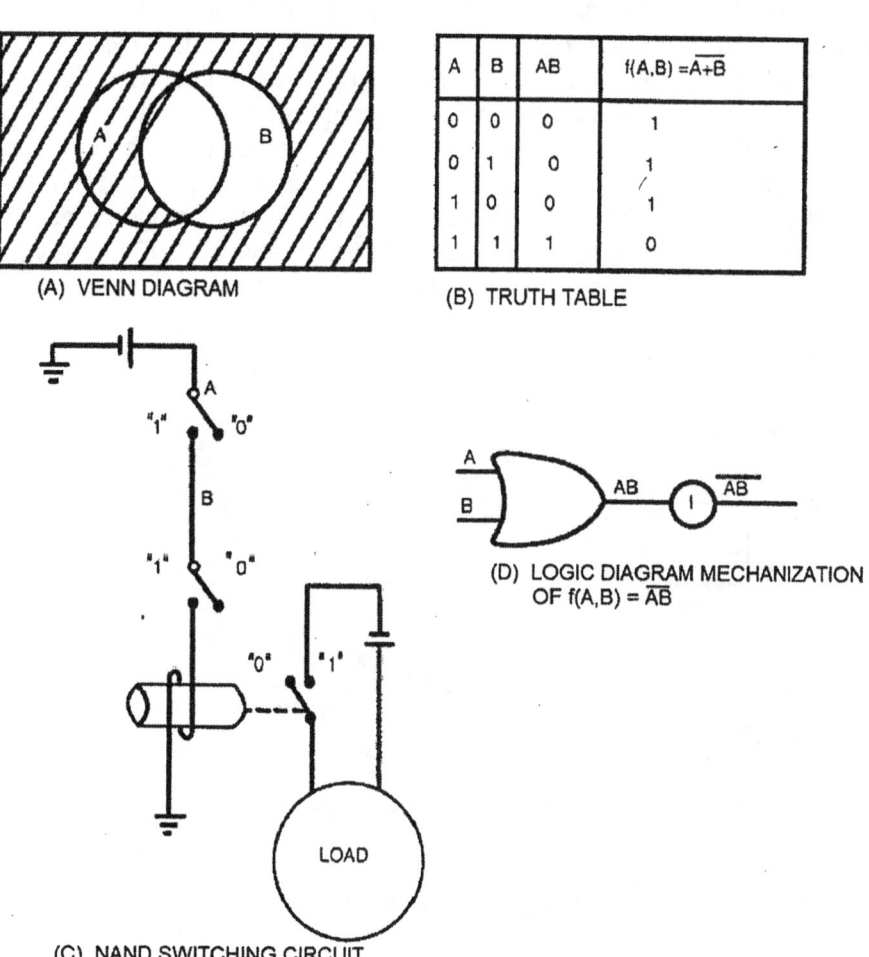

(A) VENN DIAGRAM

(B) TRUTH TABLE

(C) NAND SWITCHING CIRCUIT

(D) LOGIC DIAGRAM MECHANIZATION OF $f(A,B) = \overline{AB}$

Figure 7 - The NAND Operation

The shaded area in Figure 7(A) represents the quantity A AND B negated (NOT), and is a maxterm expression. Notice that $\overline{AB}$ is equal to the maxterm expression $\overline{A} + \overline{B}$.

The truth table is shown for the NAND operation in Figure 7(B). When A and B equal 1, then f(A,B) is equal to 0. In all other cases, the function is equal to 1.

The NAND operation is a combination of the AND operation and the NOT operation. The NAND switching circuit in Figure 7(C) is the AND circuit put in series with the NOT circuit. If either switch A or B is open, equal to 0, then current is transmitted to the load. If both switch A and B are closed, equal to 1, then there is no transmission to the load.

The logic diagram mechanization of f(A,B) equal $\overline{AB}$ (NAND operation) is shown in Figure 7(D). The AND operation logic diagram and the NOT logic diagram mechanization shows that there are two inputs, A and B, into the AND circuit producing the function in Boolean form of AB. This function is the input to the NOT circuit which gives the output, in Boolean form, of $\overline{A\ B}$. Note that the entire quantity AB is complemented and not the separate variables.

It should be noted that in the previously discussed logic diagrams that each input signal represents the operation of a switch, circuit, or other component part.

Generally, a Boolean expression that has been inverted is said to be NOTTED. While we have previously used the inverter symbol separate from the AND or OR logic diagram, it is common practice to show the NAND or NOR logic diagrams as indicated in Figure 8, in accordance with American Standard for Graphic Symbols for Logic Diagrams.

The output of a NAND or a NOR gate is a NOTTED expression. The vinculum is used to indicate that such an expression has been NOTTED. Therefore, the output of a NAND gate having inputs A,B will appear as $\overline{A+B}$ and the output of a NOR gate having inputs A,B will appear as $\overline{A+B}$. If any of the inputs to a logic gate are themselves NOTTED, a vinculum will appear over the letter representing an input. Examples are shown in Figure 8.

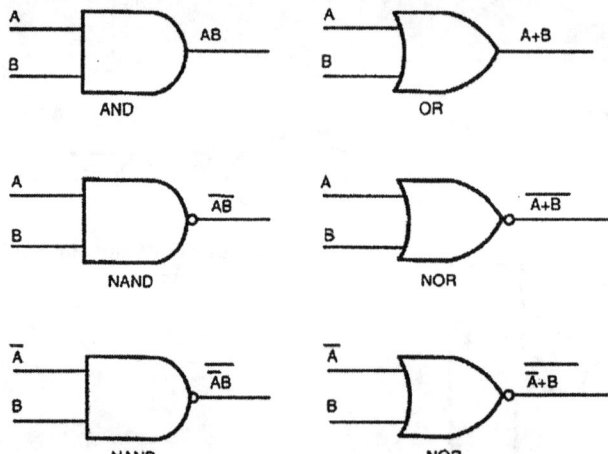

Figure 8 - American Standard Logic Symbol

OUTPUT USED AS INPUT

The output from one gate may be an input to another gate. If so, that input will contain two or more letters. Figure 9(A) shows an OR gate feeding into an OR gate. There are four possible combinations of inputs and logic symbols. These are shown in Figure 9(B,C,D,E). Notice that signs of grouping occur in all outputs except the AND input to the OR gate. The AB, in this case, is naturally grouped because the letters are written together and are separated from C by the OR sign. Figure 10 shows several different cases along with the proper output expressions.

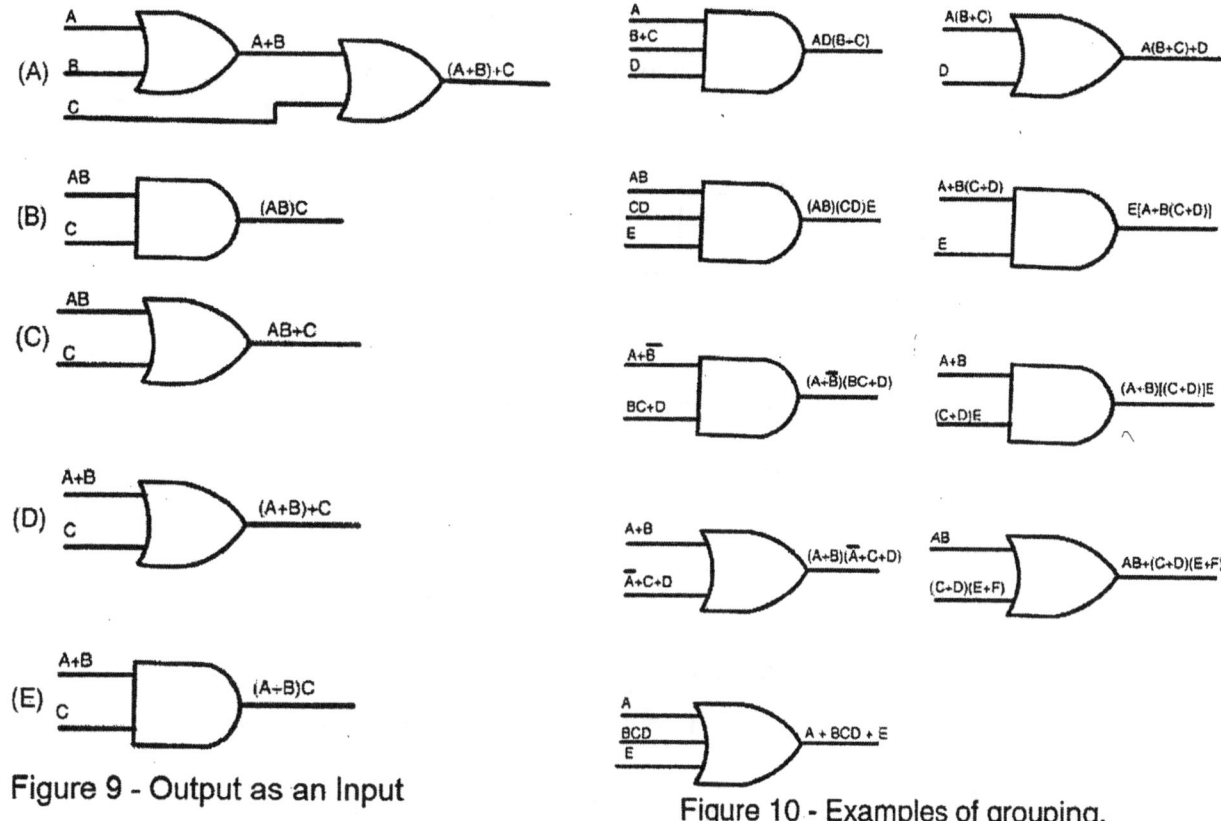

Figure 9 - Output as an Input

Figure 10 - Examples of grouping.

Although the vinculum is not used in place of parentheses or brackets, it is also a grouping sign. Consider the NOR symbol of Figure 11(A). The AB and C are the inputs to the OR circuit and form AB+C. The AB+C is then inverted to form $\overline{AB+C}$. The vinculum groups whatever portion or portions of the output expression that has been inverted. Figure 11(B,C,D) gives examples of this type output.

To determine the output of a logic diagram, find the output of each logic symbol in the diagram. You should begin with the inputs at the left and move right, using the output of each logic symbol as an input to the following symbol, as illustrated in Figure 12.

When determining the output of a logic diagram, one should be careful of the two most common mistakes which are leaving out vincula and leaving out grouping signs.

12

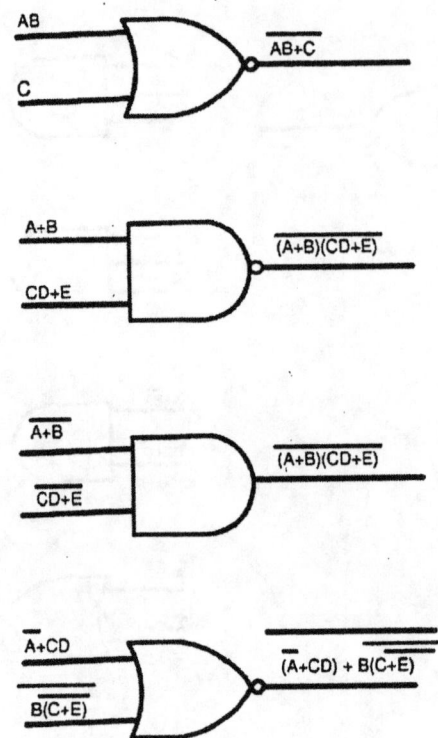

Figure 11.- Vinculum as grouping sign.

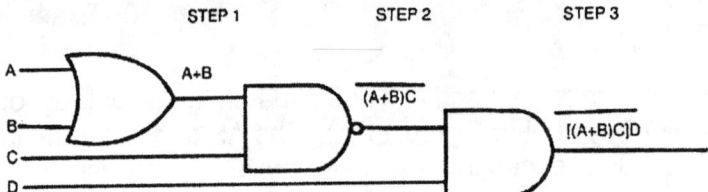

Figure 12 - Steps for Determining Output

PROBLEMS: Find the outputs of the following logic diagrams.

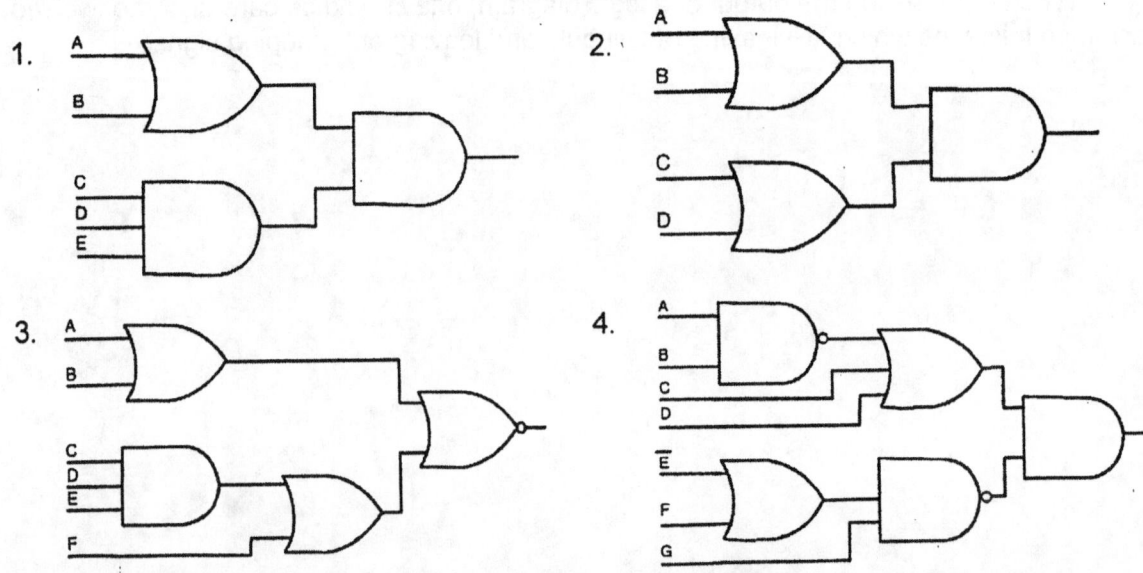

ANSWERS:
1. (A+B)(CDE)

2. (A+B)(C+D)

3. $\overline{(A+B)+(CDE+F)}$

4. $(\overline{AB}+C+D)[G(E+F)]$

DEDUCING INPUTS FROM OUTPUTS

In order to draw a logic diagram from an output expression, you should start with the output and work toward the input. Separate, in steps, the output expression until you have all single-letter inputs. If letters are grouped, first separate the group from other groups or letters, then separate the letters within groups.

To diagram the input that produces A + BC, you would first separate A from BC by using an OR logic symbol; that is,

You now draw an AND logic symbol to separate B from C, and extend all lines to a common column on the left. This is shown by the following diagram:

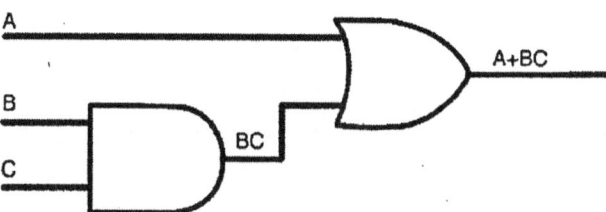

One common mistake in drawing the simplest possible diagram from an output expression is when the expression is similar to AB(C+D). The mistake is made by drawing:

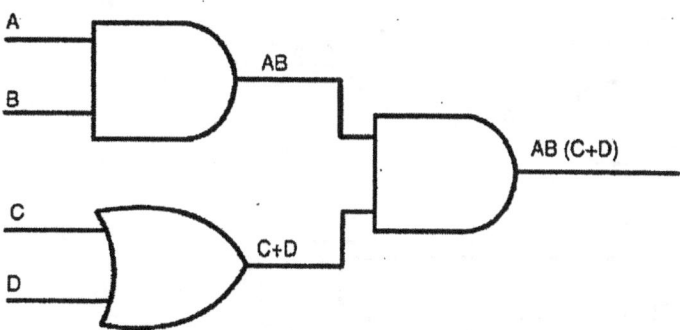

If the foregoing were your results, you would have failed to notice that A, B, and (C+D) were all ANDed together. You should have drawn:

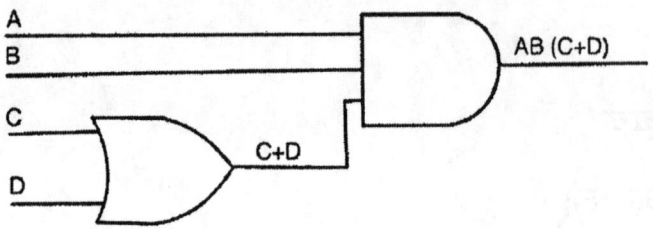

which would have saved the use of one gate. A gate is considered one circuit such as OR, AND, NOR, etc.

To diagram the expression A(B+C)(D+EF), write:

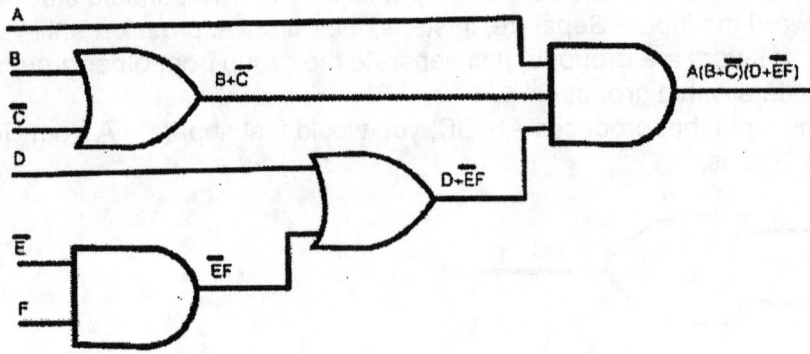

PROBLEMS: Draw the logic diagrams for the following expressions:

1. A+B(C+D)

2. (A+B+C)D+E

3. (A+B+C)DE

4. ABC(D+E)

ANSWERS:

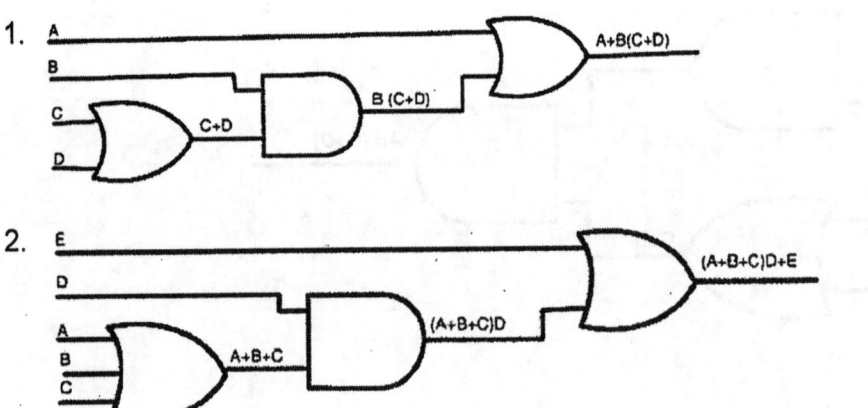

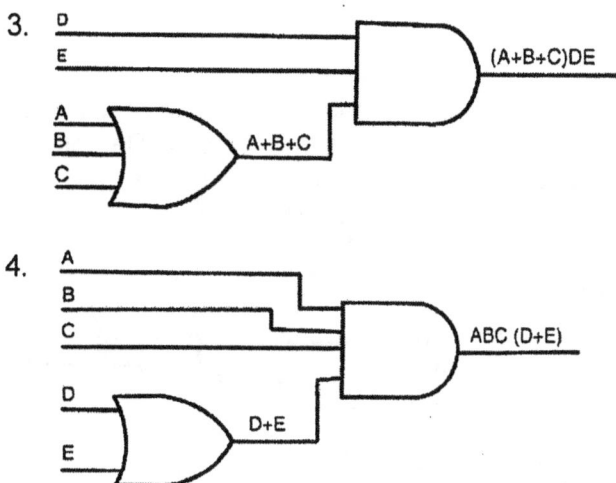

POSTULATES AND THEOREMS

In this section, we will discuss the basic laws of Boolean algebra which enables one to simplify many Boolean expressions. By applying the basic laws, the digital systems designer can be sure a circuit is in the simplest possible algebraic form.

The laws of Boolean algebra may also be used for troubleshooting defective components or for locating errors in computer programs. It should be understood that not all of the laws are similar to the laws of ordinary algebra.

LAW OF IDENTITY: This law is shown as $\dfrac{A = A}{A = A}$

and indicates that any letter, number, or expression is equal to itself. The law of identity is shown in Figure 13.

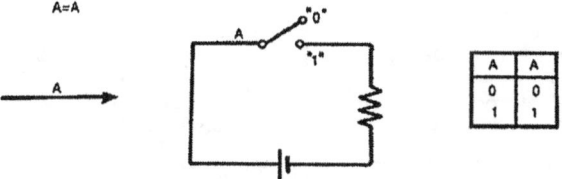

Figure 13 - Law of Identity

COMMUTATIVE LAW: The commutative law is: AB = BA and A+B = B+A, which is shown in Figure 14. This indicates that when inputs to a logic symbol are ANDed or ORed, the order in which they are written does not affect the binary value of the output; that is, R(S+T) = (S+T)R and A(BC+D+E) = (E+BC+D)A

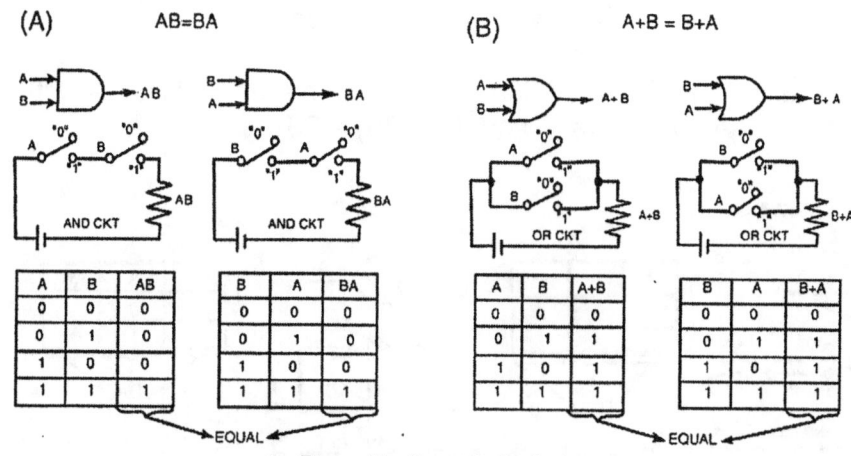

Figure 14 - Commutative Law

ASSOCIATIVE LAW: The associative law is: A(BC) = (AB)C and A + (B+C) = (A+B) + C, which is shown in Figure 15. This indicates that when inputs to a logic symbol are ANDed or ORed, the order in which they are grouped does not affect the binary value of the output; that is, ABC + D(EF) = (AB)C + DEF and C + (D+E) + (F+G) = C + D + E + F + G

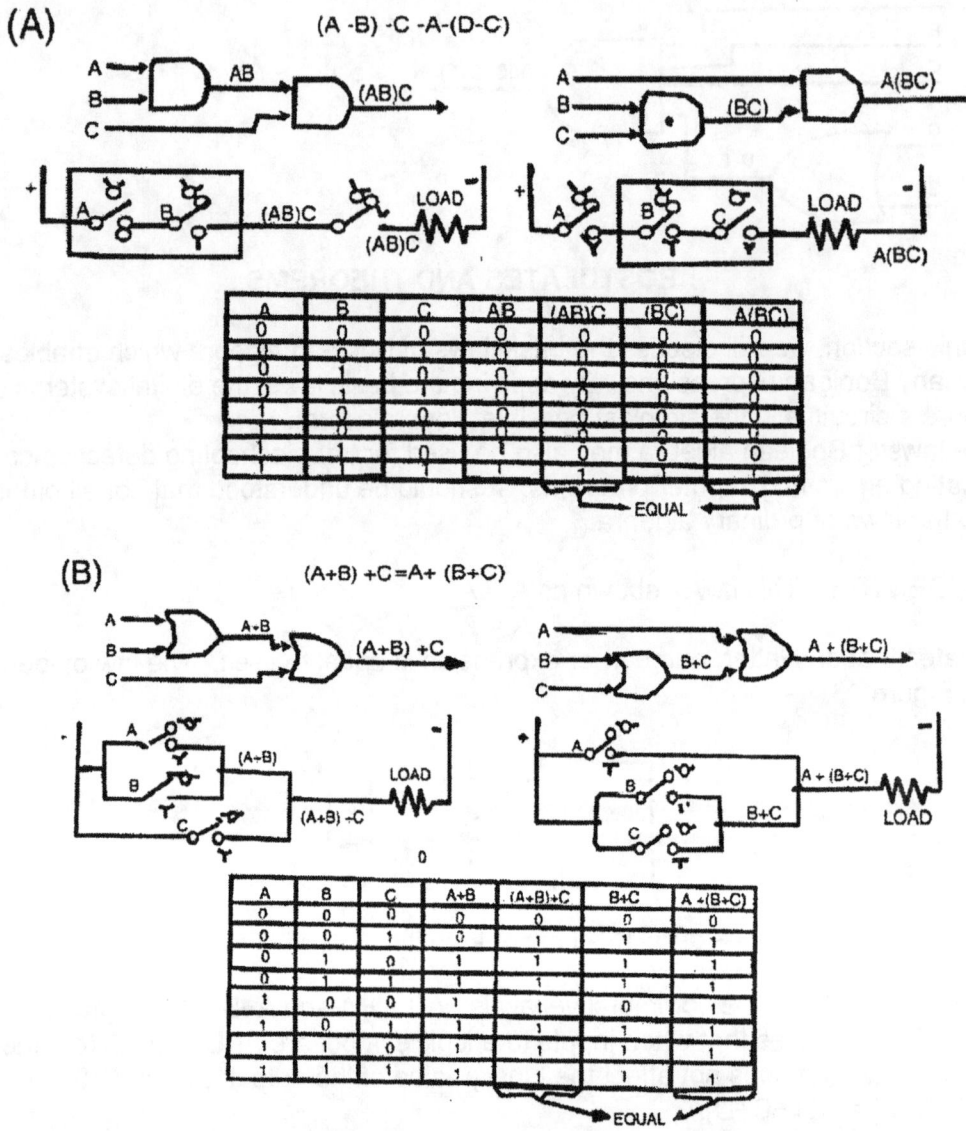

Figure 15 - Associative Law

IDEMPOTENT LAW: As seen in Figure 16, if A is ANDed with A or if A is ORed with A, the output will equal A; that is, AA = A, A+A = A and (RS)(RS) = RS.

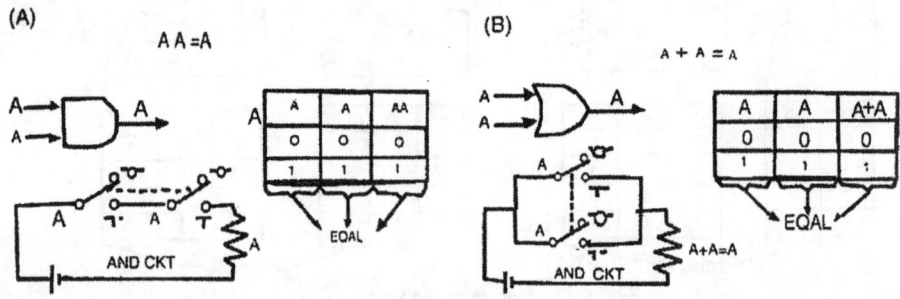

Figure 16 - Idempotent Law

LAW OF DOUBLE NEGATION: This law is $\bar{\bar{A}} = A$ which indicates that when two bars of equal length cover the same letter or expression, both may be removed. This is shown in Figure 17. Examples are: $\bar{\bar{AB}} = AB$ and $\bar{\bar{AB}} + \bar{\bar{X}} = \overline{AB} + X$

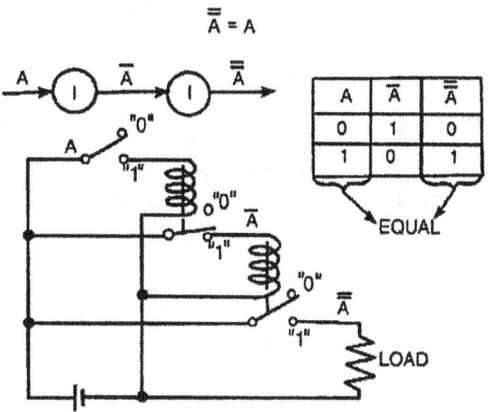

Figure 17 - Law of Double Negation

COMPLEMENTARY LAW: This law is stated as: $A\bar{A} = 0$ and $A+\bar{A} = 1$, which indicates that when any letter or expression is ANDed with its complement, the output is 0. Also, when any letter or expression is ORed with its complement, the output is 1. This is shown in Figure 18. Examples are: $CO\overline{CD} = 0$ and $\overline{ABC} + ABC = 1$.

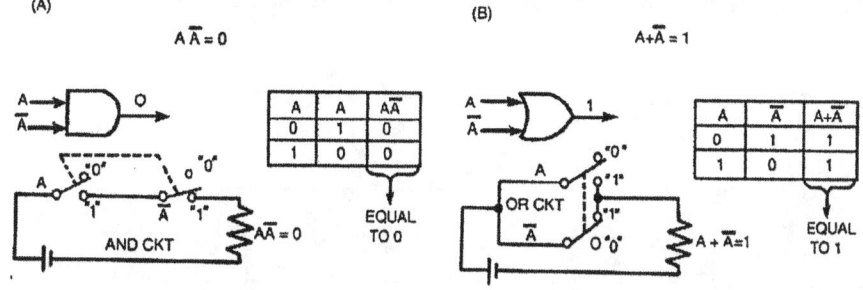

Figure 18 - Complementary Law

LAW OF INTERSECTION: As shown in Figure 19, if one input to an AND circuit has a value of 1, the output will take the value of the other input. That is, if the two inputs to an AND circuit are 1 and A, then when A is 1, the output will be 1 and when A is 0, the output will be 0. If the inputs are 0 and A, then the output will always be 0.

The law of intersection is given by the following: $A \bullet 1 = A$ and $A \bullet 0 = 0$. Examples are $AB \bullet 1 = AB$ and $CD \bullet 0 = 0$.

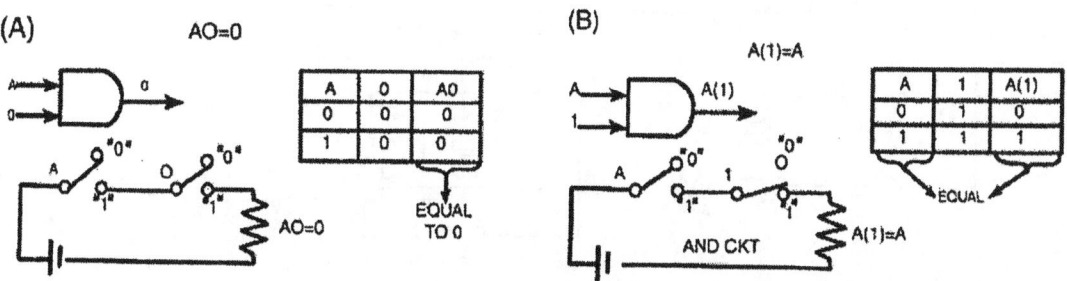

Figure 19 – Law of Intersection

LAW OF UNION: As shown in Figure 20, if one input to an OR circuit has a binary value of 1, the output will be 1. If the inputs are 0 and A, the output will be the same as the value of A. The law of union is given by the following: A + 1 = 1 and A + 0 = A.
Examples of this law are as follows: 1 + ABC = 1 and E + 0(AB) = E.

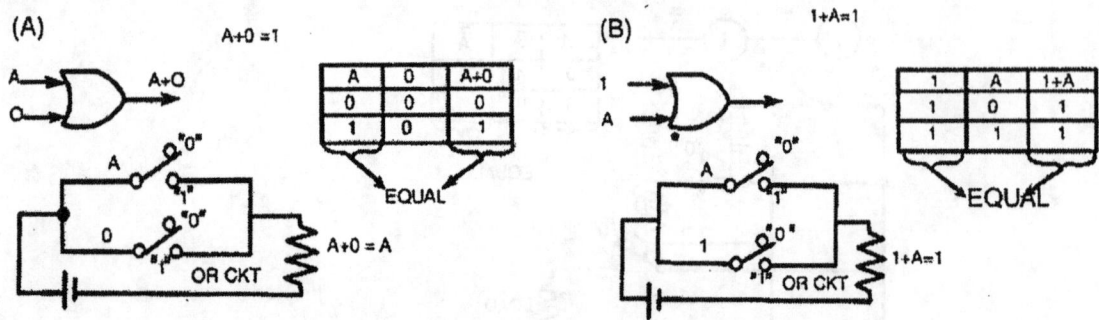

Figure 20 – Law of Union

LAW OF DUALIZATION (DeMorgan's Theorem): To split a vinculum that extends over more than one letter, and to join separate vincula into one vinculum requires the use of the law of dualization. This law is commonly referred to as DeMorgan's Theorem. This law is shown in Figure 21.
DeMorgan's Theorem may be written as follows: $\overline{AB} = \overline{A} + \overline{B}$ and $\overline{A + B} = \overline{A}\,\overline{B}$

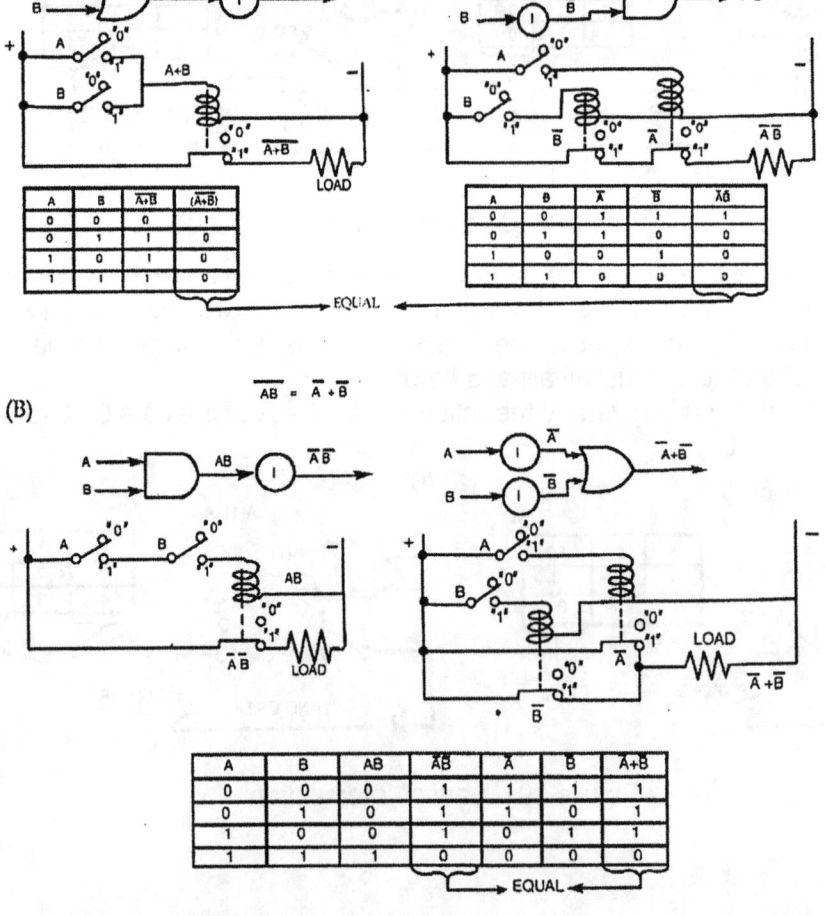

Figure 21 - Law of Dualization

Whenever you split or join a vinculum, change the sign of operation, That is, AND to OR, or OR to AND. In applying this theorem, it should be remembered that when a vinculum covers part of an expression, the signs under the vinculum change and the signs outside the vinculum do not change; that is, $\overline{ABC} + \overline{D+E} = A(\overline{B} + \overline{C}) + \overline{D}\,\overline{E}$. Notice that the grouping of letters must be maintained.

DISTRIBUTIVE LAW: There are two parts to the distributive laws as shown in Figure 22. The first identity is A(B+C) = AB + AC and in order to obtain an output of 1, the A must be 1 and either B or C must be 1. This law is similar to the law of algebra which states that multiplication distributes over addition. The second identity is A + BC = (A+B)(A+C) and in order to obtain an output of 1, at least one term in each of the parentheses must be 1.

This law does not apply to ordinary algebra. If this law did apply to ordinary algebra, it would indicate that addition distributes over multiplication. In Boolean algebra, this is true. Examples of the distributive law are as follows: A(B+C+D) = AB + AC + AD and A+(B+C)(D+E) = (A+B+C)(A+D+E).

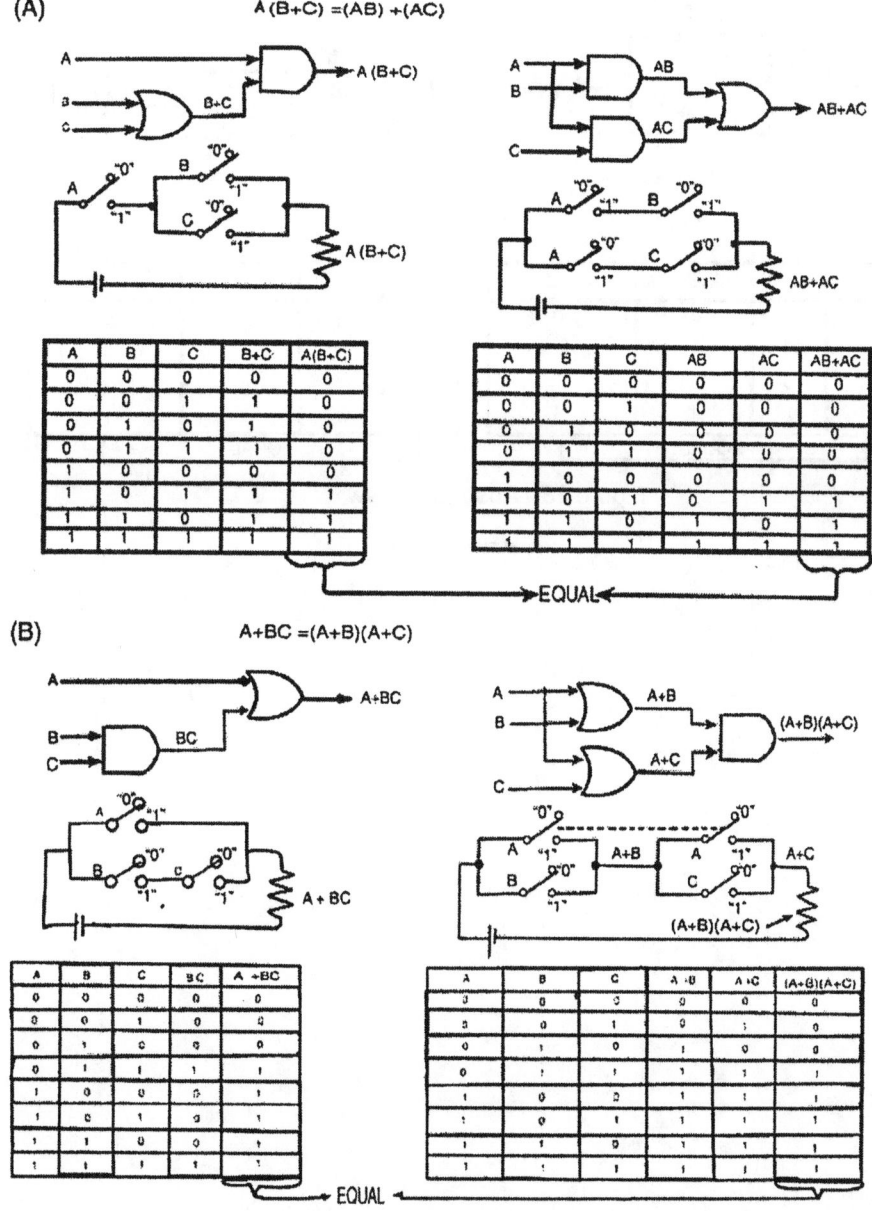

Figure 22 - Distributive Law

LAW OF ABSORPTION: The law of absorption is shown in Figure 23. This law is written as A(A+B) = A and A + AB = A and indicates that the output is 1 whenever A is 1. Examples are:
D(I+E) = D•I = D and A + AB + AC = A(1+B+C)
= A•1
= A

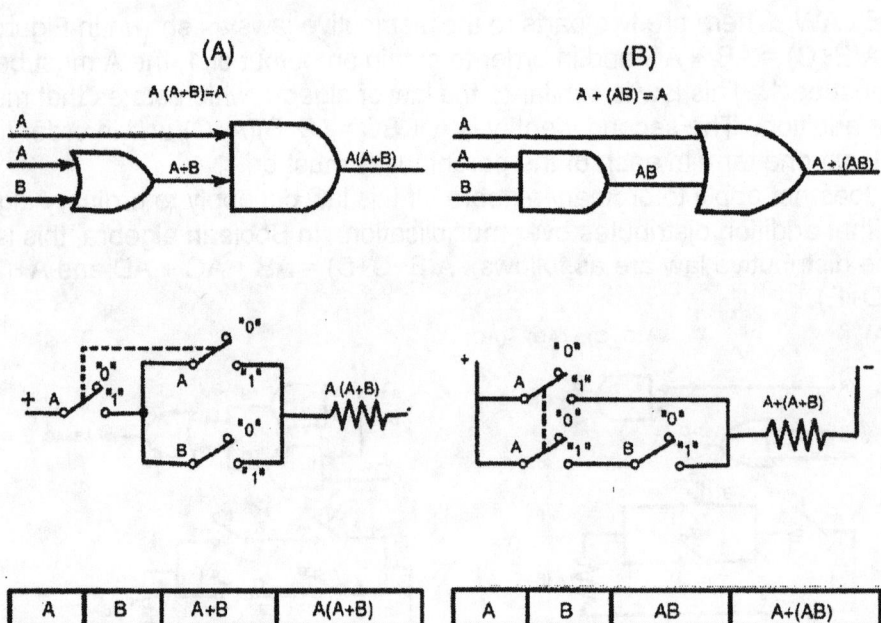

Figure 23 - Absorption Law

BASIC FUNDAMENTALS OF MATHEMATICS

TABLE OF CONTENTS

		Page
I.	Arithmetic	1
II.	Vectors	13
III.	Algebra	14
IV.	Geometry	18
V.	Trigonometry	31
VI.	Calculus	41

BASIC FUNDAMENTALS OF MATHEMATICS

I. Arithmetic

01. - Definitions. Arithmetic is that branch of mathematics dealing with computation by numbers. The principal processes involved are addition, subtraction, multiplication, and division. A number consisting of a single symbol (1, 2, 3, etc.) is a **digit.** Any number that can be stated or indicated, however large or small, is called a **finite** number; one too large to be stated or indicated is called an **infinite** number; and one too small to be stated or indicated is called an **infinitesimal** number.

The sign of a number is the indication of whether it is positive (+) or negative (-). This may sometimes be indicated in another way. Thus, latitude is usually indicated as *north* (N) or *south* (S), but if north is considered positive, south is then negative with respect to north. In navigation, the north or south designation of latitude and declination is often called the "name" of the latitude or declination. A **positive number** is one having a positive sign (+); a **negative number** is one having a negative sign (-). The **absolute value** of a number is that number without regard to sign. Thus, the absolute value of both (+)8 and (-)8 is 8. Generally, a number without a sign can be considered positive.

02. Expressing numbers. - In navigation, fractions are usually expressed as decimals. Thus, 1/4 is expressed as 0.25 and 1/3 as 0.33. To determine the decimal equivalent of a fraction, divide the **numerator** (the number above the line) by the **denominator** (the number below the line). When a decimal is less than 1, as in the examples above, it is good practice to show the zero at the left of the decimal point (0.25, not .25).

A number should not be expressed to a greater precision than justified. The precision of a decimal is indicated by the number of digits shown to the right of the decimal point. Thus, the expression "14 miles" indicates a precision to the nearest whole mile, or any value between 13.5 and 14.5 miles. The expression "14.0 miles" indicates a precision of a tenth of a mile, or any value between 13.95 and 14.05 miles.

In a number without a decimal there is sometimes doubt as to the degree of precision indicated. For example, the number 186,000 may indicate a precision to three, four, five, or six places. This ambiguity is sometimes avoided by expressing numbers as powers of 10 (art. 08). Thus, 18.6×10^4 ($18.6 \times 10,000$) indicates a precision to the nearest thousand (three places), 18.60×10^4 to the nearest hundred (four places), 18.600×10^4 to the nearest ten (five places), and 18.6000×10^4 to the nearest unit (six places). The position of the decimal is not important if the correct power of 10 is given. For example, 18.6×10^4 is the same as 1.86×10^3, 1.86×10^3, etc.

The small number above and to the right of 10 (the **exponent**) indicates the number of places the decimal point is to be moved to the *right*. If the exponent is negative, it indicates a reciprocal, and the decimal point is moved to the *left*. Thus, $1.86 \times 10^{-6} = 0.00000186$. This system is sometimes used to avoid long numbers.

Another way of indicating degree of precision is to state the number of **significant digits.** These are the digits in a number, excluding zeros at the left and sometimes those at the right. Thus, 1,325, 1,001, 1.408, 0.00005926, 625.0, and 0.04000 have four significant digits each. But in the number 312,600 there may be four, five, or six significant digits. Any doubt may be removed by expressing the number times a power of 10, as explained above.

2
MATHEMATICS

If there are no more significant digits, regardless of how far a computation is carried, this may be indicated by use of the word "exactly." Thus, 12 ÷ 4 = 3 exactly, and one nautical mile= 1,852 meters exactly; but 12 ÷ 7 = 1.7 approximately, the word "approximately" indicating that additional decimal places might be computed. Another way of indicating an approximate relationship is by placing a positive or negative sign after the number. Thus, 12 ÷ 7 = 1.7+, and ll ÷ 7 = 1.6-. This system has the advantage of showing whether the approximation is too great or too small.

In any arithmetical computation the answer is no more accurate than the least precise value used. Thus, if it is desired to add 16.4 and 1.88, the answer might be given as 18.28, but since the first term might be anything from 16.35 to 16.45, the answer is anything from 18.23 to 18.33. Hence, to retain the second decimal place in the answer is to give a false indication of accuracy, for the number 18.28 indicates a value between 18.275 and 18.285. However, additional places are sometimes retained until the end of a computation to avoid an accumulation of small errors due to rounding off (art. 04). In marine navigation it is customary to give most values to a precision of 0.1, even though some uncertainty may exist as to the accuracy of the last place. Examples are the dip and refraction corrections of sextant altitudes (arts. 1606. 1613).

In general, a value obtained by interpolation in a table should not be expressed to more decimal places than given in the table.

03. Precision and accuracy. - The word "precision" as used above is not the same as "accuracy," although the two are sometimes confused. A quantity may be expressed to a greater precision than is justified by the accuracy of the information from which the quantity is derived. For instance, if a ship steams one mile in $3^m 21^s$ its speed is $60^m \div 3^m 21^s$ = 60 ÷ 3.35 = 17.910447761194 knots, approximately. The division can be carried to as many places as desired, but if the time is measured only to the nearest second, the speed is accurate only to one decimal place in this example, because an error of 0.5 second introduces an error of more than 0.05 knot in the speed. Hence, the additional places are meaningless and possibly misleading, unless more accurate time is available. In general, it is not good practice to state a quantity to greater precision than justified by its accuracy. However, in marine navigation the accuracy of information is often unknown, and it is customary to give positions to a precision of 0:1 of latitude and longitude, although they may not be accurate even to the nearest whole minute.

The **absolute precision** of a number is indicated by its number of decimal places; its **relative precision** by its number of significant digits. Although this is an indication of precision, it may also be a measure of accuracy, and the expressions **absolute accuracy** and **relative accuracy** used. However, the term "accuracy" should not be used when "precision" only is intended. Thus, the values 186,000 and 0.00000186 may each have three significant digits, or "be correct to three digits," although the first value may be accurate ("absolute accuracy") only to the nearest 1,000, and the second to the nearest 0.00000001. If the numbers are accurate to the number of significant digits shown, each has an error ("relative accuracy") of less than "one part in 186."

Unless all numbers are exact, doubt exists as to the accuracy of the last digit in a computation. Thus, 12.3 + 9.4+4.6=26.3. But if the three terms to be added have been rounded off from 12.26, 9.38, and 4.57, the correct answer is 26.2, obtained *by* rounding off the answer of 26.21 found by retaining the second decimal place until the end. It is good practice to work with one more place than needed in the answer, when the information is available. In compu

MATHEMATICS

tations involving a large number of terms, or if great accuracy is desired, it is sometimes advisable to retain two or more additional places until the end.

04. Rounding off. - In rounding off numbers to the number of places desired, one should take the nearest value. Thus, the number 6.5049 is rounded to 6.505, 6.50, 6.5. or 7. depending upon the number of places desired. If the number to be rounded off ends in 5, the nearer *even* number is taken. Thus, 1.55 and 1.65 are both rounded to 1.6. Likewise, 12.750 is rounded to 12.8 if only one decimal place is desired. However, 12.749 is rounded to 12.7. That is, 12.749 is not first rounded to 12.75 and then to 12.8, but the entire number is rounded in one operation. When a number ends in 5, the computation can sometimes be carried to additional places to determine whether the correct value is more or less than 5.

05. Reciprocals. - The reciprocal of a number is 1 divided by that number. The reciprocal of a fraction is obtained by interchanging the numerator and denominator. Thus, the reciprocal of 3/5 is 5/3. A whole number may be considered a fraction with 1 as the denominator. Thus, 54 is the same as 54/1, and its reciprocal is 1/54. Division by a number produces the same result as multiplying by its reciprocal, or vice versa. Thus, 12 ÷ 2 = 12 X 1/2 = 6, and 12 X 2 =12 ÷ 1/2 = 24.

06. Addition. - When two or more numbers are to be added, it is generally most convenient to write them in a column, with the decimal points in line. Thus, if 31.2, 0.8874, and 168.14 are to be added, this may be indicated by means of the addition sign (+): 31.2 + 0.8874 + 168.14 = 200.2. But the addition can be performed more conveniently by arranging the numbers as follows:

$$
\begin{array}{r}
31.2 \\
0.8874 \\
\underline{168.14} \\
200.2.
\end{array}
$$

The answer is given only to the first decimal place, because the answer is no more accurate than the least precise number among those to be added, as indicated previously. Often it is preferable to state all numbers in a problem to the same precision before starting the addition, although this may introduce a small error, as indicated in article 03:

$$
\begin{array}{r}
31.2 \\
0.9 \\
\underline{168.1} \\
200.2.
\end{array}
$$

If there are no decimals, the last digit to the right is aligned:

$$
\begin{array}{r}
166 \\
2 \\
\underline{96,758} \\
96,926
\end{array}
$$

Numbers to be added should be given to the same absolute accuracy, when available, to avoid a false impression of accuracy in the result. Consider the following:

MATHEMATICS

```
   186,000
    71,832
     9,614
       728
   -------
   268,174.
```

The answer would imply an accuracy to six places. If the first number given is accurate to only three places, or to the nearest 1,000, the answer is not more accurate, and hence the answer should be given as 268,000. Approximately the same answer would be obtained by rounding off at the start:

```
   186,000
    72,000
    10,000
     1,000
   -------
   269,000.
```

If numbers are **added arithmetically,** their absolute values are added without regard to signs; but if they are **added algebraically,** due regard is given to signs. If two numbers to be added algebraically have the same sign, their absolute values are added and given their common sign. If two numbers to be added algebraically have unlike signs, the smaller absolute value is subtracted from the larger, and the sign of the value having the larger absolute value is given to the result. Thus, if + 8 and -7 are added arithmetically, the answer is 15, but if they are added algebraically, the answer is +1.

An answer obtained by addition is called a sum.

07. Subtraction is the inverse of addition. Stated differently, the *addition* of a *negative* number is the same as the *subtraction* of a *positive* number. That is, if a number is to be subtracted from another, the sign (+ or -) of the **subtrahend** (the number to be subtracted) is reversed and the result added algebraically to the **minuend** (the number from which the subtrahend is to be subtracted). Thus, 6-4=2. This may be written +6-(+4) = +2, which yields the same result as +6+ (-4). For solution, larger numbers are often conveniently arranged in a column with decimal points in a vertical column, as in addition. Thus, 3,728.41 - 1,861.16 may be written

```
   (+)3,728.41
   (+)1,861.16 (subtract)
   (+)1,867.25
```

This is the same as

```
   (+)3,728.41
   (-)1,861.16 (add algebraically)
   (+)1,867.25
```

The rule of sign reversal applies likewise to negative numbers. Thus, if -3 is to be *subtracted* from +5, this may be written +5 - (-3) = 5 + 3 = 8.

In the algebraic addition of two numbers of opposite sign (numerical subtraction), the smaller number is subtracted from the larger and the result is given the sign of the larger number. Thus, +7-4= +3, and -7+4=-3, which is the same as +4- 7 = -3.

MATHEMATICS

In navigation, numbers to be numerically subtracted are usually marked (-), and those to be numerically added are marked (+) or the sign is not indicated. However, when a sign is part of a designation, and the reverse process is to be used, the word "reversed" (rev.) is written after the number. Thus, if GMT is known and ZT in the (+)5 zone is to be found (by subtraction), the problem may be written:

```
GMT     1754
 ZD ( + ) 5   (rev.)
 ZT     1254
```

The symbol ~ indicates that an absolute difference is required without regard to sign of the *answer*. Thus, 28~13 = 15, and 13~28 = 15. In both of these solutions 13 and 28 are positive and 15 is an absolute value without sign. If the signs or names of both numbers are the same, either positive or negative, the smaller is subtracted from the larger, but if they are of opposite sign or name, they are numerically added. Thus, (+)16~(+)21 = 5 and (-)16~(-)21 = 5, but (+)16~(-)21= 37 and (-)16~ (+)21= 37. Similarly, the difference of latitude between 15° N and 20° N, or between 15° S and 20° S, is 5°, but the difference of latitude between 15° N and 20° S, or between 15° S and 20° N, is 35°. If motion from one latitude to another is involved, the difference may be given a sign to indicate the direction of travel, or the location of one place with respect to another. Thus, if B is 50 miles west of A, and C is 125 miles west of A, B and C are 75 miles apart regardless of the direction of travel. However. B is 75 miles *east* of C, and C is 75 miles *west* of B. When direction is indicated, an algebraic difference is given, rather than an absolute difference, and the symbol ~ is not appropriate.

It is sometimes desirable to consider all addition and subtraction problems as addition, with negative signs (-) given before those numbers to be subtracted, so that there can be no question of which process is intended. The words "add" and "subtract" may be used instead of signs. In navigation, "names" (usually north, south, east, and west) are often used, and the relationship involved in a certain problem may need to be understood to determine whether to add or subtract. Thus, LHA= GHA λ (west) and LHA=GHA + λ (east). This is the same as saying LHA=GHA - if west longitude is considered positive, for in this case, LHA=GHA -(- λ) or LHA = GHA+ λ in east longitude, the same as before.

If numbers are **subtracted arithmetically,** they are subtracted without regard to sign; but if they are **subtracted algebraically,** positive (+) numbers are *subtracted* and negative (-) numbers are *added*.

An answer obtained by subtraction is called a **difference.**

08. Multiplication may be indicated by the multiplication sign (X), as 154 X 28 = 4,312. For solution, the problem is conveniently arranged thus:

```
   154
 (X)28
  1232
   308
  4312.
```

MATHEMATICS

Either number may be given first, but it is generally more convenient to perform the multiplication if the larger number is placed on top, as shown. In this problem, 154 is first multiplied by 8 and then by 2. The second answer is placed under the first, but set one **place** to the left, so that the right-hand digit is directly below the 2. These steps might be reversed, multiplication by 2 being performed first. This procedure is sometimes used in estimating.

When one number is placed below another for multiplication, as shown above, it is usually best to align the right-hand digits without regard for the position of the decimal point. The number of decimal places in the answer is the sum of the decimal places in the **multiplicand** (the number to be multiplied) and the **multiplier** (the second number):

APPENDIX O:

```
       163.27
   (X) 263.9
       146943
        48981
        97962
        32654
     43086.953
```

However, when a number ends in one or more zeros, these may be ignored until the end and then added on to the number:

```
        1924
    (X) 1800
       15392
        1924
     3463200.
```

This is also true if both multiplicand and multiplier end in zeros:

```
     1924000
    (X) 1800
       15392
        1924
     3463200000.
```

When negative values are to be multiplied, the sign of the answer is positive if an *even* number of negative signs appear, and negative if there are an *odd* number. Thus, 2X3 = 6, 2 X (-3) = -6, -2 X 3 = -6, -2 X (-3) = (+) 6. Also, 2 X 3 X 8 X (-2) X 5 = -480, 2 X (-3) X 8 X (-2) X 5 = 480, 2 X (-3) X (-8) X (-2) X 5 = -480, 2 X (-3) X (-8) X (-2) X (-5) = 480, and (-2) X (-3) X (-8) X (-2) X (-5) = -480.

An answer obtained by multiplication is called a **product.** Any number multiplied by 1 is the number itself. Thus, 125X1 = 125. Any number multiplied by 0 is 0. Thus, 125X0 = 0 and 1X0=0.

MATHEMATICS

To multiply a number *by* itself is to **square** the number. This may be indicated by the **exponent** 2 placed to the right of the number and above the line as a **superior**. Thus, 15X15 may be written 15^2. Similarly, $15X15X15=15^3$, and $15X15X15X15= 15^4$, etc. The exponent (2, 3, 4, etc.) indicates the power to which a number is to be **raised**, or how many times the number is to be used in multiplication. The expression 15^2 is usually read "15 squared," 15^3 is read "15 cubed" or "15 to the third power," 15^4 (or higher power) is read "15 to the fourth (or higher) power." The answer obtained by **raising to a power** is called the "square," "cube," etc., or the "... power" of the number. Thus, 225 is the "square of 15," 3,375 is the "cube of 15" or the "third power of 15," etc. The zero power of any number except zero (if zero is considered a number) is 1. The zero power of zero is zero. Thus, $15^0 = 1$ and $0^0 = 0$.

Parentheses may be used to eliminate doubt as to what part of an expression is to be raised to a power. Thus, -3^2 may mean either $-(3 \times 3) = -9$ or $-3 \times -3 = (+)9$. To remove the ambiguity, the expression may be written $-(3)^2$ if the first meaning is intended, and $(-3)^2$ if the second meaning is intended.

09. Division is the inverse of multiplication. It may be indicated by the division sign (÷), as 376 ÷ 21 = 18 approximately; or by placing the number to be divided, called the **dividend** (376), over the other number, called the **divisor** (21), as 376/21 = 18 approximately. The expression 376/21 may be written 376/21 with the same meaning. Such a problem is conveniently arranged for solution as follows:

```
           17
     21 | 376
          21
         ---
         166
         147
         ---
          19.
```

Since the **remainder** is 19, or more than half of the divisor (21), the answer is 18 to the nearest whole number.

An answer obtained by division is called a **quotient**. Any number divided by 1 is the number itself. Thus, 65 ÷ 1 = 65. A number cannot be divided by 0.

If the numbers involved are accurate only to the number of places given, the answer should not be carried to additional places. However, if the numbers are exact, the answer might be carried to as many decimal places as desired. Thus, 374 ÷ 21 = 17.8095238095238095238095238095238095523 .... When a series of digits repeat themselves with the same remainder, as 809523 (with remainder 17) in the example given above, an exact answer will not be obtained regardless of the number of places to which the division is carried. The series of dots (...) indicates a **repeating decimal.** In a nonrepeating decimal, a plus sign (+) may be given to indicate a remainder, and a minus sign (-) to indicate that the last digit has been rounded to the next higher value. Thus, 18.68761 may be written 18.6876+ or 18.688-. If the last digit given is rounded off, the word "approximately" may be used instead of dots or a plus or minus sign.

MATHEMATICS

If the divisor is a whole number, the decimal point in the quotient is directly above that of the dividend when the work form shown above is used. Thus, in the example given above, if the dividend had been 37.6 instead of 376, the quotient would have been 1.8 approximately. If the divisor is a decimal, both it and the dividend are multiplied by the power of 10 having an exponent equal to the number of decimal places in the divisor, and the division is then carried out as explained above. Thus, if there are two decimal places in the divisor, both divisor and dividend are multiplied by $10^2=100$. This is done by moving the decimal to the right until the divisor is a whole number. If necessary, zeros are added to the dividend. Thus, if 3.7 is to be divided by 2.11, both quantities are first multiplied by 10^2, and 370 is divided by 211. This is usually performed as follows:

```
              1.75
        211| 370.00
             211
            1590
            1477
            1130
            1055
              75.
```

If *both* the dividend and divisor are positive; or if *both* are negative, the quotient is positive; but if *either* is negative, the quotient is negative. Thus. $6 \div 3 = 2$, $(-6) \div (-3) = +2$, $(-6) \div 3 = -2$, and $6 \div (-3) = -2$.

The **square root** of a number is that number which, multiplied by itself, equals the given number. Thus, $15 \times 15 = 15^2 = 225$, and $\sqrt{225} = 225^{1/2} = 15$. Either the symbol $\sqrt{}$, called the **radical sign**, or the exponent 1/2 indicates square root. Also, $\sqrt[3]{}$, or 1/3 as an exponent, indicates **cube root**. Fourth, fifth, or any root is indicated similarly, using the appropriate number. Nearly any arithmetic book explains the process of extracting roots, but this process is most easily performed by table, logarithms (art. O12), or slide rule (art. O15). If no other means are available, it can be done by trial and error. The process of finding a root of a number is called **extracting a root**.

010. **Logarithms** ("logs") provide an easy way to multiply, divide, raise numbers to powers, and extract roots. The logarithm of a number is the power to which a fixed number, called the base, must be raised to produce the value to which the logarithm corresponds. The base of **common logarithms,** (given in tables 32 and 33) is 10. Hence, since $10^{1.8}= 63$ approximately, 1.8 is the logarithm, approximately, of 63 to the base 10. In table 32 logarithms of numbers are given to five decimal **places**. This is sufficient for most purposes of the navigator. For greater precision, a table having additional places should be used. In general, the number of significant digits which are correct in an answer obtained by logarithms is the same as the number of places in the logarithms used.

A logarithm is composed of two parts. That part to the left of the decimal point is called the **characteristic**. That part to the right of the decimal point is called the **mantissa.** The principal advantage of using 10 as the base is that any given combination of digits has the same mantissa regardless of the position of the decimal point. Hence, only the mantissa is given in the main tabulation of table 32. Thus, the logarithm (mantissa) of 2,374 is given as 37548. This is correct for 2,374,000,000; 2,374; 23.74; 2.374; 0.2374; 0.000002374; or for any other position of the decimal point.

MATHEMATICS

The position of the decimal point determines the characteristic, which is not affected by the actual digits involved. The characteristic of a whole number is one less than the number of digits. The characteristic of a **mixed decimal** (one greater than 1) is one less than the number of digits to the left of the decimal point. Thus, in the example given above, the characteristic of the logarithm of 2,374,000,000 is 9; that of 2,374 is 3; that of 23.74 is 1; and that of 2.374 is 0. The complete logarithms of these numbers are:

$$\log 2{,}374{,}000{,}000 = 9.37548$$
$$\log 2{,}374 = 3.37548$$
$$\log 23.74 = 1.37548$$
$$\log 2.374 = 0.37548.$$

Since the mantissa of the logarithm of any multiple of ten is zero, the main table starts with 1,000. This can be considered 100, 10, 1, etc. Since the mantissa of these logarithms is zero, the logarithms consist of the characteristic only, and are whole numbers. Hence, the logarithm of 1 is 0 (0.00000), that of 10 is 1 (1.00000), that of 100 is 2 (2.00000), that of 1,000 is 3 (3.00000), etc.

The characteristic of the logarithm of a number less than 1 is negative. However, it is usually more conveniently indicated in a positive form, as follows: the characteristic is found by subtracting the number of zeros immediately to the right of the decimal point from 9 (or 19, 29, etc.) and following this by -10 (or -20, -30, etc.). Thus, the characteristic of the logarithm of 0.2374 is 9-10; that of 0.000002374 is 4-10: and that of 0.000000000002374 is 8-20. The complete logarithms of these numbers are:

$$\log 0.2374 = 9.37548\text{-}10$$
$$\log 0.000002374 = 4.37548\text{-}10$$
$$\log 0.000000000002374 = 8.37548\text{-}20.$$

When there is no question of the meaning, the -10 may be omitted. This is usually done when using logarithms of trigonometric functions, as shown in table 33. Thus, if there is no reasonable possibility of confusion, the logarithm of 0.2374 may be written 9.37548.

Occasionally, the logarithm of a number less than 1 is shown by giving the negative characteristic with a minus sign above it (since only the characteristic is negative, the mantissa being positive). Thus, the logarithms of the numbers given above might be shown thus:

$$\log 0.2374 = \bar{1}.37548$$
$$\log 0.000002374 = \bar{6}.37548$$
$$\log 0.000000000002374 = \overline{12}.37548.$$

In each case, the negative characteristic is one *more* than the number of zeros immediately to the right of the decimal point.

There is no real logarithm of 0, since there is no *finite* power to which *any* number can be raised to produce 0. As numbers approach 0, their logarithms approach negative infinity.

To find the number corresponding to a given logarithm, called finding the **antilogarithm** ("antilog"), enter the table with the mantissa of the given logarithm and determine the corresponding number, interpolating if necessary. Locate the position of the decimal point by means of the characteristic of the logarithm, in accordance with the rules given above.

MATHEMATICS

011. Multiplication by logarithms. - To *multiply* one number by another, *add* their logarithms and find the antilogarithm of the sum. Thus, to multiply 1,635.8 by 0.0362 by logarithms:

    log 1635.8   = 3.21373
    log 0.0362   = 8.55871-10 (add)
    log 59.216   =11.77244-10 or 1.77244.

Thus, 1.635.8X0.0362=59.216. In navigation it is customary to use a slightly modified form, and to omit the -10 where there is no reasonable possibility of confusion, as follows:

    1635.8   log 3.21373
    0.0362   log 8.55871
    59.216   log 1.77244.

To *raise a number to a power,* multiply the logarithm of that number by the power indicated, and find the antilogarithm of the product. Thus, to find 13.156^3 by logarithms, using the navigational form:

    13.156   log 1.11913
                   X   3 (multiply)
    2277.2   log 3.35739.

012. Division by logarithms. - To *divide* one number by another, subtract the logarithm of the divisor from that of the dividend, and find the antilogarithm of the remainder. Thus, to find 0.4637 ÷ 28.03 by logarithms, using the navigational form:

    0.4637   log   9.66624
    28.03   log   (-) 1.44762 (subtract)
    0.016543   log   8.21862.

It is sometimes necessary to modify the first logarithm before the subtraction can be made. This would occur in the example given above, for instance, if the divisor and dividend were reversed, so that the problem became 28.03 ÷ 0.4637. In this case 10-10 would be added to the logarithm of the dividend, becoming 11.44762-10:

    28.03   log   11.44762 -10
    0.4637   log   (-) 9.66624 -10
    60.448   log   1.78138.

One experienced in the use of logarithms usually carries this change mentally, without showing it in his work form:

    28.03   log   1.44762
    0.4637   log   (-) 9.66624
    60.448   log   1.78138.

MATHEMATICS

Any number can be added to the characteristic as long as that same number is also subtracted. Conversely, any number can be subtracted from the characteristic as long as that same number is also added.

To *extract a root* of a number, divide the logarithm of that number by the root indicated, and find the antilogarithm of the quotient. Thus, to find $\sqrt{7}$ by logarithms:

$$\begin{array}{rll} 7 & \log & \underline{0.84510} \ (\div 2) \\ 2.6458 & \log & 0.42255. \end{array}$$

To divide a negative logarithm by the root indicated, first modify the logarithm so that the quotient will have a -10. Thus, to find $\sqrt[3]{0.7}$ by logarithms:

$$\begin{array}{rll} 0.7 & \log & \underline{9.84510\text{-}30} \ (\div 3) \\ 0.88792 & \log & 9.94837\text{-}10 \end{array}$$

or, carrying the -30 and -10 mentally,

$$\begin{array}{rll} 0.7 & \log & \underline{29.84510} \ (\div 3) \\ 0.88792 & \log & 9.94837. \end{array}$$

013. Cologarithms.—The **cologarithm** ("colog") of a number is the value obtained by subtracting the logarithm of that number from zero, usually in the form 10-10. Thus, the logarithm of 18.615 is 1.26987. The cologarithm is:

$$\begin{array}{r} 10.00000\text{-}10 \\ \underline{(\text{-}) \ 1.26987} \\ 8.73013\text{-}10. \end{array}$$

Similarly, the logarithm of 0.0018615 is 7.26987-10, and its cologarithm is:

$$\begin{array}{r} 10.00000\text{-}10 \\ \underline{(\text{-})7.26987\text{-}10} \\ 2.73013. \end{array}$$

The *cologarithm* of a number is the *logarithm* of the reciprocal of that number. Thus, the cologarithm of 2 is the logarithm of 1/2. Since division by a number is the same as multiplication by its reciprocal, the use of cologarithms permits division problems to be converted to problems of multiplication, eliminating the need for subtraction of logarithms. This is particularly useful when both multiplication and division are involved in the same problem. Thus, to find $\dfrac{92.732 \times 0.0137 \times 724.3}{0.516 \times 3941.1}$ by logarithms,

one might *add* the logarithms of the three numbers in the numerator, and *subtract* the logarithms of the two numbers in the denominator. If cologarithms are used for the numbers in the denominator, all logarithmic values are added. Thus, the solution might be made as follows:

MATHEMATICS

92.732	log 1.96723	
0.0137	log 8.13672	
724.3	log 2.85992	
0.516	log 9.71265	colog 0.28735
3941.1	log 3.59562	colog 6.40438
0.45248	log 9.65560.	

014. Various kinds of logarithms. - As indicated above, **common logarithms** use 10 as the base. These are also called **Briggs' logarithms.** For some purposes, it is convenient to use 2.7182818 approximately (designated e) as the base for logarithms. These are called **natural logarithms or Naperian logarithms** ($\log_e$). Common logarithms are shown as $\log 10$ when the base might otherwise be in doubt.

Addition and subtraction logarithms are logarithms of the sum and difference of two numbers. They are used when the logarithms of two numbers to be added or subtracted are known, making it unnecessary to find the numbers themselves.

015. Slide rule. - A **slide rule** is a convenient device for making logarithmic solutions mechanically. There are many types and sizes of slide rule, some designed for specific purposes. The most common form consists of an outer "body" or "frame" with grooves to permit a "slide" to be moved back and forth between the two outer parts, so that any graduation of a scale on the slide can be brought opposite any graduation of a scale on the body. A cursor called an "indicator" or "runner" is provided to assist in aligning the desired graduations. In a **circular slide rule** the "slide" is an inner disk surrounded by a larger one, both pivoted at their common center. The scales of a slide rule are *logarithmic*. That is, they increase proportionally to the logarithms of the numbers indicated, rather than to the numbers themselves. This permits addition and subtraction of logarithms by simply measuring off part of the length of the slide from a graduated point on the body, or vice versa. Two or three complete scales within the length of the rule may be provided for finding squares, cubes, square roots, and cube roots.

Full instructions for use of a slide rule are provided with each rule, and given in some mathematical texts. Properly used, a slide rule can provide quick answers to many of the problems of navigation. However, its precision is usually limited to from two to four significant digits, and should not be used if greater precision is desired. It is frequently used to provide a quick, approximate check on answers obtained by a more laborious method.

Great care should be used in placing the decimal point in an answer obtained by slide rule, as the correct location often is not immediately apparent. Its position is usually determined by making a very rough mental solution. Thus, 2.93X8.3 is *about* 3X8=24. Hence, when the answer by slide rule is determined to be "243," it is known that the correct value is 24.3, not 2.43 or 243.

016. Mental arithmetic. - Many of the problems of the navigator can be solved mentally. The following are a few examples.

If the speed is a number divisible into 60 a whole number of times, distance problems can be solved by a simple relationship. Thus, at 10 knots a ship steams 1 mile in 60/10 = 6 minutes. At 12 knots it requires 5 minutes, at 15 knots 4 minutes, etc. As an example of the use of such a relationship, a vessel steaming at 12 knots travels 5.6 miles in 28 minutes, since $28/5 = 5\frac{3}{5} = 5.6$, or 0.1 mile every half minute.

MATHEMATICS

For relatively short distances, one nautical mile can be considered equal to 6,000 feet. Since one hour has 60 minutes, the speed in hundreds of feet per minute is equal to the speed in knots. Thus, a vessel steaming at 15 knots is moving at the rate of 1,500 feet per minute.

With respect to time, 6 minutes =0.1 hour, and 3 minutes =0.05 hour. Hence, a ship steaming at 13 knots travels 3.9 miles in 18 minutes (13X0.3), and 5.8 miles in 27 minutes (13X0.45).

In arc units, 6' = $0°.1$ and 6" = 0.1. This relationship is useful in rounding off values given in arc units. Thus, 17°23'44"= 17°23'.7 to the nearest 0:1, and 17°4 to the nearest 0.1. A thorough knowledge of the six multiplication table is valuable. The 15 multiplication table is also useful, since 15°= 1^h. Hence, 16^h= 16X15=240°. This is particularly helpful in quick determination of zone description. Pencil and paper or a table should not be needed, for instance, to decide that a ship at sea in longitude 157°18'.4 W is in the (+)10 zone.

It is also helpful to remember that 1°= 4^m and 1'=4^s. In converting the LMT of sunset to ZT, for instance, a quick mental solution can be made without reference to a table. Since this correction is usually desired only to the nearest whole minute, it is necessary only to multiply the longitude difference in degrees (to the nearest quarter degree) by four.

II. Vectors

017. Scalars and vector quantities. - A scalar is a quantity which has *magnitude* only; a **vector quantity** has both *magnitude* and *direction*. If a vessel is said to have a tank of 5,000 gallons capacity, the number 5,000 is a scalar. As used in this book, *speed* alone is considered a scalar, while *speed* and *direction* are considered to constitute *velocity,* a vector quantity. Thus, if a vessel is said to be steaming at 18 knots, without regard to direction, the number 18 is considered a scalar; but if the vessel is said to be steaming at 18 knots on course 157°, the combination of 18 knots and 157° constitutes a vector quantity. *Distance* and *direction* also constitute a vector quantity.

A *scalar* can be represented fully by a number. A *vector quantity* requires, in addition, an indication of direction. This is conveniently done graphically by means of a straight line, the length of which indicates the *magnitude,* and the direction of which indicates the *direction* of application of the magnitude. Such a line is called a **vector**. Since a straight line has two directions, reciprocals of each other, an arrowhead is placed along or at one end of a vector to indicate the direction represented, unless this is apparent or indicated in some other manner.

018. - Addition and subtraction of vectors. Two vectors can be *added* by *starting* the second at the *termination* (rather than the origin) of the first. A common navigational use of vectors is the dead reckoning plot of a vessel. Refer to figure O18. If a ship starts at *A* and steams 18 miles on course 090° and then 12 miles on course 060°, it arrives by dead reckoning at *C*. The line *AB* is the vector for the first run, and

MATHEMATICS

BC is the vector for the second. Point C is the position found by *adding* vectors AB and BC. The vector AC, in this case the *course and distance made good,* is the **resultant**. Its value, both in direction and amount, can be determined by measurement. Lines AB, BC, and AC are all **distance vectors. Velocity vectors** are used when determining the effect of, or allowing for, current (art. 807) or interconverting true and apparent wind (art. 3709).

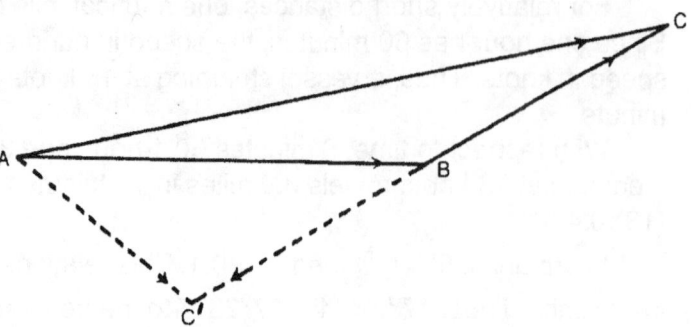

Figuer O18. Addition and subtraction of vectors.

The **reciprocal** of a vector has the same magnitude but opposite direction of the vector. To *subtract* a vector, *add* its reciprocal. This is indicated by the broken lines in figure 018, in which the vector BC' is drawn in the opposite direction to BC. In this case the resultant is AC'. Subtraction of vectors is involved in some current and wind problems.

III. Algebra

019. Definitions. - Algebra is that branch of mathematics dealing with computation by letters and symbols. It permits the mathematical statement of certain relationships between variables. When numbers are substituted for the letters. algebra becomes arithmetic. Thus if a=2b, any value may be assigned to *b,* and *a* can be found by multiplying the assigned value by 2. Any statement of equality (as *a=2b*) is an **equation.** Any combination of numbers, letters, and symbols (as 2*b*) is a **mathematical expression.**

020. Symbols. As in arithmetic, plus (+) and minus (-) signs are used, and with the same meaning. Multiplication (X) and division ($\div$) signs are seldom used. In algebra, a X b is usually written *ab,* or sometimes a.b. For division a $\div$ b is usually written $\frac{a}{b}$ or a/b. The symbol > means "greater than" and < means "less than." Thus, a>b means "a is greater than b," and a $\geq$ b or a $\geq$ b means *"a is equal to or greater than b."*

The order of performing the operations indicated in an equation should be observed carefully. Consider the equation a=b+cd-e/f. If the equation is to be solved for *a*, the value *cd* should be determined by multiplication and *e/f* by division *before* the addition and subtraction, as each of these is to be considered a single quantity in making the addition and subtraction. Thus, if cd=g and e/f=h, the formula can be written a=b+gh.

If an equation including both multiplication and division between plus or minus signs is not carefully written, some doubt may arise as to which process to perform first. Thus, a$\div$bXc or a/bXc may be interpreted to mean either that a/b is to be multiplied *by c* or that a is to be divided by bXc. Such an equation is better written *ac/b* if the first meaning is intended, or a/bc if the second meaning is in tended. **Parentheses,** ( ), may be used for the same purpose or to

MATHEMATICS

indicate any group of quantities that is to be considered a single quantity. Thus, *a(b+c)* is an indication that the sum of *b* and *c* is to be multiplied by a. Similarly, $a+(b-c)^2$ indicates that c is first to be subtracted from *b*, and then the result is to be squared and the value thus obtained added to *a*. When an expression within parentheses is part of a larger expression which should also be in parentheses, **brackets**, [ ], are used in place of the outer parentheses. If yet another set is needed, **braces,** { }, are used.

A quantity written $\sqrt{3}$ *ab* is better written *ab* $\sqrt{3}$ to remove any suggestion that the square root of 3*ab* is to be found.

021. Addition and subtraction. - A plus sign before an expression in parentheses means that each term retains its sign as given. Thus, *a+(b+c-d)* is the same as *a+b+c-d*. A minus sign preceding the parentheses means that each sign within the parentheses is to be reversed. For example, *a-(b+c-d)=a-b-c+d*.

In any equation involving addition and subtraction, similar terms can be combined. Thus, *a+b+c+b-2c-d = a+2b-c-d*. Also, $a+3ab+a^2-b-ab = a+2ab+ a^2-b$. That is, to be combined, the terms must be truly alike, for a cannot be combined with ab, or with a^2.

Equal quantities can be added to or subtracted from both members of an equation without disturbing the equality. Thus, if *a=b, a+2=b+2*, or *a+x=b+x*. If *x=y*, then *a+x=b+y*.

022. Multiplication and division. - When an expression in parentheses is to be multiplied by a quantity outside the parentheses, each quantity separated by a plus or minus sign within the parentheses should be multiplied separately. Thus, *a(b+cd-e/f)* may be written *ab+acd-ae/f*. Any quantity appearing in *every* term of one member of an equation can be separated out by **factoring,** or dividing each term by the common quantity. Thus, if $a = bc+\frac{bd}{e}-b^2+b$, the equation may be written $a=b (c+\frac{d}{e} -b+1)$.

Note that $\frac{b}{b} = 1$ and $\frac{b^2}{b}=b$. This is the inverse of multiplication: $a \times 1 = a$, but $a \times a=a^2$. Also, $a^2 \times a^3 = a^5$; and $\frac{a^7}{a^2} = a^5$. Thus, in multiplying a power of a number by a power of the same number, the powers are added, or, stated mathematically, $a^m \times a^n = a^{m+n}$. In division, $\frac{a^m}{a^n} = a^{m-n}$ or the exponents are subtracted. If *n* is greater than *m*, a *negative* exponent results. A value with a negative exponent is equal to the reciprocal of the same value with a positive exponent. Thus, $a^{-n}= \frac{1}{a^n}$ and $\frac{a^2 b^{-3}}{c} = \frac{a^2}{b^3 c}$.

In raising to a power a number with an exponent, the two exponents are multiplied. Thus, $(a^2)^3=a^{2\times3} = a^6$, or $(a^n)^m = a^{nm}$. The inverse is true in extracting a root.

MATHEMATICS

Thus, $\sqrt[3]{a^2} = a^{\frac{2}{3}} = a^{0.667}$ or $\sqrt[m]{a^n} = a^{\frac{n}{m}}$

Both members of an equation can be multiplied or divided by equal quantities without disturbing the equality, excluding division by zero or some expression equal to zero. Thus, if $a = b+c$, $2a = 2(b+c)$, or if $x = y$, $ax = y(b+c)$ and $\frac{a}{x} = \frac{a}{x} = \frac{b+c}{y}$. Sometimes there is more than one answer to an equation. Division by one of the unknowns may eliminate one of the answers.

Both members of an equation can be raised to the same power, and like roots of both members can be taken, without disturbing the equality. Thus, if $a = b + c$, $a^2 = (b + c)^2$, or if $x = y$, $a^x = (b + c)^y$. This is not the same as $a^x = b^y + c^y$. Similarly, if $a = b+c$, $\sqrt{a} = \sqrt{b+c}$, or if $x=y$, $\sqrt[x]{a} = \sqrt[y]{b+c}$. Again, $\sqrt[y]{b+c}$ is not equal to $+ \sqrt[y]{c}$, as a numerical example will indicate: $\sqrt{100} = \sqrt{64+36}$, but $\sqrt{100}$ does not equal $\sqrt{64} + \sqrt{36}$.

If two quantities to be multiplied or divided are *both* positive or *both* negative, the result is positive. Thus, $(+a) \times (+b) = ab$ and $\frac{-a}{-b} = +\frac{a}{b}$. But if the signs are opposite, the answer is negtive. Thus, $(+a) \times (-b) = -ab$, and $= -\frac{a}{b}$; also, $(-a) \times (+b) = -ab$, $\frac{+a}{-b} = -\frac{a}{b}$.

In expressions containing both parentheses and brackets, or both of these and braces, the innermost symbols are removed first.

Thus, $-\{6z - \frac{[x(x+4)-5y]}{y}\} = -\{6z - \frac{[x(x+4)-5y]}{y}\} = -\{6z - \frac{x^2}{y} - \frac{4x}{y} + 5\} = -6z + \frac{x^2}{y} + \frac{4x}{y} - 5$

023. Fractions. To add or subtract two or more fractions, convert each to an expression having the same denominator, and then add the numerators.

Thus, $\frac{a}{b} + \frac{c}{d} + \frac{e}{f} = \frac{adf}{bdf} + \frac{cbf}{bdf} + \frac{ebd}{bdf} = \frac{adf + cbf + ebd}{bdf}$. That is, both numerator and denominator of each fraction are multiplied by the denominator of the other remaining fractions.

To multiply two or more fractions, multiply the numerators by each other, and ; also multiply the denominators by each other. Thus, $\frac{a}{b} \times \frac{c}{d} \times \frac{e}{f} = \frac{ace}{bdf}$.

To divide two fractions, invert the divisor and multiply. Thus, $\frac{a}{b} \div \frac{c}{d} = \frac{a}{b} \times \frac{d}{c} = \frac{ad}{bc}$.

If the same factor appears in all terms of a fraction, it can be factored out without changing the value of the fraction. Thus, $\frac{ab + ac + ad}{ae + af} = \frac{(b+c+d)}{(e-f)}$. This is the same as factoring a from

MATHEMATICS

the numerator and denominator separately. That is, $\dfrac{ab+ac+ad}{ae+af} = \dfrac{a(b+c+d)}{a(e-f)}$ but since $\dfrac{a}{a}=1$, this part can be removed, and the fraction appears as above.

024. Transposition. - It is sometimes desirable to move terms of an expression from one side of the equals sign (=) to the other. This is called **transposition,** and to move one term is to **transpose** it. If the term to be moved is preceded by a plus or a minus sign, this sign is reversed when the term is transposed. Thus, if *a=b+c*, then *a-b = c, a - c=b, -b=c-a, -b-c=-a*, etc. Note that the signs of *all* terms can be reversed without destroying the equality, for if *a=b, b = a*. Thus, if *all* terms to the left of the equals sign are exchanged for *all* those to the right, no change in sign need take place, yet if each is moved individually, the signs reverse. For instance, if a = *b+c,- b-c=-a*. If each term is multiplied *by-* 1, this becomes *b + c=a*.

A. term which is to be multiplied or divided by *all* other terms on its side of the equation can be transposed if it is also moved from the numerator to the denominator, or vice versa.

Thus, if $a=\dfrac{b}{c}$ then *ac=b,* $c=\dfrac{b}{a}, \dfrac{1}{b}=\dfrac{1}{ac}, \dfrac{c}{b}=\dfrac{1}{a}$,etc. (Note that $a=\dfrac{a}{1}$) The same result could be obtained by multiplying both sides of an equation by the same quantity. For instance, if both sides of $a=\dfrac{b}{c}$ are multiplied by *c*, the equation becomes $ac=\dfrac{bc}{c}$ and since any number (except zero) divided by itself is unity, $\dfrac{c}{c}=1$, and the equation becomes *ac=b,* as given above. Note, also, that *both* sides of an equation can be *inverted* without destroying the relationship, for if a=b, $\dfrac{a}{1}=\dfrac{b}{1}$ and $\dfrac{1}{b}=\dfrac{1}{a}$ or $\dfrac{1}{a}=\dfrac{1}{b}$.

This is accomplished by transposing *all* terms of an equation.

Note that in the case of transposition by changing the plus or minus sign, an entire expression must bo changed, and not a part of it. Thus, if *a = bc+d, a-bc=d,* but it is not true that *a+b=c+d*. Similarly, a term to be transposed by reversing its multiplication-division relationship must bear that relationship to *all* other terms on its side of the equation. That is, if *a=bc+d,* it is *not* true that or that but $\dfrac{a}{bc+d}=1$ If *a=b (cd+e),* then $\dfrac{a}{b}=cd+e$.

025. Ratio and proportion. - If the relationship of a to 6 is the same as that of *c* to *d*, this fact can be written *a : b :: c : d,* or $\dfrac{a}{b}=\dfrac{c}{d}$. Either side of this equation, $\dfrac{a}{b} or \dfrac{c}{d}$ is called a **ratio** and the whole equation is called a **proportion**. When a ratio is given a numerical value, it is often expressed as a decimal or as a percentage. Thus, if $\dfrac{a}{b}=\dfrac{1}{4}$ (that is, *a*=1, *b*=4), the ratio might be expressed as 0.25 or as 25 percent.

Since a ratio is a fraction, it can be handled as any other fraction.

MATHEMATICS

IV. Geometry

026. Definitions. Geometry is that branch of mathematics dealing with the properties, relations, and measurement of lines, surfaces, solids, and angles. **Plane geometry** deals with plane figures, and **solid geometry** deals with three-dimensional figures.

A point, considered mathematically, is a place having position but no extent. It has no length, breadth, or thickness. A point in motion produces a **line,** which has length, but neither breadth nor thickness. A **straight** or **right line** is the shortest distance between two points in space. A line in motion in any direction except along itself produces a **surface,** which has length and breadth, but not thickness. A **plane surface** or **plane** is a surface without curvature. A straight line connecting any two of its points lies wholly within the plane. A plane surface in motion in any direction except within its plane produces a **solid,** which has length, breadth, and thickness. **Parallel** lines or surfaces are those which are everywhere equidistant. **Perpendicular** lines or surfaces are those which meet at right angles. A perpendicular may be called a **nomal,** particularly when it is perpendicular to the tangent to a curved line or surface at the point of tangency. All points equidistant from the ends of a straight line are on the perpendicular bisector of that line. The distance from a point to a line is the length of the perpendicular between them, unless some other distance is indicated.

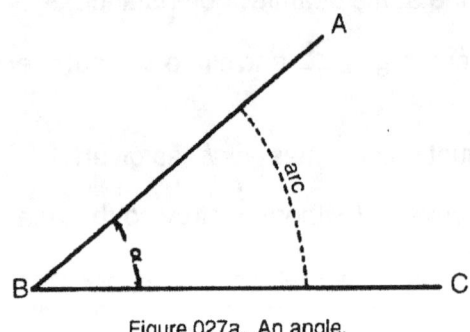

Figure 027a. An angle.

027. Angles. - An **angle** is the inclination to each other of two straight lines which meet at a point. It is measured by the arc of a circle intercepted between the two lines forming the angle, the center of the circle being at the point of intersection. Referring to figure O27a, the angle formed by lines AB and BC, measured by the arc shown, may be designated "angle B," "angle ABC," or "angle CBA", or by Greek letter (app. B), as "angle a." The first method should not be used if there is more than one angle at the point, as at G in figure O27b. When three letters are used, the middle one should always be that at the **vertex** of the angle, as G in figure O27b.

An **acute angle** is one less than a right angle (90°). In figure O27b, angles AGB, BGC, CGD, DGE, and EGF are all acute angles.

A **right angle** is one whose sides are perpendicular (90°). In figure O27b, angles AGC, BGD, CGE, and DGF are right angles.

An **obtuse angle** is one greater than a right angle (90°) but less than a straight angle (180°). In figure O27b, angles AGD, BGE, and CGF are obtuse angles. Angle AGF is also obtuse if measured counterclockwise from AG to FG.

A **straight angle** is one whose sides form a continuous straight line (180°). In figure O27b, angles AGE and BGF are straight angles.

A **reflex angle** is one greater than a straight angle (180°) but less than a circle (360°). In figure O27b, Angle AGF is reflex if measured clockwise from AG to FG. Actually, any two lines meeting at a point form two angles, one less than a straight angle of 180 (unless exactly a straight angle) and the other greater than a straight angle (180°).

MATHEMATICS

An **oblique angle** is any angle not a multiple of 90°.

Two angles whose sum is a right angle (90°) are **complementary angles,** and either is the **complement** of the other. In figure O27b, angles *AGB* and *BGC*, *BGC* and *CGD*, *CGD* and *DGE*, and *DGE* and *EGF* are complementary. The angles need not be adjacent. Angles *AGB* and *DGE*, and angles *BGC* and *EGF* are complementary.

Two angles whose sum is a straight angle (180) are **supplementary angles,** and either is the **supplement** of the other. In figure O27b, angles *AGB* and *BGE*, *AGC* and *CGE*, *AGD* and *DGE*, *BGC* and *CGF*, *BGD* and *DGF*, *BGE and EGF*, and *AGC* and *DGF* are supplementary.

Two angles whose sum is a circle (360) are **explementary angles,** and either is the **explement** of the other. The two angles formed when any two lines terminate at a common point are explementary.

Since angles *AGB* and *CGD* (fig. O27b) are each complementary to angle *BGC*, angles *AGB* and *CGD* are equal. Similarly, it can be shown that angle *EGF* is also equal to angle *CGD* (and therefore also equal to angle *AGB*) and also that angles *BGC* and *DGE* are equal to each other. Since *AGC* and *CGE* are both right angles witli a common side, *CG* is perpendicular to *AE*. Similarly, *DG* is perpendicular to *BF*. If the sides of one angle are perpendicular to those of another, the two angles are either equal or supplementary. Also, if the sides of one angle are parallel to those of another, the two angles are either equal or supplementary.

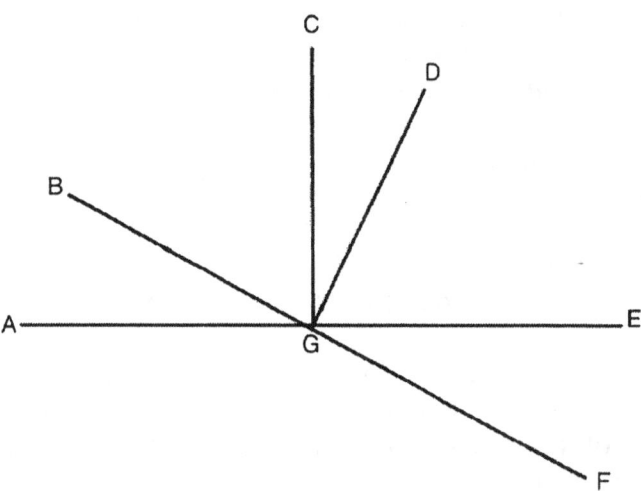

Figuer 027b. Acuet,right, and obtuse angles.

When two straight lines intersect, forming four angles, the two opposite angles, called **vertical angles,** are equal. Thus, in figure O27b, lines *AE* and *BF* intersect at *G*. Angles *AGB* and *EGF* form a pair of equal acute vertical angles, and *BGE* and *AGF* form a pair of equal obtuse vertical angles. Angles which have the same vertex and lie on opposite sides of a common side are **adjacent angles.** Adjacent angles formed by intersecting lines are supplementary, since each pair of adjacent angles forms a straight angle (fig. O27b).

A transversal is a line that intersects two or more other lines. If two or more parallel lines are cut by a transversal, groups of adjacent and vertical angles are formed,

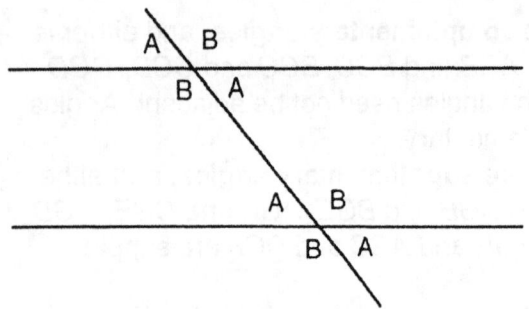

Figuer 027c. Angles formed by a transversal

as shown in figure 027c. In this situation, all acute angles *(A)* are equal, all obtuse angles *(B)* are equal, and each acute angle is supplementary to each obtuse angle.

A **dihedral angle** is the angle between two intersecting planes.

028. Triangles. - A **plane triangle** is a closed figure formed by three straight lines, called **sides,** which meet at three points called **vertices** (singular **vertex).** The vertices are usually labeled with capital letters, and the sides with lowercase letters, as shown in figure O28a.

An **equilateral triangle** is one with its three sides equal. An **equiangular triangle** is one with its three angles equal. When either of these conditions is present, the other always is, so that a triangle which is equilateral is also equiangular, and vice versa.

An **isosceles triangle** is one with two equal sides, called **legs.** The angles opposite the legs are equal. A line which bisects (divides into two equal parts) the *unequal* angle of an isosceles triangle is the perpendicular bisector of the opposite side, and divides the triangle into two equal right triangles.

A **scalene triangle** is one with no two sides equal. In such a triangle, no two angles are equal.

An **acute triangle** is one with three acute angles.

A **right triangle** is one with a right angle. The side opposite the right angle is called the **hypotenuse.** The other two sides may be called **legs.** A plane triangle can have only one right angle.

An **obtuse triangle** is one with an obtuse angle. A plane triangle can have only one obtuse angle.

An **oblique triangle** is one which does not contain a right angle.

The **altitude** of a triangle is a perpendicular line from any vertex to the opposite side, extended if necessary, or the length of this perpendicular line.

A **median** of a triangle is a line from any vertex to the center of the opposite side. The three medians of a

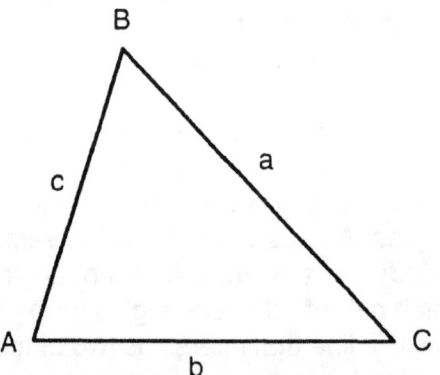

triangle meet at a point called the **centroid** of the triangle. This point divides each median into two parts, that part between the centroid and the vertex being twice as long as the other part.

Lines bisecting the three angles of a triangle meet at a point which is equidistant from the three sides, and is the center of the **inscribed circle,** as shown in figure O28b. This point is of particular interest to navigators because it is the point taken as the fix when three lines of position of equal weight and having only random errors do not meet at a common point.

MATHEMATICS

The perpendicular bisectors of the three sides of a triangle meet at a point which is equidistant from the three vertices, and is the center of the **circumscribed circle,** the circle through the three vertices and therefore the smallest circle which can be drawn enclosing the triangle. The center of a circumscribed circle is within an acute triangle, on the hypotenuse of a right triangle, and outside an obtuse triangle.

A line connecting the mid points of two sides of a triangle is parallel to the third side and half as long. Also, a line parallel to one side of a triangle and intersecting the other two sides divides these sides proportionally. This principle can be used to divide a line into any number of equal or proportional parts. Refer to figure O28c. Suppose it is desired to divide line *AB* into four equal parts. From *A* draw any line *AC*. Along C measure four equal parts of any convenient lengths *(AD, DE, EF,* and *FG)*. Draw *GB,* and through *F, E,* and *D* draw lines parallel to *GB* and intersecting *AB*. Then *AD', D'E'. E'F',* and *F'B* are equal and *AB* is divided into four equal parts.

The sum of the angles of a plane triangle is 180°. Therefore, the sum of the acute angles of a right triangle is 90°, and the angles are complementary. If one side of a triangle is extended, the **exterior angle** thus formed is supplementary to the adjacent **interior** angle and, therefore, equal to the sum of the two nonadjacent angles. If two angles of one triangle are equal to two angles of another triangle, the third angles are also equal, and the triangles are **similar.** If the area of one triangle is equal to the area of another, the triangles are **equal**. Triangles having equal bases and altitudes have equal areas. Two figures are **congruent** if one can be placed over the other to make an exact fit. Congruent figures are both similar and equal. If any side of one triangle is equal to any side of a similar triangle, the triangles are congruent. For example, if two right triangles have equal sides, they are congruent; if two right triangles have two corresponding sides equal, they are congruent. Triangles are congruent only if the sides and angles are equal.

The sum of two sides of a plane triangle is always greater than the third side; their difference is always less than the third side.

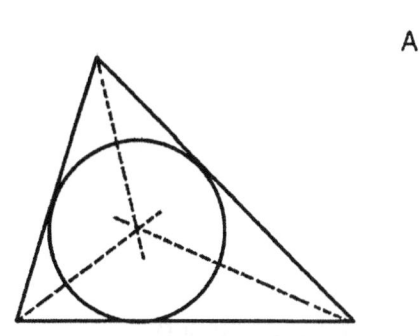

Figure 028b.   A circle inscribed in a triangle.

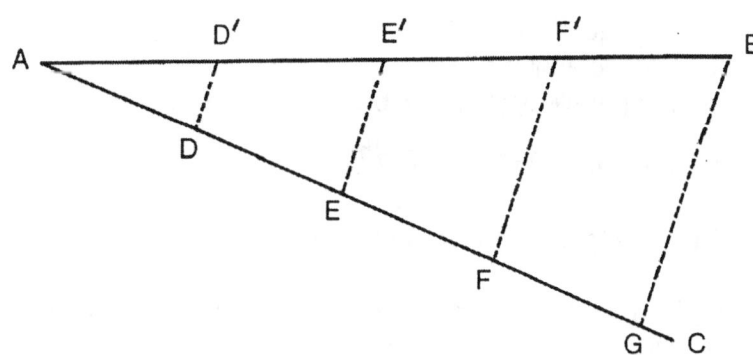

Figure 028c.   Dividing a line into equal parts.

If *A=area, b=*one of the legs of a right triangle or the base of any plane triangle, *h*=altitude, *c=*the hypotenuse of a right triangle, *a=*the other leg of a right triangle, and *S=*the sum of the interior angles:

Area of plane triangle: $A = \dfrac{bh}{2}$

MATHEMATICS

Length of hypotenuse of plane right triangle: $c = \sqrt{a^2 + b^2}$

Sum of interior angles of plane triangle: $S = 180°$.

029. Polygons. - **A polygon** is a closed plane figure made up of three or more straight lines called **sides**. A polygon with three sides is a **triangle**, one with four sides is a **quadrilateral**, one with five sides is a **pentagon**, one with six sides is a **hexagon**, and one with eight sides is an **octagon**. An **equilateral polygon** has equal sides. An **equiangular polygon** has equal interior angles. A **regular polygon** is both equilateral and equiangular. As the number of sides of a regular polygon increases, the figure approaches a circle.

A trapezoid is a quadrilateral with one pair of opposite sides parallel and the, other pair not parallel. A **parallelogram** is a quadrilateral with both pairs of opposite sides parallel. Any side of a parallelogram, or either of the parallel sides of a trapezoid, is the **base** of the figure. The perpendicular distance from the base to the opposite side is the altitude. A rectangle is a parallelogram with four right angles. (If any one is a right angle, the other three must be, also.) A square is a rectangle with equal sides. A **rhomboid** is a parallelogram with oblique angles. A **rhombus** is a rhomboid with equal sides.

The sum of the exterior angles of a convex polygon (one having no interior reflex angles), made by extending each side in one direction only (consistently), is 360°.

A diagonal of a polygon is a straight line connecting any two vertices which are not adjacent. The diagonals of a parallelogram bisect each other.

The **perimeter** of a polygon is the sum of the lengths of its sides.

If A=area, s= the side of a square, a= that side of a rectangle adjacent to the base or that side of a trapezoid parallel to the base, b=the base of a quadrilateral, h=the altitude of a parallelogram or trapezoid, S=the sum of the angles of a polygon, and n=the number of sides of a polygon:

Area of square: $A = s^2$
Area of rectangle: $A = ab$
Area of parallelogram: $A = bh$
Area of trapezoid: $A = \dfrac{(a+b)h}{2}$

Sum of angles in convex polygon: $S = (n-2)180°$.

030. Circles. - **A circle** is a plane, closed curve, all points of which are equidistant from a point within, called the **center** (*C,* fig. O30); or the figure formed by such a curve

MATHEMATICS

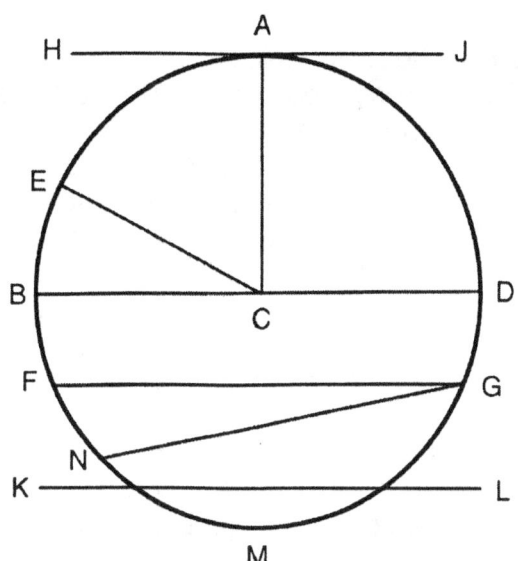

Figure 030. Elements of a circle.

The line forming the circle is called the **circumference.** The length of this line is the **perimeter,** although the term "circumference" is often used with this meaning. An **arc** is part of a circumference. A **major arc** is more than a semicircle (180°), a **minor arc** is less than a semicircle (180°). A **semicircle** is half a circle (180°), a **quadrant** is a quarter of a circle (90°), a **quintant** is a fifth of a circle (72°), a **sextant** is a sixth of a circle (60°), an **octant** is an eighth of a circle (45°). Some of these names have been applied to instruments used by navigators for measuring altitudes of celestial bodies because of the part of a circle originally used for the length of the arc of the instrument.

Concentric circles have a common center.

A **radius** (plural **radii**) or **semidiameter** is a straight line connecting the center of a circle with any point on its circumference. In figure O30, *CA, CB, CD,* and *CE* are radii.

A **diameter** of a circle is a straight line passing through its center and terminating at opposite sides of the circumference, or two radii in opposite directions *(BCD,* fig. O30). It divides a circle into two equal parts. The ratio of the length of the circumference of any circle to the length of its diameter is 3.14159+, or (the Greek letter *pi)*, a relationship that has many useful applications.

A **sector** is that part of a circle bounded by two radii and an arc. In figure O30, *BCE, ECA, ACD, ECA,* and *ECD* are sectors. The angle formed by two radii is called a **central angle.** Any pair of radii divides a circle into sectors, one less than a semicircle (180°) and the other greater than a semicircle (unless the two radii form a diameter).

A **chord** is a straight line connecting any two points on the circumference of a circle *(FG, GN* in fig. O30). Chords equidistant from the center of a circle are equal in length.

A **segment** is that part of a circle bounded by a chord and the intercepted arc *(FGMF, NGMN* in fig. O30). A chord divides a circle into two segments, one less than a semicircle (180°), and the other greater than a semicircle (unless the chord is a diameter).

A diameter perpendicular to a chord bisects it, its arc, and its segments. Either pair of vertical angles formed by intersecting chords has a combined number of degrees equal to the sum of the number of degrees in the two arcs intercepted by the two angles.

An **inscribed angle** is one whose vertex is on the circumference of a circle and whose sides are chords *(FGN* in fig. O30). It has half as many degrees as the arc it intercepts. Hence, an angle inscribed in a semicircle is a right angle if its sides terminate at the ends of the diameter forming the semicircle.

MATHEMATICS

A secant of a circle is a line intersecting the circle, or a chord extended beyond the circumference *(KL* in fig. O30).

A tangent to a circle is a straight line, in the plane of the circle, which has only one point in common with the circumference *(HJ* in fig. 030). A tangent is perpendicular to the radius at the **point of tangency** (.4 in fig. O30). The two tangents from a point to opposite sides of a circle are equal in length, and a line from the point to the center of the circle bisects the angle formed by the two tangents. An angle formed outside a circle by the intersection of two tangents, a tangent and a secant, or two secants has *half* as many degrees as the *difference* between the two intercepted arcs. An angle formed by a tangent and a chord, with the apex at the point of tangency, has half as many degrees as the arc it intercepts. **A common tangent** is one tangent to more than one circle. Two circles are tangent to each other if they touch at one point only. If of different sizes, the smaller circle may be either inside or outside the larger one.

Parallel lines intersecting a circle intercept equal arcs.

If A = area; r=radius; d=diameter; C= circumference; s=linear length of an arc; a = angular length of an arc, or the angle it subtends at the center of a circle, in degrees; β = angular length of an arc, or the angle it subtends at the center of a circle, in radians; *rad* = radians (art. O38), and sin=sine (art. O39):

Area of circle: $A = \pi r^2 = \dfrac{\pi d^2}{4}$

Circumference of circle: $C = 2\pi r = \pi d = 2\pi$

Area of sector: $A = \dfrac{\pi r^2 \alpha}{360} = \dfrac{r^2 \beta}{2} = \dfrac{rs}{2}$

Area of segment: $A = \dfrac{r^2(\beta - \sin \alpha)}{2}$

031. Polyhedrons. - A **polyhedron** is a solid having plane sides or **faces**.

A **cube** is a polyhedron having six square sides.

A **prism** is a solid having parallel, similar, equal, plane geometric figures as bases, and parallelograms as sides. By extension, the term is also applied to a similar solid having non-parallel bases, and trapezoids or a combination of trapezoids and parallelograms as sides. **The axis** of a prism is the straight line connecting the centers of its bases. A right prism is one having bases perpendicular to the axis. The sides of a right prism are rectangles. **A regular prism** is a right prism having regular polygons as bases. **The altitude** of a prism is the perpendicular distance between the planes of its bases. In the case of a right prism, it is measured along the **axis**.

A **pyramid** is a polyhedron having a polygon as one end, the **base;** and a point, the **apex,** as the other; the two ends being connected by a number of triangular sides or **faces.** The **axis** of a pyramid is the straight line connecting the apex and the center of the base. A **right pyramid** is one having its base perpendicular to its axis. A **regular pyramid** is a right pyramid having a regular polygon as its base. The **altitude** of a pyramid is the perpendicular distance from its apex to the plane of its base. A **truncated pyramid** is that portion of a pyramid between its base and a plane intersecting all of the faces of the pyramid.

MATHEMATICS

If A=area, s = edge of a cube or slant height of a regular pyramid (from the center of one side of its base to the apex), V=volume, a=side of a polygon, h=altitude, P= perimeter of base, n=number of sides of polygon, B=area of base, and r=perpendicular distance from the center of a side of a polygon to the center of the polygon:

Cube:

Area of each face: $A = s^2$
Total area of all faces: $A = 6s^2$
Volume: $V = s^3$

Regular prism:

Area of each face: $A = ah$
Total area of all faces: $A = Ph = nah$

Area of each base: $B = \dfrac{nar}{2}$

Total area of both bases: $A = nar$

Volume: $V = Bh = \dfrac{narh}{2}$

Regular pyramid:

Area of each face: $A = \dfrac{as}{2}$

Total area of all faces: $A = \dfrac{nas}{2}$

Area of base: $B = \dfrac{nar}{2}$

Volume: $V = \dfrac{Bh}{3} = \dfrac{narh}{6}$

032. - Cylinders.—A **cylinder** is a solid having two parallel plane **bases** bounded by closed congruent curves, and a surface formed by an infinite number of parallel lines, called **elements**, connecting similar points on the two curves. A cylinder is similar to a prism, but with a curved lateral surface, instead of a number of flat sides connecting the bases. The **axis** of a cylinder is the straight line connecting the centers of the bases. A **right cylinder** is one having bases perpendicular to the axis. A **circular cylinder** is one having circular bases. The **altitude** of a cylinder is the perpendicular distance between the planes of its bases. The **perimeter** of a base is the length of the curve bounding it.

If A=area, P=perimeter of base, h=altitude, r=radius of a circular base, B=area of base, and V= volume, then for a right circular cylinder:

MATHEMATICS

Lateral area: $A = Ph = 2\pi rh$
Area of each base: $B = \pi r^2$
Total area, both bases: $A = 2\pi r^2$
Volume: $V = Bh = \pi r^2 h$.

033. Cones. - A cone is a solid having a plane base bounded by a closed curve, and a surface formed by lines, called **elements,** from every point on the curve to a common point called the **apex.** A cone is similar to a pyramid, but with a curved surface connecting the base and apex, instead of a number of flat sides. The **axis** of a cone is the straight line connecting the apex and the center of the base. A **right cone** is one having its base perpendicular to its axis. A **circular cone** is one having a circular base. The **altitude** of a cone is the perpendicular distance from its apex to the plane of its base. A **frustum** of a cone is that portion of the cone between its base and any parallel plane intersecting all elements of the cone. A **truncated cone** is that portion of a cone between its base and any nonparallel plane which intersects all elements of the cone but does not intersect the base.

If A=area, r=radius of base, s=slant height or length of element, B= area of base, h=altitude, and V= volume, then for a right circular cone:

Lateral area: $A = \pi rs$
Area of base: $B = \pi r^2$
Slant height: $s = \sqrt{r^2 + h^2}$
Volume: $V = \dfrac{Bh}{3} = \dfrac{pr^2 h}{3}$

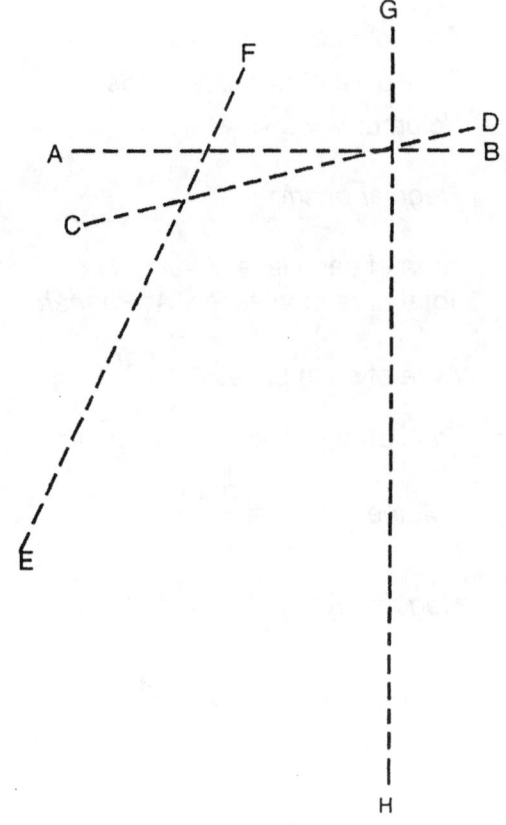

Figure 034a. Conic sections

034. Conic sections. - If a right circular cone of indefinite extent is intersected by a plane perpendicular to the axis of the cone (AB, fig. O34a), the line of intersection of the plane and the surface of the cone is a **circle,** discussed in article O30.

If the intersecting plane of figure O34a is tilted to some position such as CD, the intersection is an **ellipse** or flattened circle, figure O34b. The longest diameter of an ellipse is called its **major axis,** and half of this is its **semimajor axis, a.** The shortest diameter of an ellipse is called its **minor axis,** and half of this is its **semiminor axis, b.** Two points, F and F', called **foci** (singular **focus**) **or focal points,** on the major axis are so located that the sum of their distances from any point P on the curve is equal to the length of the major axis. That is, $PF+PF' = 2a$ (fig. O34b). The **eccentricity** (e) of an ellipse is equal to c/a where c is the dis

MATHEMATICS

tance from the center to one of the foci *(c=CF=CF')*, It is always greater than 0 but less than 1.

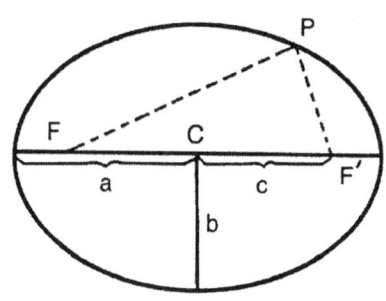

Figure 034b. An ellipse.

If the intersecting plane of figure O34a is parallel to one element of the cone, as at *EF*, the intersection is a **parabola**, figure O34c. Any point *P* on a parabola is equi-distant from a fixed point *F*, called the **focus** or **focal point**, and a fixed straight line, *AB*, called the **directrix**. Thus, for any point *P*, *PF=PE*. The point midway between the focus *F* and the directrix *AB* is called the **vertex**, *V*. The straight line

through *F* and *V* is called the **axis**, *CD*. This line is perpendicular to the directrix *AB*. The **eccentricity** *(e)* of a parabola is 1.

If the elements of the cone of figure O34a are extended to form a second cone having the same axis and apex but extending in the opposite direction, and the intersecting plane is tilted beyond the position forming a parabola, so that it intersects both curves, as at *GH*, the intersections of the plane with the cones is a **hyperbola,** figure O34d. There are two intersections or branches of a hyperbola, as shown. At any point *P* on either branch, the *difference* in the distance from two fixed points called **foci or focal points,** *F* and *F'*, is constant and equal to the shortest dis-

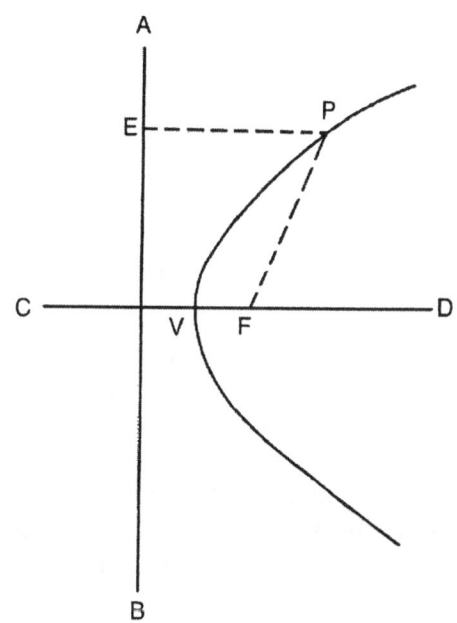

Figure 034c. A parabola.

tance between the two branches. That is, $PF-PF' = 2a$ (fig. O34d). The straight line through *F* "and *F'* is called the **axis**. The **eccentricity** *(e)* of a hyperbola is the ratio - (fig. O34(d). It is always greater than 1. Each branch of a hyperbola approaches ever closer to. but never reaches, a pair of intersecting straight lines, *AB* and *CD*, called **asymptotes**. These intersect at *G.*

MATHEMATICS

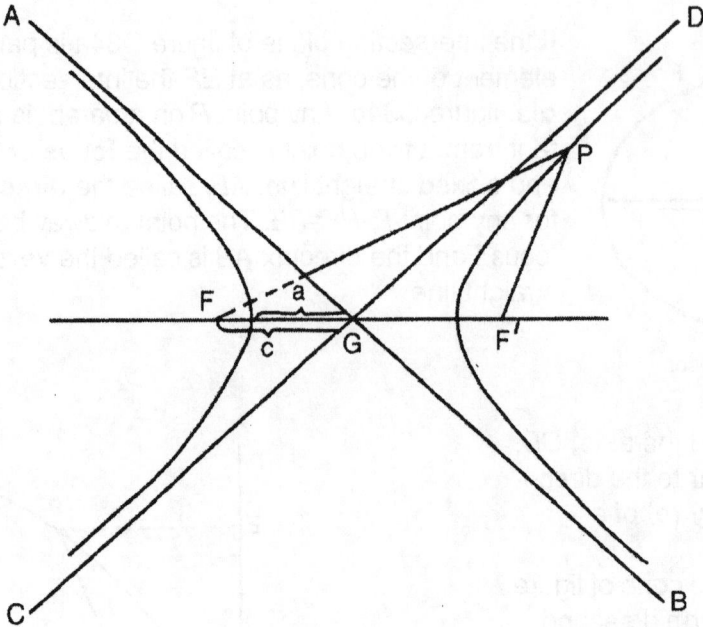

Figure 034d. A hyperbola.

The various conic sections bear an eccentricity relationship to each other. The eccentricity of a circle is 0, that of an ellipse is greater than 0 but less than 1, that of a parabola or straight line (a limiting case of a parabola) is 1, and that of a hyperbola is greater than 1.

If e=eccentricity, A=area, a=semimajor axis of an ellipse or half the shortest distance between the two branches of a hyperbola, b=the semiminor axis of an ellipse, and c=the distance between the center of an ellipse and one of its focal points or the distance between the focal point of a hyperbola and the intersection of its asymptotes:

Circle:
   Eccentricity: $e=0$
   Other relationships given in article O30.

Ellipse:
   Area: $A = \pi\,ab$

   Eccentricity: $e = \dfrac{c}{a}$, greater than 0, but less than 1.

Parabola:
   Eccentricity: $e=1$.

Hyperbola:

   Eccentricity: $e = \dfrac{c}{a}$, greater than 1.

MATHEMATICS

When cones are intersected by some surface other than a plane, as the curved surface of the earth, the resulting sections do not follow the relationships given above, the amount of divergence therefrom depending upon the individual circumstances. Thus, a "hyperbolic" line of position (art. 1109) is not a true hyperbola.

035. - Spheres. A sphere is a solid bounded by a surface even- point of which is equidistant from a point within, called the **center.** It may be formed by rotating a circle about any diameter.

A **radius** or **semidiameter** of a sphere is a straight line connecting its center with any point on its surface. A **diameter** of a sphere is a straight line through its center and terminated at both ends *by* the surface of the sphere. The poles of a sphere are the ends of a diameter.

The intersection of a plane and the surface of a sphere is 'a circle, a **great circle** if the plane passes through the center of the sphere, and a **small circle** if it does not. The shorter arc of the great circle between two points on the surface of a sphere is the shortest distance, on the surface of the sphere, between the points. Every great circle of a sphere bisects every other great circle of that sphere. The **poles** of a circle on a sphere are the extremities of the sphere's diameter which is perpendicular to the plane of the circle. All points on the circumference of the circle are equidistant from either of its poles. In the case of a great circle, *both* poles are 90° from any point on the circumference of the circle. Any great circle may be considered a **primary,** particularly when it serves as the origin of measurement of a coordinate. The great circles through its poles are called **secondaries.** Secondaries arc perpendicular to their primary.

A **spherical triangle** is the figure formed on the surface of a sphere by the intersection of three great circles. The lengths of the sides of a spherical triangle are measured in degrees, minutes, and seconds, as the angular lengths of the arcs forming them. The sum of the three sides is always less than 360°. The sum of the three angles is always *more* than 180 and *less* than 540°.

A **lune** is that part of the surface of a sphere bounded by halves of two great circles.

A **spheroid** is a flattened sphere, which may be formed by rotating an ellipse about one of its axes. An **oblate spheroid,** such as the earth, is formed when an ellipse is rotated about its minor axis. In this case the diameter along the axis of rotation is less than the major axis. A **prolate spheroid** is formed when an ellipse is rotated about its major axis. In this case the diameter along the axis of rotation is greater than the minor axis.

If A=area, r=radius, d=diameter, and V=volume of a sphere:

Area: $A = 4pr^2 = pd^2$

Volume: $V = \dfrac{4pr^3}{3} = \dfrac{pd^3}{6}$

If A=area, a=semimajor axis, b = semiminor axis, e = eccentricity, and V= volume of an oblate spheroid:

Area: $A = 4pr^2(1 - \dfrac{e^2}{3} - \dfrac{e^4}{15} - \dfrac{e^6}{2} \ldots\ldots)$

MATHEMATICS

Eccentricity: $e = \sqrt{\dfrac{a^2 - b^2}{a^2}}$

volume: $V = \dfrac{4pa^2 b}{3}$

036. Coordinates are magnitudes used to define a position. Many different types of coordinates are used.

If a position is known to be at a stated point, no magnitudes are needed to identify the position, although they may be required to locate the point. Thus, if a vessel is at port A, its position is known if the location of port A is known, but latitude and longitude may be needed to locate port A.

If a position is known to be on a given line, a single magnitude (coordinate) is needed to identify the position if an origin is stated or understood. Thus, if a vessel is known to be *south* of port B, it is known to be on a line extending southward from port B. If its distance from port B is known, and the position of port B is known, the position of the vessel is uniquely defined. If a position is known to be on a given surface, two magnitudes (coordinates) are needed to define the position. Thus, if a vessel is known to be on the surface of the earth, its position can be identified by means of latitude and longitude. Latitude indicates its angular distance north or south of the equator, and longitude its angular distance east or west of the prime meridian. If nothing is known regarding a position other than that it exists in space, three magnitudes (coordinates) are needed to define its position. Thus, the position of a submarine may be defined by means of latitude, longitude, and depth below the surface.

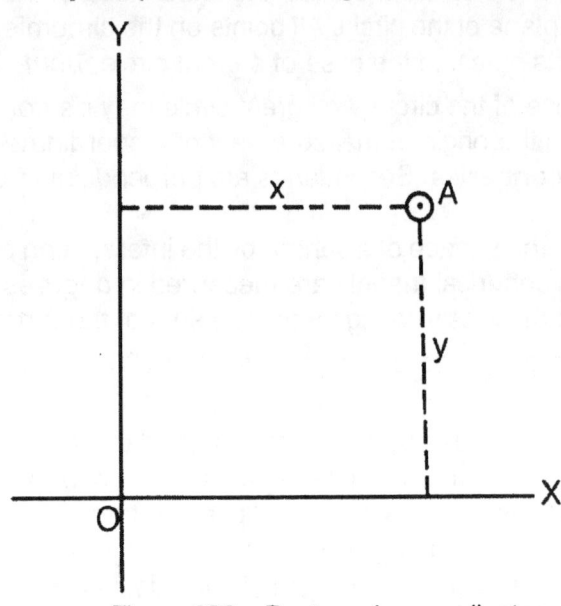

Figure 036a. Rectangular coordinates

Each coordinate requires an origin, either stated or implied. If a position is known to be on a given plane, it might be defined by means of its distance from each of two intersecting lines, called **axes**. Thus, in figure O36a the position of point A can be defined by stating that it is x units to the right of line OY and y units upward from line OX. These are called **rectangular coordinates**. The coordinate along OY is called the **ordinate,** and the coordinate along OX is called the **abscissa.** Point 0 is the origin, and lines OX and OY the **axes** (called the X and Y axes, respectively). Point A is at position x, y. If the axes are not perpendicular but the lines x and y are drawn parallel to the axes, **oblique coordinates** result. Either type are **Cartesian coordinates.** A three-dimensional system of Cartesian coordinates, with X, Y, and Z axes, is called **space coordinates.**

MATHEMATICS

Another system of plane coordinates in common usage consists of the *direction* and *distance* from the origin (called the **pole**), as shown hi figure O36b. A line extending in the direction indicated is called a **radius vector.** Direction and distance from a fixed point constitute **polar coordinates,** sometimes called the rho- (the Greek *p,* to indicate distance) theta (the Greek θ, to indicate direction) system. Navigators more commonly call it the "bearing-distance" system. An example of its use is with respect to a radar PPI (art. 1208).

Spherical coordinates are used to define a position on the surface of a sphere or spheroid by indicating angular distance from a primary great circle and a reference secondary great circle. Familiar examples are latitude and longitude, altitude and azimuth, and declination and hour angle.

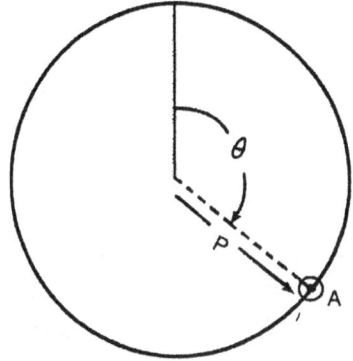

Figure O36b. Polar coordinates.

V. Trigonometry

037. Definitions. - **Trigonometry** is that branch of mathematics dealing with the relations among the angles and sides of triangles. **Plane trigonometry** is that branch dealing with plane triangles, and **spherical trigonometry** is that branch dealing with spherical triangles.

038. - Angular measure. A circle may be divided into 360 **degrees** (°), which is the **angular length** of its circumference. Each degree may be divided into 60 **minutes** ('), and each minute into 60 **seconds** ("). The angular length of an arc is usually expressed in these units. By this system a right angle or quadrant has 90° and a straight angle or semicircle 180°. In marine navigation, altitudes, latitudes, and longitudes are usually expressed in degrees, minutes, and tenths (27°14!4). Azimuths are usually expressed in degrees and tenths (164°7). The system of degrees, minutes, and seconds indicated above is the **sexagesimal system.** In the **centesimal system,** used chiefly in France, the circle is divided into 400 **centesimal degrees** (sometimes called **grades**) each of which is divided into 100 **centesimal minutes of 100 centesimal seconds** each.

A **radian** is the angle subtended at the center of a circle by an arc having a linear length equal to the radius of the circle. A radian is equal to 57°2957795131 approximately, or 57°17'44".80625 approximately. The radian is sometimes used as a unit of angular measure.

A circle (360°) = 2π radians, a semicircle (180°) = π radians, a right angle (90°)= $\dfrac{\pi}{2}$ radians, 1°=0.0174532925 radians approximately, l' = 0.0002908882 radians approximately, and 1"=0.0000048481 radians approximately.

MATHEMATICS

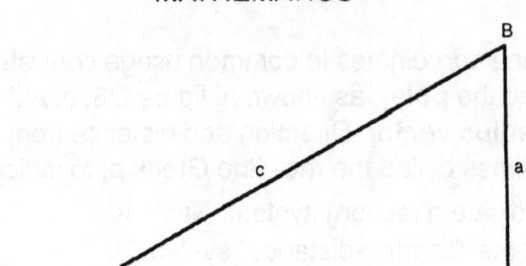

Figure 039a. A right triangle.

039. Trigonometric functions are the various proportions or ratios of the sides of a plane right triangle, defined in relation to one of the acute angles. In figure O39a, A, B, and C are the angles of a plane right triangle, the right angle being at C. The sides are a, b, c, as shown. The six principal trigonometric functions of angle A are:

$$\text{sine } A = \sin A = \frac{\text{side opposite}}{\text{hypotenuse}} = \frac{a}{c}$$

$$\text{cosine } A = \cos A = \frac{\text{side adjacent}}{\text{hypotenuse}} = \frac{b}{c}$$

$$\text{tangent } A = \tan A = \frac{\text{side opposite}}{\text{side adjacent}} = \frac{a}{b}$$

$$\text{cotangent } A = \cot A \frac{\text{side adjacent}}{\text{side opposite}} = \frac{b}{a}$$

$$\text{secant } A = \sec A = \frac{\text{hypotenuse}}{\text{side adjacent}} = \frac{c}{b}$$

$$\text{cosecant } A = \csc A = \frac{\text{hypotenuse}}{\text{side opposite}} = \frac{c}{a}$$

Certain additional relations are also classed as trigonometric functions:
 versed sine A=versine A=vers A=ver A= 1- cos'A
 versed cosine A=coversed sine A= coversine A=covers A=cov A=1- sin A
 haversine A=hav A=1/2 ver A=1/2 (1- cos A).

The numerical value of a trigonometric function is sometimes called the **natural function** to distinguish it from the logarithm of the function, called the **logarithmic function.** Numerical values of the six principal functions are given at 1' intervals in table 31. Logarithms are given at the same intervals in table 33. Both natural and logarithmic haversines are given in table 34

MATHEMATICS

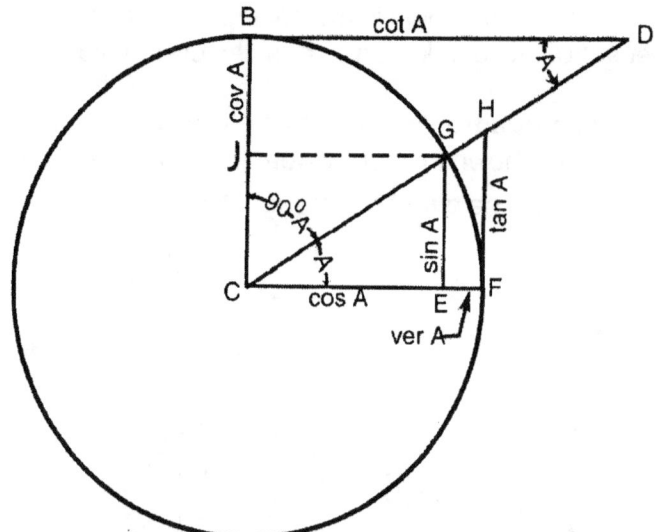

Figure O39b. Line definitions of trigonometric functions.

Various functions may be represented by lines associated with a circle, as shown in figure 039b. The radius of the circle is considered 1. Angle *BDC*= angle *ECG*= angle *A*.

sin A = GE	cot A = BD
cos A = CE	sec A = CH
tan A = HF	esc A = CD
ver A = EF	cov A = BJ.

Some relationships apply only to plane trigonometry and others to both plane and spherical trigonometry. Those which apply to both are called **fundamental identities.** Examples are given below.

Of the six principal functions, the second three are the reciprocals of the first three. Thus,

$$\sin A = \frac{1}{\csc A} \qquad \csc A = \frac{1}{\sin A}$$

$$\cos A = \frac{1}{\sec A} \qquad \sec A = \frac{1}{\cos A}$$

$$\tan A = \frac{1}{\cot A} \qquad \cot A = \frac{1}{\tan A}$$

From figure O39a:

$$\sin B = \frac{b}{c} = \cos A \qquad \cot B = \frac{a}{b} = \tan A$$

$$\cos B = \frac{a}{c} = \sin A \qquad \sec B = \frac{c}{a} = \csc A$$

$$\tan B = \frac{b}{a} = \cot A \qquad \csc B = \frac{c}{b} = \sec A$$

MATHEMATICS

Since *A* and *B* are *complementary,* these relations show that the sine of an angle is the cosine of its complement, the tangent of an angle is the cotangent of its complement, and the secant of an angle is the cosecant of its complement. Thus, the **co** function of an angle is the function of its complement.

040. The functions in various quadrants. - The sign (+ or -) of the functions varies with the quadrant of an angle. This is shown in figure O40a. In the left-hand diagram a radius is imagined to rotate in a counterclockwise direction through 360°

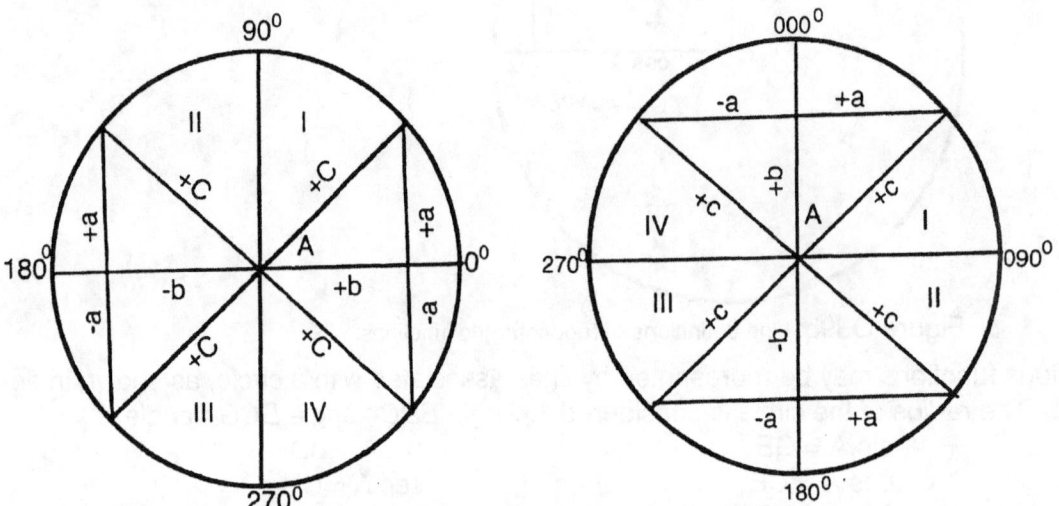

Figure O40a. Trigonometric fuction in the four quadrants. *Left,* mathematical convention; *right* navigational convention.

from the horizontal position at 0. This is the mathematical convention. In the right-hand figure this concept is shown in the usual navigational convention of a compass rose, starting with 000 at the top and rotating clockwise. In either diagram the angle *A* between the original position of the radius and its position at any time increases from 0 to 90° in the *first quadrant* (I), 90° to 180° in the *second quadrant* (II), 180° to 270° in the *third quadrant* (III), and 270° to 360 in the *fourth quadrant* (IV). If the values of *a* and *b* are considered positive in the directions they extend in the first quadrant *(upward* and to the *right)* and negative in the opposite directions, and if *c* is regarded as always positive, the signs of the functions can be determined by considering the signs of the sides involved, as shown in the following table:

Functions	I	II	III	IV
sine and cosecant	+	+	-	-
cosine and secant	+	-	-	+
tangent and cotangent	+	-	+	-
versine, coversine, and haversine	+	+	+	+

TABLE 040a. Signs of trigonometric functions by quadrant.

MATHEMATICS

The numerical values vary as shown in the following table and in figure O40b:

Functions	I	II	III	IV
sine	0 to +1	+1 to 0	0 to -1	-1 to 0
cosecant	+∞ to +1	+1 to +∞	-∞ to -1	-1 to -∞
cosine	+1 to 0	0 to -1	-1 to 0	0 to +1
secant	+1 to +∞	-∞ to -1	-1 to -∞	+∞ to +1
tangent	0 to +∞	-∞ to 0	0 to +∞	-∞ to 0
cotangent	+∞ to 0	0 to -∞	+∞ to 0	0 to -∞
versine	0 to +1	+1 to +2	+2 to +1	+1 to 0
coversine	+1 to 0	0 to +1	+1 to +2	+2 to +1
haversine	0 to +1/2	1/2 to +1	1 to +1/2	+1/2 to 0

TABLE O40b. Values of trigonometric functions in various quadrants. These relationships are showngraphically in figure O40b.

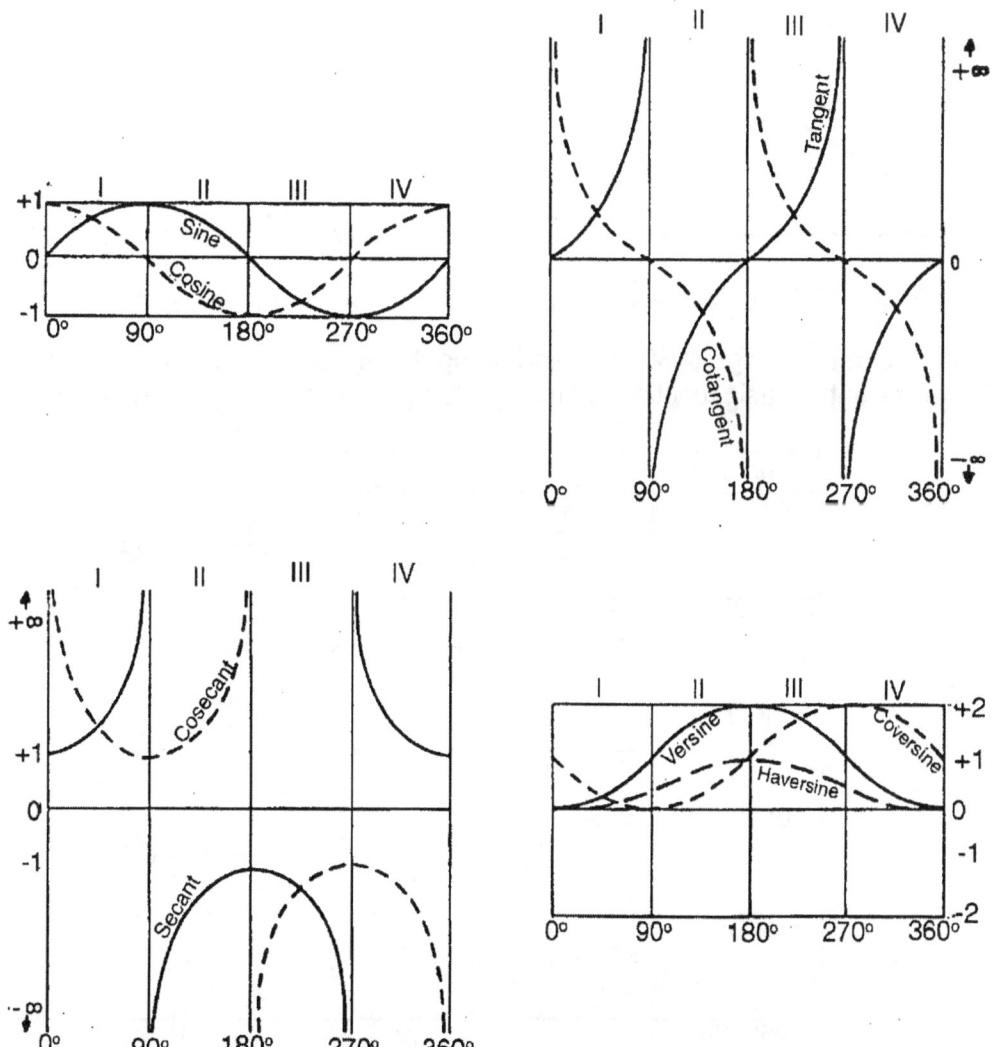

FIGURE O40b. Graphic representation values of trigonometric function in various quadrants.

MATHEMATICS

The functions of any angle in the second, third, and fourth quadrants are numerically equal to the same functions of some angle in the first quadrant, as follows:

Quadrant	Corresponding angle in first quadrant
II	180°-angle
III	angle-180°
IV	360°-angle

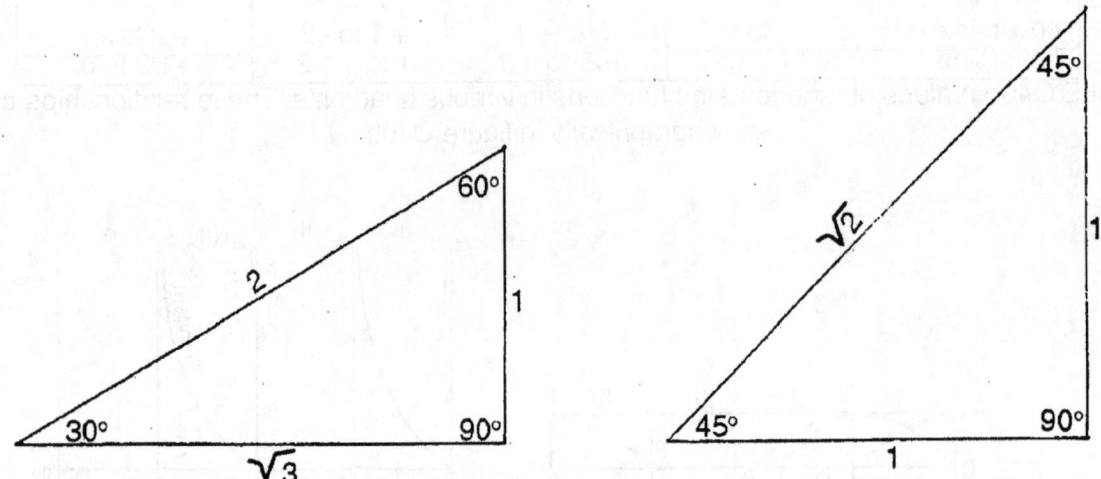

FIGURE O40c. Numerical relationship of sides of 30°-60° and 45° triangles.

Since the relationships of 30°-60° and 45 right triangles are as shown in figure O40c, certain values of the basic functions can be stated exactly as shown in the following table:

Function	30°	45°	60°
sine	$\dfrac{1}{2}$	$\dfrac{1}{\sqrt{2}} = \dfrac{1}{2}\sqrt{2}$	$\dfrac{\sqrt{3}}{2} = \dfrac{1}{2}\sqrt{3}$
cosine	$\dfrac{\sqrt{3}}{2} = \dfrac{1}{2}\sqrt{3}$	$\dfrac{1}{\sqrt{2}} = \dfrac{1}{2}\sqrt{2}$	$\dfrac{1}{2}$
tangent	$\dfrac{1}{\sqrt{3}} = \dfrac{1}{3}\sqrt{3}$	$\dfrac{1}{1} = 1$	$\dfrac{\sqrt{3}}{1} = \sqrt{3}$
cotangent	$\dfrac{\sqrt{3}}{1} = \sqrt{3}$	$\dfrac{1}{1} = 1$	$\dfrac{1}{\sqrt{3}} = \dfrac{1}{3}\sqrt{3}$
secant	$\dfrac{2}{\sqrt{3}} = \dfrac{2}{3}\sqrt{3}$	$\dfrac{\sqrt{2}}{1} = \sqrt{2}$	$\dfrac{2}{1} = 2$
cosecant	$\dfrac{2}{1} = 2$	$\dfrac{\sqrt{2}}{1} = \sqrt{2}$	$\dfrac{2}{\sqrt{3}} = \dfrac{2}{3}\sqrt{3}$

TABLE O40c. Values of various trigonometric functions for angles of 30°, 45°, and 60°.

MATHEMATICS

041. Inverse trigonometric functions. - The angle having a given trigonometric function may be indicated in any of several ways. Thus, sin $y = x$, $y = $ arc sin x, and $y = \sin^{-1} x$ have the same meaning. The superior - 1 is not an exponent in this case. In each case, y is "the angle whose sine is x." In this case, y is the **inverse sine** of x. Similar relationships hold for all trigonometric functions.

042. Solution of triangles. - A triangle is composed of six parts: three angles and three sides. The angles may be designated A, B, and C; and the sides opposite these angles as a, b, and c, respectively. In general, when three parts are known, the other three parts can be found, unless the known parts are the three angles of a plane triangle.

Right plane triangles. - In a right plane triangle it is only necessary to substitute numerical values in the appropriate formulas representing the basic trigonometric functions (art. O39) and solve. Thus, if a and b are known:

$$\tan A = \frac{a}{b}$$
$$B = 90° - A$$
$$c = a \csc A$$

Similarly, if c and B are given:

$$A = 90° - B$$
$$a = c \sin A$$
$$b = c \cos A.$$

Oblique plane triangles. - In solving an oblique plane triangle, it is often desirable to draw a rough sketch of the triangle approximately to scale, as shown in figure O42a. The following laws are helpful in solving such triangles:

Law of sines: $$\frac{a}{\sin A} = \frac{b}{\sin B} = \frac{c}{\sin C}$$

Law of cosines: $$a^2 = b^2 + c^2 - 2bc \cos A.$$

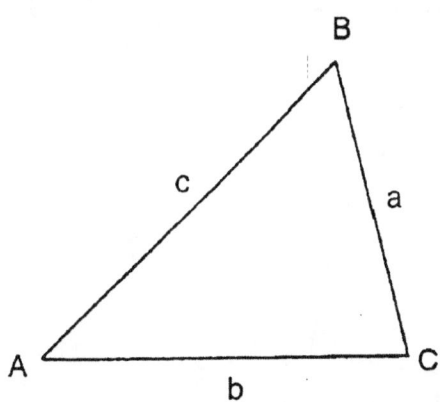

Figure O42a. A plane oblique triangle

MATHEMATICS

The unknown parts of oblique plane triangles can be computed by the formulas of table O42a, among others. By reassignment of letters to sides and angles, these formulas can be used to solve for all unknown parts of oblique plane triangles.

Known	To find	Formula	Comments
a, b, c	A	$\cos A = \dfrac{c^2 + b^2 - a^2}{2bc}$	Cosine law
a, b, A	B	$\sin B = \dfrac{b \sin A}{a}$	Sine law. Two solutions if $b>a$
	C	$C = 180° - (A + B)$	$A + B + C = 180°$
	c	$c = \dfrac{a \sin C}{\sin A}$	Sine law
a, b, C	A	$\tan A = \dfrac{a \sin C}{b - a \cos C}$	
	B	$B = 180° - (A + C)$	$A + B + C = 180°$
	c	$c = \dfrac{a \sin C}{\sin A}$	Sine law
a, A, B	b	$\sin b = \dfrac{a \sin B}{\sin A}$	Sine law
	C	$C = 180° - (A + B)$	$A + B + C = 180°$
	c	$c = \dfrac{a \sin C}{\sin A}$	Sine law

TABLE O42a. Formulas for solving oblique plane triangles

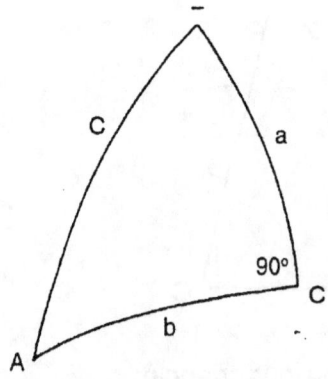

FIGURE O42b. Parts of a right spherical triangle as used in Napier's rules.

MATHEMATICS

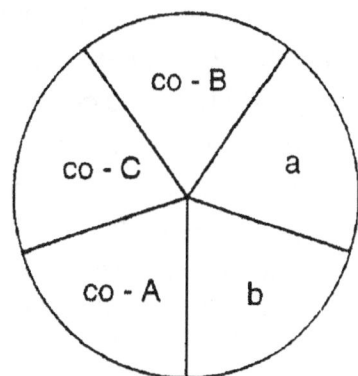

FIGURE O42c. Diagram for Napier's rules.

Right spherical triangles can be solved with the aid of **Napier's rules,** devised by John Napier. If the right angle is omitted, the triangle has five parts: two angles and three sides, as shown in figure 042b. The triangle can be solved if any two parts are known. If the two sides forming the right angle, and the *complements* of the other three parts are used, these elements (called "parts" in the rules) can be arranged in five sectors of a circle in the same order in which they occur in the triangle, as shown in figure O42c. Considering *any* part as the *middle* part, the two parts nearest it in the diagram are considered the *adjacent* parts, and the two farthest from it the *opposite* parts. The rules are:

The sine of a middle part equals the product of (1) the tangents of the adjacent parts or (2) the cosines of the opposite parts.

In the use of these rules, the *co* function of a complement can be given as the function of the element. Thus, the cosine of co-.A is the same as the sine of A. From these rules the following formulas can be derived:

$$\sin a = \tan b \cot B = \sin c \sin A$$
$$\sin b = \tan a \cot A = \sin c \sin B$$
$$\cos c = \cot A \cot B = \cos a \cos b$$
$$\cos A = \tan b \cot c = \cos a \sin B$$
$$\cos B = \tan a \cot c = \cos b \sin A.$$

The following rules apply:
1. An oblique angle and the side opposite are in the same quadrant.
2. Side *c* (the hypotenuse) is less than $90°$ when *a* and *b* are in the same quadrant, and more than $90°$ when *a* and *b* are in different quadrants.

If the known parts are an angle and its opposite side, two solutions are possible.

A quadrantal spherical triangle is one having one side of $90°$. A **biquadrantal spherical triangle** has two sides of $90°$. A **triquadrantal spherical triangle** has three sides of $90°$. A biquadrantal spherical triangle is isosceles and has two right angles opposite the $90°$ sides. A triquadrantal spherical triangle is equilateral, has three right angles, and bounds an octant (one-eighth) of the surface of the sphere. A quadrantal spherical triangle can be solved by

MATHEMATICS

Napier's rules provided any two elements in addition to the 90° side arc known. The 90° side is omitted and the other parts are arranged in order in a five-sectored circle, using the complements of the three parts farthest from the 90° side. In the case of a quadrantal triangle, rule 1 above is used, and rule 2 restated: angle C (the angle opposite the side of 90°) is *more* than 90° when A and B are in the same quadrant, and *less* than 90° when A and B are in different quadrants. If the rule requires an angle of more than 90° and the solution produces an angle of less than 90°, subtract the solved angle from 180°.

Oblique spherical triangles. An oblique spherical triangle can be solved by dropping a perpendicular from one of the apexes to the opposite side, extended if necessary, to form two right spherical triangles. It can also be solved by the following formulas, reassigning the letters as necessary.

Known	To find	Formula	Comments
a, b, c	A	$\text{hav } A = \dfrac{\text{hav } a - \text{hav}(b-c)}{\sin b \sin c}$	
A, B, c	a	$\text{hav } a = \dfrac{-\cos S \cos(S-A)}{\sin B \sin C}$	$S = \frac{1}{2}(A+B+C)$
a, b, c	c	$\text{hav } c = \text{hav}(a \sim b) + \sin a \sin b \text{ hav } C$	
	A	$\tan A = \dfrac{\sin D \tan C}{\sin(b-D)}$	$\tan D = \tan a \cos C$
	B	$\sin B = \dfrac{\sin C \sin b}{\sin C}$	
c, A, B	C	$\cos C = \sin A \sin B \cos c - \cos A \cos B$	
	a	$\tan A = \dfrac{\tan c \sin E}{\sin(B+E)}$	$\tan E = \tan A \cos c$
	b	$\tan b = \dfrac{\tan c \sin F}{\sin(A+F)}$	$\tan F = \tan B \cos c$
a, b, A	c	$\sin(c+G) = \dfrac{\cos a \sin G}{\cos b}$	$\cot G = \cos A \tan b$ Two solutions
	B	$\sin B = \dfrac{\sin A \sin b}{\sin a}$	Two solutions
	C	$\sin(c+H) = \sin H \tan b \cot a$	$\tan H = \tan A \cos b$ Two solutions

a, A, B	C	$\sin(C - K) = \dfrac{\cos A \sin K}{\cos B}$	$\cot K = \tan B \cos a$ Two solutions
	b	$\sin b = \dfrac{\sin A \sin B}{\sin A}$	Two solutions
	c	$\sin(c - M) = \cot A \tan B \sin M$	$\tan M = \cos B \tan a$ Two solutions

TABLE O42b. Formulas for solving oblique spherical triangles.

VI. Calculus

043. Definitions. - Calculus is that branch of mathematics dealing with the rate of change of one quantity with respect to another.

A **constant** is a quantity which does not change. If a vessel is making good a course of 090°, the latitude does not change and is therefore a constant.

A **variable**, where continuous, is a quantity which can have an infinite number of values, although there may be limits to the maximum and minimum. Thus, from latitude 30° to latitude 31° there are an infinite number of latitudes, if infinitesimally small units are taken, but no value is less than 30° nor more than 31°. If two variables are so related that for every value of one there is a corresponding value of the other, one of the values is known as a **function** of the other. Thus, if speed is constant, the distance a vessel steams depends upon the elapsed time. Since elapsed time does not depend upon any other quantity, it is called an **independent variable.** The distance depends upon the elapsed time, and therefore is called a **dependent variable.** If it is required to find the time needed to travel any given distance at constant speed, distance is the independent variable and time is the dependent variable.

The principal processes of calculus are differentiation and integration.

044. Differentiation is the process of finding the rate of change of one variable with respect to another. If x is an independent variable, y is a dependent variable, and y is a function of x, this relationship may be written $y=f(x)$. Since for every value of x there is a corresponding value of y, the relationship can be plotted as a curve, figure O44. In this figure, A and B arc any two points on the curve, a short distance apart

42
MATHEMATICS

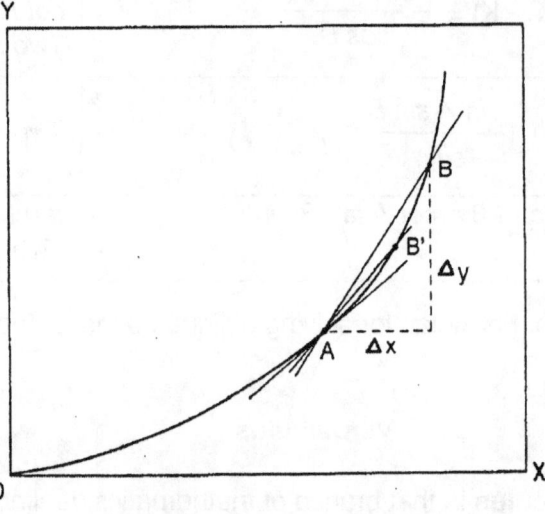

FIGURE O44. Differentiation.

The difference between the value of x at A and at B is Δx (delta x), and the corresponding difference in the value of y is Δy (delta y). The straight line through points A and B is a secant of the curve (art. O30). It represents the rate of change between A and B, for anywhere along this line the change of y is proportional to the change of x.

As B moves closer to A, as shown at B', both Δx and Δy become smaller, but at a different rate, and $\frac{\Delta y}{\Delta x}$ changes. This is indicated by the difference in the slope of the secant. Also, that part of the secant between A and B moves closer to the curve and becomes a better approximation of it. The limiting case occurs when B reaches A or is at an infinitesimal distance from it. As the distance becomes infinitesimal, both Δy and Δx become infinitely small, and are designated dy and dx, respectively. The straight line becomes tangent to the curve, and represents the rate of change, or slope, of the curve at that point. This is indicated by the expression dy/dx called the **derivative** of y with respect to x.

The process of finding the value of the derivative is called **differentiation.** It depends upon the ability to connect x and y by an equation. For instance, if $y = x^n$, $dy/dx = nx^{-1}$ If n = 2, $y = x^2$, and $\frac{dy}{dx} = 2x$. This is derived as follows: If point A on the curve is$z, y;$ point B can be considered $x + \Delta x, y + \Delta y$. Since the relation $y=x^2$ is true anywhere on the curve, at B:

$$y + \Delta y = (x + \Delta x)^2 = x^2 + 2x \Delta x + (\Delta x)^2$$

Since $y = x^2$, and equal quantities can be subtracted from both sides of an equation without destroying the equality:

$$\Delta y = 2x \Delta x + (\Delta x)^2.$$

Dividing by Δx: $\quad \frac{\Delta y}{\Delta x} = 2x + \Delta x.$

As B approaches A, Δx becomes infinitesimally small, approaching 0 as a limit. Therefore approaches 2x as a limit.

MATHEMATICS

This can be demonstrated by means of a numerical example. Let $y=x^2$. Suppose at A, x=2 and y=4, and at B, x=2.1 and y=4.41. In this case $\Delta x=0.1$ and $\Delta y = 0.41$, and

$$\frac{\Delta y}{\Delta x} = \frac{0.41}{0.1} = 4.1$$

From the other side of the equation:

$$2x + \Delta x = 2 \times 2 + 0.1 = 4.1.$$

If Δx is 0.01 and Δy is 0.0401, $\frac{\Delta y}{\Delta x}$ =4.01. If Δx is 0.001, $\frac{\Delta y}{\Delta x}$ =4.001; and if Δx is 0.0001, $\frac{\Delta y}{\Delta x}$ = 4.0001. As Δx approaches 0 as a limit, $\frac{\Delta y}{\Delta x}$ approaches 4, which is therefore the value $\frac{dy}{dx}$. Therefore, at point A the *rate* of change of y with respect to x is 4, or y is increasing in value 4 times as fast as x.

An example of the use of differentiation in navigation is the Ad value in H.O. Pub. No. 214. This is the change of altitude for a change of 1' of declination. In this case, declination is the independent variable, altitude is the dependent variable, and both meridian angle (H.A.) and latitude are constants. The rate of change at the tabulated value is desired, so that the table can be entered with the *nearest* tabulated value of declination, and interpolation performed in either direction (either larger or smaller values of declination).

045. Integration is the inverse of differentiation. Unlike the latter, however, it is not a direct process, but involves the recognition of a mathematical expression as the differential of a known function. The function sought is the **integral** of the given expression. Most functions can be differentiated, but many cannot be integrated.

Integration can be considered the summation of an infinite number of infinitesimally small quantities, between specified limits. Consider, for instance, the problem of finding an area below a specified part of a curve for which a mathematical expression can be

MATHEMATICS

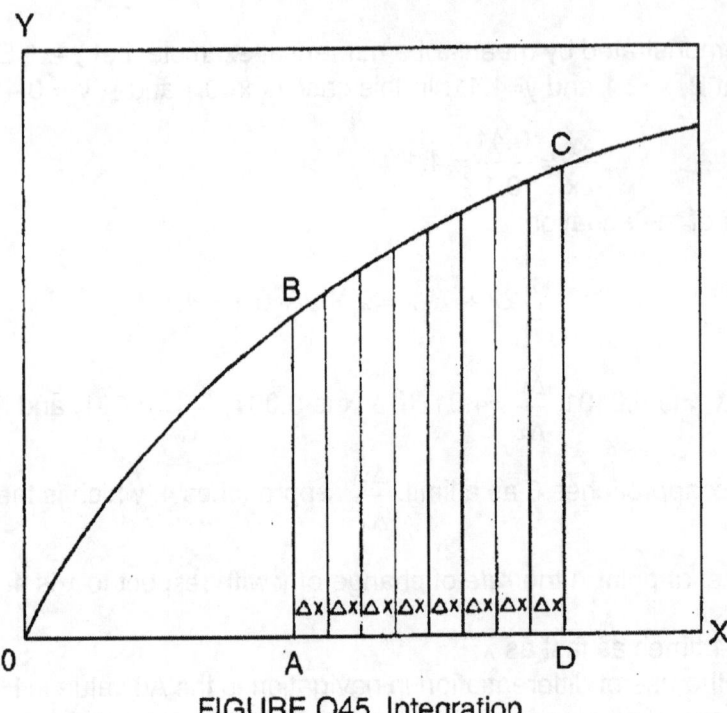

FIGURE O45. Integration.

written. Suppose it is desired to find the area *ABCD* of figure O45. If vertical lines are drawn dividing the area into a number of vertical strips, each Δx wide, and if *y* is the height of each strip at the midpoint of Δx, the area of each strip is approximately $y \Delta x$; and the approximate total area of all strips is the sum of the areas of the individual strips. This may be written $\sum_{l_1}^{l_2} y \Delta x$, meaning the sum of all $y \Delta x$ values between x_1 and x_2. The symbol Σ is the Greek letter *sigma,* the equivalent of the English *S*. If Δx is made progressively smaller, the sum of the small areas, becomes ever closer to the true total area. If Δx becomes infinitely small, the summation expression is written $\int_{l_1}^{l_2} y dx$, the symbol *dx* denoting an infinitely small Δx.

The symbol $\int$, called the "integral sign," is a distorted *S*.

An expression such as $\int_{l_1}^{l_2} y dx$ is called a **definite integral** because limits are specified (x_1 and x_2). If limits are not specified, as in $\int y dx$, the expression is called an **indefinite integral.**

A navigational application of integration is the finding of meridional parts, table 5. The *rate* of change of meridional parts with respect to latitude changes progressively. The formula given in the explanation of the table is the equivalent of an integral representing the sum of the meridional parts from the equator to any given latitude.

MATHEMATICS

046. Differential equations. -An expression such as *dy* or *dx* is called a **differential**. An equation involving a differential or a derivative is called a **differential equation.**

As shown in article O44, if $y = x^2, \dfrac{dy}{dx} = 2x$. Neither *dy* nor *dx* is a finite quantity, but both are limits to which Ay and Ax approach as they are made progressively smaller. Therefore is merely a ratio, the limiting value of and not one finite number divided by another. However, since the ratio is the same as would be obtained by using finite quantities, it is possible to use the two differentials *dy* and *dx* independently in certain relationships. Differential equations involve such relationships.

www.ingramcontent.com/pod-product-compliance
Lightning Source LLC
Chambersburg PA
CBHW082038300426
44117CB00015B/2528